331.89

PAY, POLITICS, AND ECONOMIC PERFORMANCE IN IRELAND 1970–1987

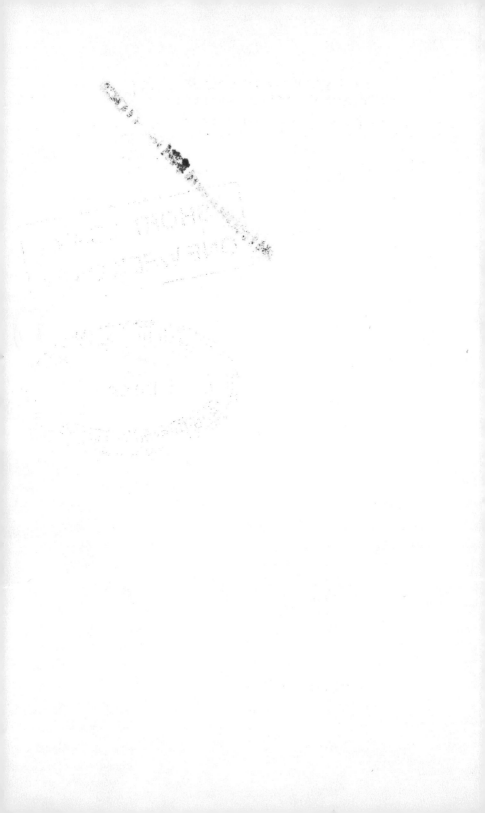

PAY, POLITICS, AND ECONOMIC PERFORMANCE IN IRELAND 1970–1987

NIAMH HARDIMAN

CLARENDON PRESS · OXFORD
1988

Oxford University Press, Walton Street, Oxford OX2 6DP
Oxford New York Toronto
Delhi Bombay Calcutta Madras Karachi
Petaling Jaya Singapore Hong Kong Tokyo
Nairobi Dar es Salaam Cape Town
Melbourne Auckland
and associated companies in
Berlin Ibadan

Oxford is a trade mark of Oxford University Press

Published in the United States
by Oxford University Press, New York

British Library Cataloguing in Publication Data
Hardiman, Niamh
Pay, Politics, and Economic
Performance in Ireland 1970–1987
1. Ireland. (Republic). Collective
bargaining, 1970–1987
I. Title
331.89'09417
ISBN 0–19–827533–1

Library of Congress Cataloging in Publication Data
Hardiman, Niamh.
Pay, Politics, and Economic Performance
in Ireland, 1970–1987/Niamh Hardiman.
p. cm.
Bibliography: p.
Includes index.
1. Collective bargaining—Ireland. I. Title.
HD6670.3.H37 1988 331.89'09417—dc 19 88–25257
ISBN 0–19–827533–1

Typeset by Cambrian Typesetters, Frimley, Surrey
Printed and bound in
Great Britain by Biddles Ltd,
Guildford and King's Lynn

Acknowledgements

I<small>T</small> is a pleasure to acknowledge my great debt to John Goldthorpe, whose intellectual stimulus has been invaluable to me in developing this work. It is a pleasure also to thank Bill Cox, whose critical insight and editorial advice have made this a far better book than it might otherwise have been, and whose support I appreciate more than can be acknowledged here. I wish to express my thanks to all those who generously gave their time in interviews. I would like to thank Donal Nevin of ICTU, Jim O'Brien of FUE, and Des Byrne of Irish Marketing Surveys Ltd. for making various documentation available to me, and the officials in the Department of Labour and the Department of the Public Service who kindly helped me with information and documentation. I wish also to express my gratitude to Basil Chubb, Colin Crouch, Michael Fogarty, and Chris Whelan for their helpful comments on my doctoral thesis. I am grateful to the Economic and Social Research Institute, Dublin, for making it possible for me to undertake this research, and to Nuffield College, Oxford, where most of it was written. I owe a special debt of gratitude to my parents for their unfailing support and encouragement. I have been fortunate in benefiting from the expertise and insight of a number of people whose judgement I respect, in the course of my work on this book. However, I have not always followed their advice, and I must accept full responsibility for shortcomings of any sort.

N.H.

Contents

List of Figures

List of Tables

Abbreviations

PAYE	pay-as-you-earn
PD	Progressive Democratic Party/Progressive Democrats
PRSI	pay-related social insurance
PSBR	public sector borrowing requirement
QEC	*Quarterly Economic Commentary*
RTE	Radio Telefís Éireann (state-sponsored broadcasting service)
SDC	Special Delegate Conference
SIMI	Society of the Irish Motor Industry
TD	Teacha Dála (Dáil deputy or member of parliament)
VAT	value added tax

2. TRADE UNIONS

AGEMOU	Automobile, General Engineering and Mechanical Operatives' Union
ASTI	Association of Secondary Teachers of Ireland
ASTMS	Association of Scientific, Technical and Managerial Staffs
ATGWU	Amalgamated Transport and General Workers' Union
AUEW	Amalgamated Union of Engineering Workers
AUEW–TASS	Amalgamated Union of Engineering Workers–Technical, Adminstrative and Supervisory Section
CPSSA	Civil and Public Services' Staff Association
CSEU	Civil Service Executive Union
EETPU	Electrical, Electronic, Telecommunication and Plumbing Union
ETU	Electrical Trades Union
FWUI	Federated Workers' Union of Ireland
IBOA	Irish Bank Officials' Association
INTO	Irish National Teachers' Organisation
ITGWU	Irish Transport and General Workers' Union
IPOEU	Irish Post Office Engineering Union
IUDWC	Irish Union of Distributive Workers and Clerks
LGPSU	Local Government and Public Services Union
MPGWU	Marine Port and General Workers' Union
NEETU	National Engineering and Electrical Trade Union
NGA	National Graphical Association

NUJ	National Union of Journalists
POWU	Post Office Workers' Union
PTWU	Postal and Telecommunications Workers' Union
TUI	Teachers' Union of Ireland
UCATT	Union of Construction, Allied Trades and Technicians

Introduction

THE primary subject of this book is the period of centralized wage bargaining in the Republic of Ireland between 1970 and 1980. During this period a series of centralized wage agreements was negotiated between the peak federations of unions and employers and, as the decade progressed, government became more directly involved in facilitating the negotiation of agreements. From the outset the centralized agreements were intended to make a substantial contribution to improving general economic performance, and they were hailed as a major breakthrough in collective bargaining when the first agreement was negotiated in 1970. The increasing involvement of government underlined the extent to which pay policy was seen as a key element of government's approach to economic management. But by the end of the 1970s and the early 1980s all sides were disillusioned with the agreements, if to varying extents, and centralized collective bargaining was quietly abandoned in 1981.

The book has two objectives. It aims to illuminate some central aspects of the particular Irish experience with centralized collective bargaining during the 1970s, and to investigate why the agreements were initiated, how they functioned, and what the consequences were for all concerned. It also seeks to make a contribution to a more general literature on the political economy of wage regulation, with particular reference to the comparative performance of small states. While both sets of concerns are advanced simultaneously, it may be that sections of the book will prove to be of greater or lesser interest to readers for whom one or other interest is primary.

It has often been argued that the small open economies of Western Europe (of which Ireland is one) experienced a special incentive to develop integrated political agreements whereby wage regulation takes place on terms which are specifically intended to improve aspects of national economic performance. Because of the exposed position of small open economies in the international economic order consequent upon the liberalization of trade since the Second World War, the representatives of employers and of employees may, under certain conditions, come to see advantages in avoiding complete reliance on market processes of wage formation through collective bargaining. Each may prefer, for their own reasons, to look to state policy to advance some of their interests, in other words to rely increasingly on *political* rather than on *market* processes to achieve certain of their objectives. In this fashion the conduct and outcomes of collective bargaining become more closely integrated into, and dependent upon, general government strategies for management of the economy. Governments' discretionary powers to 'manage' small open economies are typically more highly constrained than in the larger economies, because of the vulnerability of small economies to fluctuations in trading conditions. Thus the management of small open economies has been likened to small-boat sailing, in which progression depends on skilful tacking to prevailing winds, in contrast to the more familiar image of economic 'steering'. To continue the analogy, employer and trade union commitment to 'politicized' wage regulation agreements, that is to a form of incomes policy, may be likened to co-operation among the crew of a small craft, bent upon a common purpose.

One of the themes developed in this book is that the conditions under which a common framework of economic analysis and a common economic strategy may be agreed between trade union and employer federations are considerably more complex than much of the literature on small open economies would suggest. Small size and economic vulnerability may well provide certain incentives to adapt collective bargaining in this manner. But the identification of a need implies nothing for the probability that that need will be met effectively. The options available to potential participants in centralized agreements may dispose them to make quite different rational choices. Thus one of the purposes of this book is to show that not all small open economies may be in a position to develop the solutions adopted with some success in small states such as Sweden, Norway, Austria, or Switzerland.

Chapter 1 sets out the general theoretical focus of the book, and readers primarily interested in the Irish case may skip over this discussion without losing any vital information. This chapter sets out the logic of why, under certain conditions, it may be to the advantage of unions and their members to enter into centralized bargaining agreements which are designed to improve general economic performance and, to this end, are backed up in some way by government commitments. Agreements of this sort have often been termed 'neo-corporatist' or 'concertative', referring to the facilitating role of the state in 'concerting' the conflicting interests of the central organizations of the trade unions and the employers. Chapter 1 also identifies some of the main organizational, political, and economic conditions which have been advanced as being the most conducive to concertative agreements. These facilitating conditions provide the framework for explaining Ireland's experience with centralized bargaining.

Many have suggested that a 'consensual' approach to collective bargaining should be fairly easily negotiable in Ireland, either because it is a small society, or because 'consensus' is manifestly needed to improve economic performance for all, or because social relations between government and economic interests tend often to be conducted informally in Ireland. This view was characteristic of successive Irish governments during the 1970s. However, few would now argue that such a 'social partnership', in any lasting sense, was achieved during these years. One of the main puzzles addressed in this study is how the agreements were viewed by each of the parties to them, that is, trade unions, employers, and, increasingly, government: why each side participated in them, and why each side eventually withdrew its commitment to them.

In fact the Irish case can be understood quite well drawing on lines of explanation suggested by comparative studies of neo-corporatism. The organizational and political conditions which would tend to be conducive to sustaining neo-corporatist agreements were not well developed in Ireland, therefore concertative wage bargaining could not develop very far. In particular, the trade union movement's authoritative centralization was limited, and it was constrained in its ability to devise a central strategy and secure the compliance of all affiliates. Similarly, employers' ability to devise a centralized strategy was limited by, among other factors, the variations in economic conditions prevailing in different sectors of the economy. However, we may well ask why each of the parties to the agreements did not develop a greater interest in strengthening their organizational and institutional structures. The answer to this question is complex, rooted in the traditions and preferences of the organizations in question. But, in part at least, it may be sought by examining their respective understandings of how best to advance their interests in the context of the economic conditions prevailing in the 1970s.

This leads us back to the 'small open economy' thesis. Several aspects of Ireland's economic situation in the 1970s distinguished it quite markedly from other West European small open economies. Ireland industrialized late and was still experiencing a structural shift in economic composition of quite major proportions while the centralized agreements were in effect. Furthermore, for much of the period during which the economy was experiencing the upheavals of trade liberalization, it was heavily dependent in various ways on British economic performance. Both of these conditions radically affected the context of centralized collective bargaining. Most importantly, they resulted in the trade union movement and the employers and industrialists perceiving their interests as divergent rather than convergent.

The development of the argument falls into three parts. The first section comprises the first three chapters. The contents of Chapter 1 have already been sketched: this chapter sets out some of the main lines of enquiry to be explored in relation to the Irish case in subsequent chapters. Chapter 2 outlines the scale of economic transformation in Ireland and sets out an analysis of the role of wage regulation agreements as a means of addressing some of the problems of a small open economy such as Ireland. Chapter 3 charts the development of government involvement in the centralized agreements. It shows that although in retrospect they appear to follow one another in a series there was nothing automatic about their continuation and that a great deal depended on the role of government.

The second section is a single chapter, Chapter 4. This examines various aspects of the functioning of the centralized agreements: the reasons why both unions and employers (including government as employer) were dissatisfied with the outcomes are each explored in turn. One aspect of both unions' and employers' grievances concerned the role of government in wage formation. This chapter therefore also surveys some of the contradictory objectives to which governments were committed, and in particular the tensions between taxation policy, the state's commitments in industrial policy, and the efforts of successive governments to secure wage regulation agreements.

In the third section, comprising Chapters 5, 6, and 7, more detailed explanations are developed for the strategies each party adopted in relation to the centralized agreements. Each of these chapters tries to explain more fully why each party to the agreements adopted its particular course of action. Chapter 5 examines the structure and ideological orientation of the trade union movement and the nature of inter-union relations which contributed to its distinctive approach to centralized bargaining. Chapter 6 undertakes what is in some ways a parallel enquiry in connection with employers' associations. The employers' approach to collective bargaining is related to the discussion in Chapter 2 of changes in the structure of the economy. In Chapter 7 the political context of government policy-making and economic management, which in the course of earlier chapters were seen to be problematic in various respects, is discussed at greater length. Two features of the political system are involved in explaining the contribution of government to overall pay policy in the 1970s. First, the historical constitution of political parties is analysed in order to explain the lack of correspondence between social cleavages and the party system. The distinctive party system articulated the political interests of working people in a manner which turned out not to be particularly conducive to the negotiation of cross-class 'com-promises' as required by neo-corporatist arrangements. Secondly, the responses of policy-makers to pressures from diverse interests is discussed. Various features of the political system contributed to a tendency for governments to accommodate and absorb prevailing pressures, even where they involved an expensive attempt to satisfy conflicting interests, rather than attempt to facilitate a compromise agreement on new terms between these conflicting interests.

Finally, Chapter 8 gives a brief account of the course of collective bargaining and the political economy of wage determination during the years of decentralized bargaining in the 1980s. This was a decade marked by deep international and domestic recession and severe problems in managing domestic public finances. As the relative balance of power in collective bargaining between em-ployers and trade unions altered, the dominant government strategy between 1982 and 1987 also shifted. For much of the decade wage formation assumed a more thoroughly market-based pattern: no trade-off was deemed to be possible between fiscal policy and wage negotiations. However, the two main problems of the 1980s, control of the public finances and the very high levels of unemployment, both proved difficult to tackle. Increasingly support grew for a consensually agreed approach to economic and social recovery. In this context, a new centralized agreement was negotiated in 1987—but the terms on which it was concluded were very different from the agreements of the 1970s. Chapter 8 traces the reasons why all sides became interested in returning to a centralized framework at this time. Finally, the main explanatory themes of the book are drawn together in a short Conclusion.

The Logic of 'Concertative' Economic Policies

The Context of 'Concertation' in Post-War Political Economy

In the years following the end of the Second World War Keynesian policies of demand management gained widespread acceptance in the countries of Western Europe. Governments were expected to maintain high levels of employment and to co-ordinate economic performance through counter-cyclical intervention; their responsibilities for economic management became considerably extended.

But the economic problems encountered by governments in the post-war years were different from those to which Keynesianism had been the response. Inflation rather than unemployment emerged as the crucial defining problem. There had, of course, been many earlier periods of inflation. But post-war observers noted that, in contrast with previous experience, recessionary episodes did not now bring any significant decline in the general price level. Indeed, sometimes prices even continued to rise during these episodes: inflation 'persisted' (Cagan, 1979: ch. 1; cf. Sachs, 1980; Olson, 1982: 219–20). Even before the general experience of 'stagflation' in the 1970s, it could be observed that the upward trend in price increases was not necessarily halted during recessions. The difficulties encountered in the 1970s should not be seen, therefore, as resulting primarily from inadequate policy responses to unpredictable 'external shocks' (OECD, 1977). Rather, they had much deeper roots in the political economy of Western nations (see also Keohane, 1978; Thurow, 1980; Bispham and Boltho, 1982: 323).

Two reasons for the persistence of inflation may be stated in broad outline. First, governments of Western Europe were, by and large, committed to policies of full employment and this increased the labour market strength of trade unions. Second, while the post-war years saw a significant growth in trade union membership in

European countries (Bain and Price, 1980; Korpi, 1983), other groups beside trade unions were also becoming more effectively organized. The density of organization increased among producer groups and professionals; public servants came increasingly to adopt the norms of other trade unionists. A great many more groups acquired the ability to protect themselves against the consequences of inflation by relying on their strength in the market (Scitovsky, 1978, 1980; Olson, 1982). The resulting phenomenon has been termed 'distributive dissent' (Goldthorpe, 1978, 1984, 1987). In consequence, inflation may be seen as the monetary expression of distributive conflict.

This analysis should not be taken to suggest that trade unions, through cost-push inflation, 'cause' inflation in any simple sense. Their actions are far from being the only element of distributive conflict and theirs is not the only influence on government monetary policies. But in many countries the process of wage determination took on a new significance for governments, since, if this could be regulated, inflationary pressures could more easily be contained.

Three kinds of policy approach may be identified among Western governments. First, where trade unions were weak, because they had a low membership density or were internally divided, governments could simply 'exclude' them from policy calculations. This was the case, for example, in France, and in Italy until the late 1960s and early 1970s. Second, where trade unions were well organized but had primarily a pressure-group or 'pluralist' relationship with government, the early responses of government involved efforts to implement incomes policies, with varying degrees of consultation with the trade union movement, but little direct negotiation. Britain would afford an example of this kind of approach, although it was not very successful (see Crouch, 1977, 1978a; Panitch, 1976). Third, unions' and employers' interests could develop close connections with government, through which government would facilitate the negotiation of a pay agreement on terms other than those which 'free' collective bargaining and the market were likely to produce. In other words, participation in incomes regulation could in some sense be made 'worth while' for trade unions. This approach has been termed 'neo-corporatist' or 'concertative' (Lehmbruch, 1984) and will be discussed further in the course of this chapter. A 'concertative' approach emerged at a relatively early date in countries such as Austria and Sweden. By the 1960s and 1970s several governments were attempting a comparable approach to developing negotiated agreements between the peak associations of unions and employers (Shonfield, 1965; Crouch, 1978*b*, 1979*a*: ch. 8; Flanagan, Soskice, and Ulman, 1983). *In the post-war years*

Governments were keen to have incomes regulation of some sort to curb the wage–price inflationary spiral because restraint of inflation was identified as a public good in Olson's (1965) sense: that is, as something which if achieved—at a cost—would be to everyone's benefit (cf. Commission of the European Communities, 1980: 34). Economists who took a narrow view of economic management as the business of solving essentially technical problems argued that trade union behaviour was 'irrational' (Kahn, 1976): unions engaged in strikes to secure wage increases which would only add to the thrust of inflation. If unions would forbear from exerting their market power to the full in the pursuit of 'confetti money', everyone would gain. But in many countries it became clear that trade unions did not accept that their behaviour was in any way irrational. Trade union leaders might well agree that a rapid rate of price increases was not in unions' interests: it made it more difficult for them to obtain real wage increases. But, given inflationary conditions, their view would be that it was altogether rational for them to seek to protect their members' living standards. This conflict in perceptions led to a greater concern on the part of Western governments, following an analysis advanced by OECD advisers, to promote 'consensus' between unions and employers on the main problems besetting the economy.[1]

But a call for a consensual approach to economic analysis has little chance of success if all that is meant is aggregating the views of what came to be called the 'social partners' (Hardiman, 1984*a*), a

---

[1] A change is detectable in OECD thinking towards the end of the 1970s. In the early part of the decade, its reports tended to favour the consultative, 'consensual' approach to collective bargaining. The publication of the McCracken Report (OECD, 1977) marked a break with the earlier view. This report recommended that governments should henceforth supplement a better demand management policy with a policy of 'non-accommodation' of inflationary pressure, entailing the consequence that government could no longer accept responsibility for maintaining a high level of employment. However, many OECD experts, especially those working in the field of labour relations, continued to favour the 'consensual' view. See e.g. OECD, 1980; OECD, 1982.

term which, in this context, means the peak federations of unions and employers. Distributive conflict is integral to the relationship between capital and labour in the organization of production. But if control of inflation is a public good for labour then the costs of engaging in collective action to secure that public good have to be taken into account. Trade unions' options between different strategies may usefully be modelled by rational choice theory. Trade unions, on this reckoning, face a classic 'prisoners' dilemma' (see Olson, 1965; Barry and Hardin, 1982; Heath, 1976; also Crouch, 1982a), that is, an impasse where it is not rational for any individual actor to contribute to the action required to bring about a public good.

Rational choice theory explores the ways in which individual actors calculate how to obtain the best outcome when obliged to choose between different courses of action under conditions of uncertainty. The classic 'prisoners' dilemma' is that of two accomplices in some criminal act who are being questioned separately by the police. Each is offered a reduced punishment if he confesses and implicates the other. If both remain silent, both escape punishment because neither has been indicted. If one stays silent while the other confesses, the first risks incurring the maximum punishment, an outcome which each wishes to avoid. Although co-operation would produce the best outcome for each, neither can risk relying on the other and so it is rational for each to confess, even though the outcome achieved is not the optimal one.

A public good, as already noted, is defined as something which requires some effort or cost to bring about but which, once obtained, is enjoyed by all. But control of inflation is not like, for example, a public park which could be funded by a single wealthy benefactor. Many public goods, including control of inflation, require collective action in order to bring them about. If a curb on wage pressures contributes to control of inflation, all unions must co-operate in this strategy. All must bear some cost towards achieving the public good. But for any particular union, according to the assumptions of rationality involved here, there is a strong incentive to 'free-ride' on other unions' wage restraint and still to press for sectional wage increases for its own members. It could then enjoy the benefits of more stable price levels while avoiding the costs borne by the others. But this incentive is the same for all unions. The logical implication is that no union should rationally be prepared to risk the costs of restraint. Appeals by policy-makers for a consensual approach to economic problems do nothing to address this impasse.

Of course it is possible to deny that the control of inflation *is* a public good for trade unions and their members and to argue that any incomes policy is exclusively an instrument 'related to certain basic imperatives or needs of capitalism to reproduce the conditions for its existence and continually to accumulate further resources' (Schmitter, 1979: 24). This is a view shared by Marxist or neo-Marxist authors (e.g. Jessop, 1978, 1979; Panitch, 1976, 1979, 1981; see also the discussion of these authors in Crouch, 1979b). An argument which often follows is therefore that trade unions can only become involved in negotiated agreements with employers and government as a strategy of despair during periods of economic crisis, when the state backs employers' interests to secure stabilization. A Michelsian analysis may also be drawn upon to explain the apparent 'incorporation' of the trade union leadership into the opposing class and its values, and internal union discipline may be regarded as an aspect of its oligarchical control over the membership (Sabel, 1981). Thus concertative policies and the neo-corporatist integration of economic interests in the political process are by definition opposed to the true interests of workers and necessarily entail 'zero-sum' outcomes. Industrial militancy ought not to be relinquished at the level of the workplace, and the trade union movement and the political parties representing labour interests are generally seen as properly operating in quite separate arenas of conflict.

But recent work by Przeworski and Wallerstein (1982) has put forward a game-theoretical analysis of labour–capital relations which casts doubt on the explanatory value of the Marxist or neo-Marxist approach. They demonstrate that under certain conditions it may be entirely rational for labour (as a collective actor) to participate in wage regulation agreements with capital in a strategy of 'positive-sum' class compromise, because it will result in medium-term outcomes for each side which are superior to those which would result from more militant bargaining strategies. Furthermore, if trade unions can act collectively, they can engage in a 'political exchange' with government (Pizzorno, 1978)—an essential feature of 'concertative' agreements. Trade unions would restrain their wage militancy, thus reducing strike levels and weakening inflationary pressures; and in exchange for this 'under-utilization of market power' public policy would be used to mediate market uncertainties. Various forms of government intervention in the economy and various aspects of social policy would be directed towards protecting other trade union interests, particularly full employment.

Moreover, during the 1960s and 1970s, no Western government succeeded in combining optimal levels of performance in all the dimensions usually looked to, such as inflation, unemployment, growth, and the balance of payments deficit (Scharpf, 1981), and they varied also in the nature of the social and welfare policies pursued (e.g. Korpi, 1983; Uusitalo, 1983). The manifest priorities of governments must of course be seen as the product of distinctive political processes within the constraints of different class con-figurations and different political and economic institutional arrangements (Keohane, 1978; Scharpf, 1981; Esping-Andersen and Friedland, 1982). But the Marxist or neo-Marxist position does not offer an adequate account of the empirically observable variations in performance in different countries. Recent cross-national studies of economic performance have provided evidence of the advantages which may accrue to labour through engaging in concertative policies. These studies have suggested, among other things, that it may be possible simultaneously to protect employ-ment levels *and* control the rate of inflation during recession (Cameron, 1984; Schmidt, 1981, 1982; Allsopp, 1982; Johannesson and Schmid, 1980; see also Schmitter, 1981). Again, comparative studies of Britain and Sweden have contrasted the dominance of private capital and the political influence of the working class in the two countries, to the advantage of the latter with its concertative policies (Scase, 1977; Castles, 1978; see also Edgren, Faxén, and Odhner, 1973; Martin, 1979; Crouch, 1980). The implications of such contrasts have led some to conclude that in the advanced Western societies a peaceful 'transition to socialism' could be effected (Stephens, 1979). The projection of an untroubled transition to socialism certainly under-estimates the structural limitations to such a strategy within a capitalist economy. But it helps to draw attention to the degree to which the 'fulcrum of the see-saw' of relative advantage may be shifted through the conjunction of political and economic action by organized labour and its political allies (Hodgson, 1982).

These considerations thus support the view that, contrary to Marxist claims, it may under certain conditions be to the advantage of organized labour to participate in bargained agreements of a concertative sort. This strategy may therefore be seen as a 'positive-sum game'. If, then, union control of wage militancy can be a public good for labour, and trade unions' participation in concertative arrangements is not necessarily to their disadvantage, the question follows of what those conditions might be. This will be discussed shortly. But first the trade unions' version of the 'prisoners' dilemma' must be considered in more detail.

The Logic of Trade Union Action

Rational self-interest paradoxically produces sub-optimal collective outcomes. If the prisoners in the 'prisoners' dilemma' could rely on one another, the best outcome for each could be obtained. The solution lies in having recourse to a norm. 'Honour among thieves' is such a norm. If each prisoner knew that the other subscribed to that norm, both could select the optimizing but high-risk course of action, that is, remain silent. The norm would have a better chance of being observed if it was also backed by some sanction, enforced by the 'community of thieves'. If there existed a generalized sanction, then observance of the norm would not merely be a matter of personal trust between two individuals, but could be included with greater confidence in their respective rational deliberations.

It is not altogether obvious which norm, or ideology, would provide a solution to the trade unions' problem of collective action. The trade unions' problem is that the advantage potentially to be obtained through participation in a collective anti-inflation strategy might never come about because it is not rational for any individual union to participate, and even if many participate it is still rational to seek to free-ride on the efforts of others.

One solution sometimes suggested is an appeal to patriotism and the national interest. In this view, trade union members would be inspired by a dedication to the common good to forgo their own perceived interests. But this assumes away the free-rider problem instead of analysing how it might be overcome. There would seem to be little grounds for believing that this naively optimistic view would prevail. Another solution might be to suggest that trade union leaderships should impose compliance on their recalcitrant memberships. But this, too, would be a problematic solution. The trade union federation, it is true, must have sufficient authority to be able to commit its membership to the course of action implied by the 'political exchange', and it is likely that this would require some ability to override dissident views (cf. Sabel, 1981). The inclination to free-ride will probably persist for those in the strongest labour-market positions or most profitable industrial sectors who stand to lose most and gain least in relative terms from a strategy of political exchange. But, although the activities of trade unions may be supported by various statutory measures, in liberal democracies they are voluntary associations, not coercive or authoritarian associations. Unless the federation's strategy were also perceived as legitimate by the mass of the membership of affiliated unions, defections from its strategy and its authority would quickly occur. Its strategy must be capable of commanding the assent of the membership.

However, it may be noted that if a strategy of bargained 'class compromise' can produce public goods for labour collectively there may be no fundamental opposition between individual workers' preferences and the collective strategy. Lange (1984) has developed the argument as to why it may be individually as well as collectively rational for workers to support their unions' involvement in wage regulation. He contends that the 'game' of wage regulation is not a one-off game. It is '*just one in a series of bargains* (wage-regulating and not) between unions and employers' (Lange, 1984: 102, emphasis in original). The 'iteratively played' game introduces the possibility of envisaging medium- to long-term outcomes instead of one-off outcomes. This alters the rational calculus and broadens the strategic possibilities for each individual because 'it means that players can, rationally, play *contingently co-operative* strategies' (Lange, 1984: 103, emphasis in original). The rational commitment of 'conditional players' to participate depends on the material benefits which follow and the degree of certainty with which their attainment can be expected, while the possibility of communication between individuals, over time, means that participation does not depend solely on the structure of the pay-offs in the present game. If enough contingently conditional players find that participation will satisfy their rational self-interests, a 'largely cooperative equilibrium could be established . . . and a wage-regulation outcome could be stabilised' (Lange, 1984: 103).

Lange's analysis sets out the rational grounds for employees' participation in a wage regulation policy which contributes to the 'politics of the virtuous circle', that is, where 'wage regulation becomes part of a mutually reinforcing relationship between policies which support economic growth and the expansion of social welfare programmes, labour restraint in the market, and stable, dominant electoral support for the governments involved' (Lange, 1984: 121 n. 1). The material benefits of compliance, even at an immediate cost, may then still be rationally compelling. Prior experience of the benefits of the 'virtuous circle' may help to prevent defection from the strategy. Government may make available 'side-payments', in the form of immediate fiscal or other benefits, to help strengthen the credibility and authoritative role of the trade union federation and as an indication of its own commitment to securing its side of the agreement, that is, the systematic direction of various aspects of public policy to the benefit of the working class. By the same token, if a leftist political party is in power, it may give the trade unions greater confidence in the reliability of the government's commitments.

However, the most striking feature of Lange's elaboration of the rationality of consent to wage regulation agreements is the contingency and fragility of the strategy. It depends on workers' expectations regarding future economic performance, and on the certainty with which longer-term as against short-term or one-off calculations may be made (see also Schwerin, 1979, 1981). The likelihood of improving the net benefits obtainable through political exchange will not always outweigh in the short term the benefits which significant sections of the trade union movement could with greater certainty obtain by defecting from the strategy and relying on their market strength. The longer-term perspective may keep the strategy functioning, but this depends on union members having a reasonable expectation that the benefits will eventually materialize (Przeworski, 1980b). Thus the economic climate must be propitious for growth and employment expansion, but not so certain as to invite defection with impunity. Neither must a period of recession be so severe as to bring into question the efficacy of government stabilization policies. The institutions of the state itself and the links between state and economy also have a bearing on the calculus for the same reason, since workers must have confidence in the capacity of government to perform its side of the agreement efficiently.

The logic of a functioning 'virtuous circle' may be reinforced by a form of political inertia. Once the political costs of the strategy have been negotiated and the respective commitments of unions' and employers' peak federations and government established, it may prove easier for government to continue to follow that strategy even when economic conditions have changed (Scharpf, 1984). Thus, where the trade union movement has established solid claims for labour interests, employers may wish to withdraw from the agreements during recession, but government may continue to be committed to defence of those interests, costly though this might be.

However, a virtuous circle has to be initiated in some way, and some norm or ideology is required with respect to which employees will assent to their unions' participation in a federation-wide strategy of collective action. What would seem crucial here is which reference-group they take to be of primary significance. Employees may have a range of interests arising from their market situation and employment conditions, but not all interests will be equally relevant as a focus of organization. Much depends on the political and economic circumstances in which interests acquire organizational expression (Berger, 1981a). Thus it may be said that 'identity precedes interest' (cf. Pizzorno, 1978): different collective identities will entail different bundles of perceived interests. Trade union members may be seen as having rather complex economic interests (Offe and Wiesenthal, 1980; Bowles and Eatwell, 1983). A perception of their interests in terms of class will not necessarily predominate any more than class is necessarily the most compelling basis of political identity. Several major political cleavages may be identified in Western societies, often cross-cutting one another (cf. Lipset and Rokkan, 1967), and it can be observed that 'workers' often see their political interests in other than class terms. It is also possible for workers to 'see society as composed of individuals; they view themselves as members of collectivities other than class; they behave politically on the basis of religious, ethnic, regional or some other affinity. They become Catholics, Southerners, Francophones or simply "citizens" ' (Przeworski, 1980b: 43). Correspondingly, workers may well perceive their economic interests to be defined by membership of a particular firm or industry or by possession of a particular craft or skill, or by a status-based distinction made against another group of employees.

Workers may therefore be said to have two 'orders' of economic interests. Their interests are at stake in different ways in workplace or company collective bargaining and in the priorities established in public policy. In the first case, interests are immediate and short-range and relate overwhelmingly to issues of wages and conditions of employment in particular circumstances. The collective action required to secure these gains need not be broad-based but may well be sectional and competitive with other unions' collective action. The second order of interests includes a high level of employment, a low rate of inflation, and extensive welfare provisions. These are also material interests. But they are collective interests which employees share as members of a class: they are public goods for workers. They must be obtained through collective action by an 'encompassing' organization (Olson, 1982) whose membership spans the whole class (cf. Elster, 1985: ch. 6), and through involvement in processes of political bargaining.

This distinction between two orders of interest requiring different strategies of collective action may be clarified by drawing upon Offe and Wiesenthal's (1980) work. They argue that labour and capital have different class-based logics of collective action. They argue that labour's task in articulating collective interests and engaging in collective action is more complex than that of capital. Labour's efforts to define its collective interests are refracted by the market because of its dependent position in productive relations. The most immediate, sectional interests are quite obvious, but the interests which follow from the basic capital–labour divide are less obvious and must be discovered through class-based mobilization. Thus labour has both a 'monological' and a 'dialogical' task: the former designates immediate interests and an immediate area of collective action, and the latter entails the need to forge a new collective identity and collective strategy as a class. Capital, they contend, only needs to engage in 'monological' representation of its interests. The case of employers' interests is taken up again in Chapter 6.

The ultimate solution to the problem of generating collective action involving the whole trade union movement would seem, on this analysis, to lie in an appeal to collective class-interests. Trade unions could become conditional participants in concertative agreements if they had access to an ideology capable of sustaining this 'new collective identity' (Pizzorno, 1978). Participation must still be seen as contingent upon many factors, particularly on a reasonable degree of success in obtaining the public goods in question. The trade union leadership may need to have a degree of sanctioning power in order to curb the free-riding tendencies of some groups, but neither its authoritative resources nor its ideology alone can be an adequate substitute for real 'pay-offs' to the material interests of the different sections of the trade union movement. Unless the benefits are forthcoming, the leadership and its strategy will lose their claim to legitimacy.

An abiding class-wide collective identity is, perhaps, a near-impossibility, given the primary purposes of trade unionism and the complexity of social differentiation in capitalist society. But some organizational, political, and ideological conditions may make its approximation more likely than others. The most conducive conditions will be looked at in outline in the following section.

Conditions Facilitating Concertation

The organizational conditions facilitating political linkages between functional interests and government received new attention during the 1970s in the literature on neo-corporatism (see Schmitter and Lehmbruch, 1979; Lehmbruch and Schmitter, 1982). But the term 'neo-corporatism' was used to refer to a wide variety of phenomena (Panitch, 1980; Martin, 1983a, 1983b; Crouch, 1983; Beyme, 1983). We shall confine our attention to accounts which have dealt with the conditions facilitating wage regulation agreements, or neo-corporatism understood in the sense of 'concertation'. Three features have emerged from the literature as being of particular importance (see Lehmbruch, 1984). The first is the organizational basis of unions' and employers' authoritative leadership: this may be seen as a problem of 'vertical' co-ordination. The second concerns the institutional conditions which best facilitate the negotiation of union–employer agreement in the context of government's input: this is a problem of 'horizontal' co-ordination. The third concerns the partisan colouring of the governing party or parties.

ORGANIZATIONAL FACILITATING CONDITIONS

In the last section it was argued that both the trade unions' peak federation(s) and the peak federation(s) of employers' associations must have adequate authority to be able to formulate and advance a concertative strategy in collective bargaining. This means that there must be an adequate degree of 'vertical' co-ordination of interests, or intra-organizational aggregation. The problem is likely to be greatest for the trade unions because they must redirect a tendency to engage in wage militancy towards a strategy of political bargaining. /

Headey's (1970) analysis of conditions facilitating incomes policies may be taken as a useful starting point. He put forward a set of formal conditions concerning the number of unions and the unity and centralization of the peak organization. This analysis was broadened by Schmitter (1974, 1979, 1982), among others. It was linked with the trend towards the corporatist 'intermediation' of interests in contrast with a pluralist, lobbying relationship between functional economic interests and government. The peak federations of unions and employers, it was argued, develop relations of intermediation of interests with government through which, as a result of its central and unchallenged position, each not only functions as a channel for the articulation of collective interests to government but also mobilizes its own members so as to implement the policies they had helped to make. Lehmbruch (1984) has termed 'sectoral corporatist' these linkages between the centralized interest organizations of the economic interests and government.[2] These linkages may then facilitate 'the "social partnership" of organised labour and business aimed at regulating conflicts between these groups in co-ordination with government policy' (Lehmbruch, 1984: 61).

The organizational conditions which seem to be most important for 'trans-sectoral concertation' concern both the peak union federation and the organizational structure of the trade union movement. There should be a single peak federation and it should have a monopoly on representation of trade unions. Industrial trade unions are generally regarded as most conducive to developing

[2] Recent debate about 'neo-corporatism' contributed to a critique of pluralist assumptions about the representation of interests and the institutional separation of political and economic spheres. But neither a 'sectoral corporatist' form of representation nor that related phenomenon, the 'attribution of public status to interest groups' (Offe, 1981), was new in itself. Monopoly representation and a 'public status' had long been the objective of many interest groups, and this tendency had previously been noted by authors writing within the pluralist tradition (e.g. Eckstein, 1960; Martin, 1980).

a centralized collective strategy. Not only are there likely to be relatively few unions to mobilize, but in industrial unions sectional differences between occupational groups are easier to contain within the organization. The problems of union aggregation may therefore be reduced where the bases of union differentiation are least complex. A high membership density is desirable so the trade union movement will have significant organizational strength in the economy, and so the federation can aspire to an 'encompassing' character. ⁄

Korpi, (1978, 1983) and Korpi and Shalev (1979, 1980) gave an explicitly class-theoretical rationale for these organizational conditions. Industrial unionism, in their view, by facilitating the federation's central co-ordination of the trade union movement, offers the best possible organizational conditions for class-action. These organizational conditions thus maximize the 'capacity for strategy' (Pizzorno, 1978) of the trade union movement.

Some qualification might be entered concerning the need for a single trade union federation. In Italy, for example, the three union federations have succeeded at times in devising a common strategy and thus in overcoming the disadvantages of multiplicity (Regini and Esping-Anderson, 1980; Regini, 1982, 1984; Lange, Ross and Vannicelli, 1982). The formal structures appear in this case to have been less important than the political will to pursue a particular strategy. However, organizational features are an important limiting factor to the chances of success of a centralized collective strategy. It would appear that the 'vertical' co-ordination of interests is most effective when the organization is highly structured and when the authoritative role of the trade union leadership is supported by the organizational conditions outlined above.

INSTITUTIONAL FACILITATING CONDITIONS

Institutionalized tripartism has often been taken to be the distinguishing feature of concertative agreements, not least by policy-makers anxious to produce 'consensus' between unions, employers, and government. But the existence of formal tripartite arrangements does not necessarily mean that they function as an integral part of the policy process, and offers relatively little guidance to understanding how decisions are really made (Lehmbruch, 1982, 1984). Negotiation of concertative agreements may be said to be consensus-orientated, but these are first and foremost bargained agreements. The bargaining process, between unions and employers and between unions and government, is not necessarily best promoted by formal institutional frameworks.

Formal institutional structures may play a useful part, none the less, at one stage in the whole process. Concertative policies are not consensual in any straightforward sense. But there is a sense in which 'consensus' of a sort may be important, that is, in defining the economic problems which need to be addressed. It is important that employers and unions should share a view of these issues which leaves their respective policy priorities within negotiating distance of one another. It may therefore be useful (though not essential) to have available formal channels for discussing and monitoring economic performance.

A survey of the process of 'horizontal' co-ordination in different countries produces fewer reliable generalizations about facilitating conditions than the above examination of intra-organizational 'vertical' co-ordination. The process of 'horizontal' co-ordination involved in the negotiation of a concertative agreement may be very differently achieved in different societies. Lehmbruch (1979*b*) distinguishes, for example, between 'two-step' bargaining and 'one-step' bargaining. In the former case the 'autonomous groups' first bargain among themselves and this is followed later by bargaining with government; but in the latter case these steps are merged in a 'one-step' bargaining process where government serves actively as a mediator. Indeed the distinctive feature of concertative agreements is the role of the state in the mediation of conflict between employers and labour through its input to centralized negotiations. It may be easiest for government to facilitate a bargained agreement between the two federations if they already have 'sectoral corporatist' links in the policy process. The government thus makes possible a 'trans-sectoral concertation' of interests (Lehmbruch, 1984).

Overall, it would appear that the most effective arrangements are those where institutionalization is minimal and the maximum flexibility is available to secure the trade-offs and mutual commitments needed. Where the 'vertical' co-ordination of interests is well established and the peak federations are disposed to engage in a concertative strategy, the political problems of working it out can be tackled in a number of different ways, depending on the wider institutional features and political culture of the society in question. Formally institutionalized tripartism is one possible forum for this process. But it is neither the only nor necessarily the most effective one (see Lehmbruch, 1982, 1984). Sweden and Austria, for example, each combine 'vertical' formality with 'horizontal' informality, in different ways (see, for example, Korpi, 1978; Marin, 1983). 'Horizontal' co-ordination depends upon effective prior 'vertical' co-ordination, but once that condition is met informal linkages would appear to have certain advantages over formal.

PARTY POLITICAL CONDITIONS

Efforts to systematize some of the most favourable political conditions have given rise to two models of party political arrangements, which overlap in some respects but which nevertheless represent discernibly different facilitating conditions. These may be termed the 'Social Democratic hegemony' model and the 'consociational' model. The Scandinavian countries (chiefly Sweden, but Norway and Finland as well) may be taken as examples of the first model and Austria and the Netherlands as examples of the second.

Headey (1970) may again be taken as a useful starting point for a discussion of the conditions facilitating incomes policies. He identified the participation in government of leftist political parties as a facilitating factor. The prima-facie reason seems uncontroversial, since the governing party must be willing to make various commitments both in the shape of immediate fiscal commitments and in terms of more general and long-term policy priorities. A leftist government would be expected to be more sympathetic to a concertative strategy and more committed than other parties to the consequent 'pro-worker' priorities, and to have better relations with the trade union movement.

Subsequent research extended the analysis of this association between functioning wage regulation policies and leftist parties in government (e.g. Armingeon, 1981; Cameron, 1984). Scholars also began to relate the electoral, parliamentary, and governmental strength of leftist parties to systematic differences in various aspects of public policy germane to wage regulation policies—such as the volume of government revenue and expenditure and its redistributive role (e.g. Hibbs, 1976, 1977, 1978; Cameron, 1978,

1982). A more fully worked out rationale for these relationships was provided by Korpi (1978, 1983) and Korpi and Shalev (1979, 1980). They argued that wage regulation agreements and political bargaining could together be seen as an advanced form of class-wide action to promote working-class interests. This depends on a high level of 'working-class mobilization', the organizational bases for which include effective 'vertical' co-ordination of the trade union movement and Social Democratic hegemony in parliamentary politics. The degrees of working-class mobilization in different countries could be compared according to this model, depending on how they ranked in these two dimensions. For Korpi and Shalev, then, under conditions of 'Social Democratic hegemony' wage regulation agreements were to be seen as the most effective means of advancing the collective interests of labour—a view diametrically opposed, of course, to that of the Marxists and neo-Marxists earlier discussed.

The model of wage regulation as an integral element of 'Social Democratic hegemony' was developed out of reflection primarily on the experience of the Scandinavian countries. But as a general model for explaining the conditions under which concertative agreements and wage regulation policies might be put into effect this approach over-stresses some features and underemphasizes others.[3] It is unsatisfactory as a general account in two areas in particular: first, in the exclusive interest it takes in the proportion of votes and cabinet seats obtained by leftist parties, to the exclusion of other aspects of the party political system; and, secondly, in its neglect of the nature of the links between the trade union movement and the rest of the political system.

A low level of ideological polarization of the political system may be important for the possibility of a stable understanding with both the union and the employer federations. The expectation that elected governments would be sympathetic to labour would favourably influence the trade unions' calculations about 'iterative plays' (see also Faxén, 1982); but it may be less important that a strong party of the left be in power than that the government in question be prepared to seek a concertative agreement. A relatively

---

[3] In Korpi and Shalev's index of class mobilization the key dependent variable was the incidence of strike action, since they regarded exertion of market power as a less efficient means of deploying working class power resources than action through political channels, spearheaded by the parliamentary representatives of labour interests.

stable and continuous set of policy priorities, even with changes of government, would clearly be more favourable than the dramatic oscillation of policies with the advent of opposing parties to power. Once again, it would appear that once class cleavages have been given organizational expression the political conditions in which concertative policies may be implemented are under-determined, and that more depends on what is done than on which party or type of party actually undertakes and implements the relevant commitments.

The second subject omitted from Korpi and Shalev's discussion is the nature of the connections between the trade union movement and the rest of the political system. The kind of connections they have in the 'policy universe' (see Richardson, 1982; Scharpf, 1981, 1984) may have important implications for the possibility of concertation. Among those countries which rate less well in the rank-ordering of working-class mobilization, there may be considerable differences in other features which would be more or less conducive to policies of bargained co-operation—for example, in the degree of institutional integration of the trade union movement in the industrial relations system (Gourevitch, Lange, and Martin, 1981).

The countries which present the greatest explanatory problems for Korpi and Shalev also tend to be those which fit most comfortably into a model of concertation based on consociational patterns of policy-making, the second model to be discussed here.

The characteristic feature of consociational societies, according to Lijphart (1968), is a commitment to central negotiation over political differences in societies which are deeply divided. The political cleavage may cut right across social classes. The Netherlands and Austria provided the prototypical models of consociational politics. Political negotiations were seen as conducted by élites which had a strong authoritative position with regard to their constituencies (strengthened in the Dutch case by the denominational 'pillarization' of society). During the 1970s scholars became increasingly interested in the degree to which the success of élite negotiations depended on neo-corporatist patterns of representation and a commitment to government-backed wage regulation policies (see, for example, Scholten, 1980; Lehmbruch, 1979a, 1979b). It is true that the post-war Dutch incomes policy collapsed in the 1960s (see Flanagan et al, 1982), and that this is often linked with the departure from the coalition government of the leftist political party. But other commentators have argued that the nature of the connections between the trade unions and the policy-making process continued to prevent sustained industrial militancy from developing thereafter. The model of a 'social coalition' was still relevant in the 1970s, it is argued, whereby the trade unions bargained indirectly with government while defending their own interests as devised through intra-organizational processes of aggregation (see Akkermans and Grootings, 1978: 185). The Austrian case may be seen as a more unequivocal instance of 'two-step bargaining'. This is strengthened by the relative 'functional independence' of the institutions of employer–labour negotiation which have displayed great stability through changes in government composition (Lehmbruch, 1979b; Marin, 1983).

The West German model of industry-level bargaining within the context of a 'social market economy' is different again (Markovits, 1982). Policy-making processes have tended to be highly structured and controlled (Dyson, 1982). During the 1950s and 1960s economic growth contributed to the stability of this system. But although the 'search for a new class compromise' (Müller-Jentsch and Sperling, 1978: 274–5) from the late 1960s led to increasing intra-union tensions (Streeck, 1982; Sabel, 1981; also Streeck, 1984), the case of Germany during the period of 'Konzertierte Aktion' may perhaps be likened to the model of 'consociational' concertative arrangements (see Hudson, 1980).

The 'consociational' model of concertation does not depend on a strong leftist party in government, whether alone or in coalition. But the success of the 'consociational' model would also appear to depend centrally on the parties' ability to contribute to class-compromise negotiations.

THE CONTINGENCY OF CONCERTATIVE AGREEMENTS

The different political features stressed by the Scandinavian or Social Democratic model and by the consociational model would tend to caution against any too rigid specification of prerequisites for concertative agreements. The most important facilitating conditions would appear to be adequate authority on the part of the peak federations (especially the trade unions) to commit their memberships to a consistent strategy, and an ideological disposition on the part of the unions and on the part of an adequate bloc of political opinion to engage in concertative bargaining. It would appear that class-oriented mobilization would be the most likely to secure enduring and stable agreements./But stable wage regulation agreements also depend on other variable factors. To some degree workers' expectations regarding economic performance are shaped by social institutions such as the trade unions and government, and are therefore open to moulding by the political leadership. But fluctuations in economic performance may alter expectations and consequently the chances of worker compliance. Other pressures on government policies, whether international or domestic, may have the same effect. Concertative policies may be seen to depend, therefore, on 'a variety of contingent problematic conditions' (Lange, 1984).

Given these constraints and contingencies, it may be wondered that so much effort was expended in many Western nations, at least until the recession of the early 1980s, on sustaining or initiating concertative solutions to problems of political economy. But where trade unions exerted their strength in market-based activity, 'punching their full weight' in collective bargaining (Goldthorpe, 1978), the implications for economic performance were grave, and bargaining 'games' could result in 'negative-sum outcomes'. The trade union movements of different countries did not necessarily perceive their interests to lie in participation in concertative agreements. But where they did, it was a strategy which, under certain conditions, could be to their advantage. Where trade union market power was strong, governments frequently perceived a need to seek to involve the trade unions in some form of political process on issues of economic management. One author, commenting on the constraints governments experienced in dealing with the pervasive problems of political economy in Western societies between the 1950s and the 1970s, aptly concluded that:

The alternative to collective action through class-based organization is hardly the free market in the classical sense, as one might be led to believe from much of the debate on this issue. In Western democracies, where the right to organize exists, it is collective action in some more fragmentary and differentiated form which is the alternative. (Åberg, 1984: 230.)

2

The International Context of the Irish Case

Political Adaptation in Small Open Economies

Almost all the West European countries in which neo-corporatist political arrangements have functioned successfully in the post-war period are small nations: the Scandinavian countries (Sweden, Norway, Denmark), the Low Countries (the Netherlands, Belgium) and the central European countries (Austria, and the unusual case of Switzerland). Only the Federal Republic of Germany need be added to complete the list (Schmitter, 1981; Lehmbruch, 1979b, 1982, 1984; Stephens, 1979; Cameron, 1984). The high correlation between country size and neo-corporatist political arrangements has appeared to many to be more than coincidental, and has stimulated research into the relationship between the situation of such small states in the international economy and the adaptation of domestic political structures. (On the general debate about the international influences on domestic politics, see Gourevitch, 1978; Keohane, 1978, 1984; Katzenstein, 1978; Ruggie, 1982; on small states in particular, see Katzenstein, 1980a, 1983, 1984, 1985).

Ireland is a small state with an open economy, and it may be shown that the logic of neo-corporatist or concertative adaptation was relevant to the Irish case, as well as to the other small open economies of Western Europe. But if smallness may be said to be a predisposing factor in the development of neo-corporatist practices, it is far from being a sufficient condition. Few would claim Ireland as a successful case of neo-corporatist policy-making and implementation. In this chapter, then, the logic of neo-corporatist adaptation in the Irish case is explored. Later chapters examine and explain the reasons why such adaptation was less effective than might initially have been expected.

By locating the economic difficulties of small states in the context of the international economy it is possible to identify a shared logic in the adoption of neo-corporatist practices. All too frequently small size is isolated as the chief explanatory variable and the social and political conflicts which characterize larger societies are presumed not to be particularly relevant. Small states are credited with 'mystical forms of social coherence and common purpose' (Katzenstein, 1983: 116). But the invariant factor of size cannot explain the variability of political arrangements observable across different small societies (Castles, 1978: 121). Nor can it account for the deviance from the apparent norm of stable neo-corporatism in small societies which is evinced by the case of Ireland. It is important therefore to analyse 'how power is organised' (Katzenstein, 1983) within these states, and to discuss this in the context of unequal international economic relations.

Small states share the common feature of vulnerability to changes in international economic trading conditions. Lacking a large domestic market, their industrial structure is typically quite highly export-oriented and not very diversified (although these features will vary according to the degree of openness or protection adopted, among other factors). Correspondingly, they tend to be highly dependent on imports. A marked difference is evident in small open economies between the competitive sector, much of which is strongly export-oriented and most of which is exposed to competition at world prices on the domestic market, and the sheltered sector of non-tradable goods. This high degree of exposure to international trade fluctuations increases the cost of distributional conflict and of failure to adjust domestic industrial and economic strategy. The economic structure presents conditions such that the politics of 'class compromise' may offer advantages over other possible strategies for each of the major actors. Hence the small open economies have mostly adopted a strategy of support for international liberalization of trade allied with a domestic strategy of 'compensation' (Katzenstein, 1983, 1984) through increased state intervention in economic management.

The question why it should be that small states seem to share a common tendency toward devising concertative arrangements has produced diverse and not always compelling explanations. In the preceding chapter it was argued that far from depending solely on the innate social coherence of a society, or on a patriotic sense of common national purpose, concertative arrangements depend primarily on the adequacy of the organizational, political, and ideological conditions to support a strategy of concertation on the part of all relevant actors. Thus authors such as Ingham (1974) and

Cameron (1978, 1982, 1984), who look to intervening variables between the small size or openness of an economy and the development of neo-corporatist practices, are closer to providing adequate causal explanations, because these variables can then be seen as the product of strategic responses by the various economic actors.

The smallness and openness of the economy provide the context within which certain sorts of economic difficulties may be experienced. But the manner in which different societies adapt to these pressures may vary. The political and economic interests within a society are faced with a changing set of constraints and opportunities within which they formulate their strategy. But they do so in a context shaped by earlier decisions and existing organizational and political interest in the 'foundation conditions' of concertative strategies. Lehmbruch (1984), as noted in Chapter 1, has stressed that the success of a concertative strategy depends fundamentally on employers and unions sharing, to some degree, a frame of reference within which economic problems are analysed, such that unions' and employers' analyses are within negotiating distance of one another. It has been argued that in many countries, the bases for post-war concertative policies were laid down during the 1930s and 1940s, when the experience of shared crisis (for example, the Depression, Fascism, war, or occupation) sharpened the sense of national vulnerability (Maier, 1984; Katzenstein, 1983, 1984). Such experiences contributed to a clear preference on the part of unions and employers respectively for avoiding the real possibility of 'negative-sum outcomes', and a commitment to bargained co-operation to achieve 'positive-sum outcomes' in economic management. In some cases the new orientation was strengthened by a prior tradition of accommodation of ethnic or religious cleavages through élite negotiation and compromise.

It is sometimes argued that the scale of economic activity in small economies is conducive to concertation, because it makes the functioning of the economy more 'transparent' to the trade unions. The damaging consequences of unrestrained industrial militancy are more easily perceived and thus further incentive is given to devise suitable alternative policies. Once a neo-corporatist strategy has been established, small societies are expected to find relatively little difficulty in maintaining effective policy networks. Communication may easily be sustained, much of it through face-to-face encounters.

The precise form of the strategy of adaptation to external economic conditions will vary from one country to the next. The formation of what may be termed the 'dominant strategy' depends to a considerable extent on the nature of trade union organization and its political orientation, which was discussed in Chapter 1; it also depends on the coherence and degree of organization of employers' interests. Thus, more generally, the dominant strategy of political adaptation to economic pressures depends on the composition and orientation of the 'social coalitions' in each country and the terms on which they are established historically (Esping-Andersen and Friedland, 1982). The nature of social coalitions depends to some degree, of course, on the industrial structure in relation to which classes were formed. The pattern of interest organization should therefore be understood in the context of the nature and phasing of industrialization (Ingham, 1974; Esping-Andersen, 1985; Hardiman, 1987a, 1987b). Furthermore, the industrial and economic structure itself presents a set of constraints which tend to favour some strategies relatively more than others.

The concentration of industry may facilitate the centralization of both trade unions and employers' associations (Ingham, 1984; Windmuller and Gladstone, 1976; Stephens, 1979: ch. 4). Industrial concentration is likely to be associated with an internationally-oriented business community, high export intensities, and an 'offensive' approach to competition and industrial adaptation. These features have been identified in the cases of Sweden, the Netherlands, and Switzerland. A greater concentration of traditional industries and low-value-added services may be associated with a relatively greater reliance on domestic markets and a somewhat greater reliance on industrial protection. Countries sharing these features are Austria, Denmark, and Norway (Katzenstein, 1980). There is no direct correlation between industrial structure, social coalitions, and the prevailing policy 'mix' adopted within each country. But the structure of the economy is important as a constraining variable, underlying the organizational opportunities and 'capacity for strategy' (Pizzorno, 1978) of the trade union movement and shaping the possibilities for social coalitions in concertative arrangements.

Notwithstanding these differences, the small states of Western Europe experience common pressures to adapt domestic political structures to withstand the rigours of international trade. Most of the small open economies have responded with some sort of integrated policy network linking state and society through a concertative approach to pay determination.

The Irish Case: An Introduction

Ireland, like other small open economies, encountered pressures to adapt domestic political structures in response to the competitive demands of the international economy. The growing openness of the Irish economy in the course of the 1960s and 1970s provided a strong incentive to devise new patterns of collective bargaining, as will be seen later in this chapter. Furthermore, several features of the political and social structure would appear to have been conducive to the reorientation of collective bargaining along concertative lines.

Ireland is a small society, the population of which totalled slightly less than three and a half million in the late 1970s. It is ethnically and religiously homogeneous, as a consequence of the partition of Ireland in 1920, prior to the establishment of an independent state (later the Republic) in the twenty-six counties. It is a society in which informal networks of communication can easily be maintained. Moreover, the observation is frequently made that, in contrast with Britain for example, class differences are less systematically reinforced by symbols of social status (such as accent or type of schooling). This may be attributable, in some measure, to an egalitarian strain in Irish nationalism; it is often cited as a feature of Irish society which facilitates informal relations between politicians and the leadership of the various economic interests.

THE STRUCTURE OF ECONOMIC INTERESTS

If, as Chapter 1 suggested, the existence of single peak federations on both the trade union and the employer sides is conducive to developing bargained neo-corporatist agreements, then Ireland would appear to be in as good a position as many other West European countries, if not better, to facilitate these kinds of agreements.[1]

[1] Agricultural interests are not discussed in this work because their relation with government took a very different form on the whole, particularly during the 1970s when farm prices were negotiated for the EEC as a whole and farmers' interests tended to centre on the terms and conditions of the EEC's Common Agricultural Policy.

A single federation, the Irish Congress of Trade Unions (ICTU), accounts for almost all trade union members in the Republic—only 5–7 per cent of trade union members in the 1970s belonged to unions which were not affiliated to ICTU. Trade union density, that is, actual trade union membership as a proportion of all potential members, was quite high in comparative terms (see Chapter 5). No ideological or confessional differences divided the trade union movement. It had divided into two federations in the mid-1940s, primarily on issues related to the status and organizing rights of the long-established unions with head offices in Britain. But work towards reconciliation was relatively quickly undertaken, and the trade union movement was reunified in 1959. Throughout the 1960s and 1970s ICTU was the sole recognized federation, representing the trade union movement in relations with government and with employers.

On the employers' side, a single overarching federation of employers' associations, the Irish Employers' Confederation (IEC), was established in the late 1960s. This was intended to be the employers' equivalent to ICTU; it was given a particular brief to engage in centralized collective bargaining. Over the course of the 1970s, however, the IEC was a fairly loosely constituted body, and the individual employers' associations retained their own identity and autonomy. The dominant employers' body for purposes of collective bargaining and industrial relations was unquestionably the Federated Union of Employers (FUE), and the FUE tended to play a leading role in the IEC (see Chapter 6).

POLITICAL PARTIES

Although Ireland has no strong leftist party, several features of its political system would seem to approximate to other conditions which, as Chapter 1 argued, may be equally conducive to a neo-corporatist pattern of wage formation. Three main parties dominated party politics from the early 1930s; from the late 1950s to the 1980s the smallest parties disappeared from the political scene and the three main parties were the only ones represented in the Dáil or parliament. General elections must be held at least every five years in accordance with the Constitution, but throughout the 1960s and 1970s they were held at regular four-yearly intervals. In the four elections of 1965, 1969, 1973, and 1977 the three main parties won between 97 per cent and 99 per cent of all seats (Chubb, 1982: 101).

The main leftist party, the Labour Party, has always been by far the smallest of the three main parties. Of the two larger parties, Fianna Fáil has always been the largest and Fine Gael the second largest, ever since the consolidation of the party system in the late 1920s and early 1930s. The relative extents of support for the three parties varied somewhat over time, but never enough to alter their respective positions in terms of parliamentary strength (see Gallagher, 1976, 1985; Manning, 1972; O'Leary, 1979).

Fianna Fáil is not only the single largest party, it is also hitherto the only party which may expect to win a majority of seats and form a government alone. The Irish party system is, in Sartori's terms, a 'predominant party system' (Sartori, 1976: 192–201). In the period of fifty years between 1932 and 1981 Fianna Fáil formed the government for thirty-eight, including two uninterrupted spans of sixteen years each (1932–48 and 1957–73). Over this period the only realistic alternative to unbroken Fianna Fáil rule was coalition between Fine Gael and the Labour Party. Two such coalition governments held power, with the support of minor parties, between 1948 and 1957 (1948–51 and 1954–7), and a Fine Gael–Labour Party coalition formed the government between 1973 and 1977.[2]

The cleavage structure of Irish politics is unusual compared with other European countries, and is discussed further in Chapter 7. Social class plays a minor role in structuring political behaviour, as the small size of the Labour Party testifies. The principal divide between the two larger parties originated in the nationalist and constitutional conflicts which accompanied the foundation of the state in 1922. Both parties were formed as a consequence of the split in the nationalist Sinn Féin movement, a split which resulted in bitter civil war in 1922–3. The civil war cleavage cut across class divisions. During the 1960s and 1970s, although there were some systematic differences in the bases of support for each party and in the prevailing images of Fianna Fáil and Fine Gael, no fundamental ideological differences divided the two parties.

The OECD, in its annual *Economic Surveys* of the Irish economy, regularly exhorted the Irish government to address

[2] Fine Gael–Labour Party coalitions have also held power twice in the 1980s (June 1981–Feb. 1982 and Nov. 1982–Mar. 1987).

economic problems through promotion of a prices and incomes policy. In its view Ireland was 'as well-suited to developing such a policy as other small nations of Western Europe such as Austria, the Netherlands and the Scandinavian countries'. The features specifically noted as being conducive in the Irish case included the 'absence of entrenched ideological positions', the weakness of a class-based cleavage in the political system, and the smallness and conservatism of the left in Irish politics; these conditions, according to the *Economic Survey* of 1973, made possible the sort of 'excellent informal relations between the social partners' which should facilitate a centralized, bargained consensus (OECD, 1973: 46).

It will become clear in the course of the present study that the conditions identified here might not be as conducive as supposed by the OECD to the successful negotiation of concertative agreements. But the case argued by the OECD complemented governments' own analyses. From the 1960s on each government subscribed to the view that a closer integration of pay policy with overall economic management objectives was desirable. In the course of the 1970s, therefore, government came to play a more active role in facilitating the conclusion of centralized agreements, through the implication of budgetary concessions and government policy commitments in the terms on which pay agreements were concluded. Both the Coalition government which held power between 1973 and 1977 and the Fianna Fáil government which took office in 1977 thus adopted an approach which may be seen to be consistent with the logic of concertation; in other words, they shared a 'concertative intent'. A basic ideological continuity was thus apparent across both governments.

The Economic Context of Pay Policy in Ireland

The reasons why a concertative intent was most highly favoured by Irish governments during the 1970s may be clarified by examining the context in which they formulated economic policy. Drawing on the lines of analysis set out above, it can be seen that trade liberalization altered the context of domestic policy formation and wage determination. From the late 1950s on government policy was committed to effecting the progressive integration of the Irish economy into the broader European economy. The changed orientation of economic policies contributed to a rapid transformation in the structure of the Irish economy and Irish society (see Rottman and O'Connell, 1982a). Thus Ireland came to experience many of the economic pressures common to small open economies, and the need to adapt some of its domestic structures, particularly in the area of wage regulation, began to become apparent. As in the case of other small open economies, the logic of concertation appeared to have certain advantages as a means of overcoming the consequences of distributive conflict.

TRADE LIBERALIZATION AND ECONOMIC ADAPTATION

Towards the end of the 1950s the Irish government initiated a major departure in economic policy, substituting trade liberalization for protectionism. At this time the Irish economy was still protected by high tariff barriers. Agricultural produce accounted for the greater part of exports. The long post-war boom was producing rapid growth in other Western economies, but the Irish economy was stagnating and the annual rate of emigration rose to an average of more than fourteen per thousand of population during the 1950s (see Meenan, 1970: 206). The small industrial sector chiefly served the domestic market, and in the absence of much foreign competition was commonly recognized to be inefficient and undynamic.

The decision to embark upon this new policy of trade liberalization was taken at a time when other changes likely to affect Ireland's trading relations were taking place. In the latter part of the 1950s Britain was negotiating for membership of the European Economic Community (EEC). It seemed that if Britain joined Ireland would have little option but to join as well, given the very high level of dependence on the British economy at this time. Throughout the period since the independence of the state in 1922 the Irish economy had been closely linked with that of Britain. This was evident not only in the monetary union whereby the Irish pound was maintained at parity with sterling, but also in the fact that Britain was overwhelmingly the most important trading partner, and in the free mobility of both capital and labour between Ireland and Britain. But whether or not Britain joined the EEC considerable adjustments to trade liberalization would be needed by Irish industry.

The new approach in economic policy was directed towards the progressive integration of the Irish economy into the international economy.[3] Full free trade with Britain was accomplished by 1966. In 1973 the accession of Ireland, along with Britain and Denmark, to the EEC, resulted in free trade with member countries, with certain limited exceptions during the specified adjustment period. Greater freedom of trade was intended to stimulate greater domestic competition and hence more rapid growth (see Chubb and Lynch, 1969; Donaldson, 1966; Fitzgerald, 1968; Kennedy and Foley, 1978; Bristow, 1979). Central to the growth strategy was the reorganization of Ireland's industrial policy, involving an increase in the incentives provided for direct capital investment (see Bew and Patterson, 1982; Raymond, 1983; Whitaker, 1983a). Particular reliance was placed on attracting foreign investment, since Ireland had traditionally had a marked insufficiency of native investment capital. Direct grant-aid and generous company tax-relief measures were the principal incentives made available to overseas investors. Foreign companies which came to Ireland during the 1960s were also attracted by the relatively low wage rates which prevailed at that time. And Ireland's membership of the EEC proved an additional investment incentive in the next decade, as foreign companies could thus gain access to European markets.

Industrial policy brought about far-reaching changes in the composition of industry over the course of the 1970s. Because of these, the need for a new form of collective bargaining was felt all the more acutely; but at the same time the nature of the industrial transformation itself created new constraints on the strategies that were possible in the realm of collective bargaining. The main features of industrial change are set out in the following paragraphs, and the implications are traced in the course of the coming chapters.

CHANGES IN THE STRUCTURE OF ECONOMIC ACTIVITY

The new orientation of economic and industrial policies resulted in rapid shifts in the pattern of economic activity in Ireland. Whereas

[3] Development plans included a modest degree of economic 'programming', specifications for which were set out in the Programmes for Economic Expansion. The need for more joint consultation was stressed in the early planning documents. Tripartite consultative bodies established in the early 1960s included the Committee on Industrial Organisation (CIO), the Employer–Labour Conference (ELC), the Irish National Productivity Committee (INPFC), and the National Industrial and Economic Council (NIEC).

in the early 1960s Ireland was still a country primarily reliant on agriculture and small-scale industry oriented to the domestic market, by the end of the 1970s manufacturing industry and services had greatly increased in importance, both in terms of overall employment and in terms of the proportion of GNP accounted for by each sector. Table 2.1 shows the changing composition of employment over the period in question. Agriculture experienced continuous decline in absolute numbers involved as well as in the proportion of the total labour force accounted for. The numbers engaged in manufacturing increased steadily until 1980, but after that date they began to decline as unemployment mounted. Services grew most rapidly, as may be seen in Table 2.2. A striking feature of this development is that most of this expansion occurred in the public sector (including public administration, defence, health, and education services, but excluding commercial semi-state bodies). This is a reflection of the growth in public sector expenditure as a proportion of GNP, which will be examined further in Chapter 4. The rate of increase of public sector employment was high in relation to overall employment growth, though the trend roughly matches that in other OECD countries during this period (Conniffe and Kennedy, 1984: 261). Total employment in services grew by 12% between 1961 and 1971, but in the public sector it grew by 28% and in other sectors by 6%. A similar trend is evident during the 1970s: total services employment grew by 30%, but public services employment grew by 56% and other services by 18%. These data help to explain why public sector pay came to assume greater direct importance for government,

TABLE 2.1. *Sectoral Composition of the Workforce in 1961, 1971, 1981 (%)*

	1961	1971	1981
Agriculture	34	24	16
Manufacturing	18	22	21
Building	6	7	7
Services	38	42	47
Total employed	96	95	91
Unemployed	4	5	9
TOTAL	100	100	100
N ('000s)	1060.2	1079.9	1264.0

Source: Adapted from Conniffe and Kennedy, 1984: 11.

TABLE 2.2. *Employment in Services in 1961, 1971, 1981 (%)*

	1961	1971	1981
Public services	29	33	40
Other services	71	67	60
Total services	100	100	100
N ('000s)	405.2	454.3	590.0

Source: Conniffe and Kennedy, 1984: 11.

because of its implications for levels of current expenditure; this issue will be taken up again in Chapter 4.

The apparently less dramatic increase in employment within the manufacturing sector conceals extensive change in the composition of industrial employment.[4] Over the period in question the extent of reliance on direct foreign investment contributed to the differential development of manufacturing industry. It contributed to the emergence of what have been seen as two sectors in manufacturing, a high-profit sector, strongly orientated to export, and a relatively low-profit sector which was mainly orientated to the domestic market. While it would be over-simple to identify these sectors exclusively with foreign and domestic ownership respectively, most of the industry which had developed during the protectionist period was Irish-owned, and the 'new' export industries which were built up during the 1970s were largely foreign-owned.

Within the Irish-owned sector, the older 'traditional' industries included many low-wage, labour-intensive employments and were usually not very technologically sophisticated. These were the industries most exposed to the effects of free trade—food, footwear, textiles, clothing, and furniture among others. During the 1970s indigenously-owned industry accounted for the greater part of total industrial employment (though the proportion declined somewhat from three-quarters at the start of the decade to two-thirds by 1980, due to the growth in levels of employment in the foreign-owned sector). But the composition of indigenously-owned industry changed somewhat over time. By 1980 about one-quarter of employment in Irish-owned manufacturing industry was in sectors which formed part of the 'new' industrial base, principally

[4] The following paragraphs draw extensively from information presented in NESC Report No. 64 (1982).

in metals and engineering, but also in chemicals and other industries. Besides, some firms in the 'traditional' industries, in which employment levels were declining overall, managed to adapt to free-trading conditions and to expanded export opportunities.

Much of the new multinational investment came from 1973 onwards, following Ireland's accession to EEC membership. In a major study of industrial policy undertaken in the early 1980s it was found that over 80% of the foreign companies surveyed came to Ireland 'primarily because it provided a tax shelter for penetrating the EEC' (NESC, 1982: 135; see also Moore, Rhodes, and Tarling, 1978). A relatively small foreign-owned sector had developed in Ireland during the protectionist period, particularly in the food and automobile industries, but many of these firms closed following the advent of free trade between Britain and Ireland in the mid-1960s and EEC entry in the 1970s. In 1973 foreign-owned firms were responsible for just over one-quarter of total manufacturing employment, a share which grew to about one-third in 1980 (the number increased from about 58,000 people to about 80,000). This foreign investment was concentrated in 'new' industries such as electronics, engineering, chemicals, pharmaceuticals, and information technology.

During the 1970s both domestic and foreign-owned industry experienced similar proportions of job losses; the rate of creation of new employment in existing firms was about the same in domestic and foreign-owned companies. But a proportionately higher level of extra employment was generated by new projects from foreign-owned companies. These new projects came mostly from American, British, German, and Dutch companies. The American share of total employment in foreign-owned firms increased rapidly during the 1970s, from just over one-quarter in 1973 to two fifths in 1980.[5] Thus prospects for employment expansion in the 1970s seemed to depend to an important degree on Ireland's success in attracting new foreign, especially American, investment. This consideration was never far from the forefront of government statements on pay and industrial relations developments in the course of the decade.

[5] Between 1974 and 1978 the average rate of return on US manufacturing investments in Ireland was 29.9%, over twice the EEC and world averages. (US Dept. of Commerce, Survey of Current Business, Aug. 1979; information from the IDA).

The move to free trade and the heavy reliance on foreign investment did not result in any dramatic concentration of industry. Much indigenous industry was quite small-scale anyway, and few of the new projects were large employers by international standards. Besides, the thrust of industrial policy was away from low-grade, labour-intensive employment. More highly-skilled, sustainable industrial employment was preferred by the Industrial Development Authority (IDA), the state-sponsored body which co-ordinated promotional campaigns and administered the grant-aid schemes. However, the new industries tended not to develop integrated production units in Ireland, and research and development and other functions tended to be located elsewhere. With its small domestic market, Ireland was more attractive to foreign companies as a manufacturing 'satellite' for the EEC market, and the nature of employment opportunities created tended to reflect that orientation. Thus when compared with the very rough characterization of the typical industrial structures of other small European economies in the first section of this chapter, it can be seen that Ireland represents an intermediate case, since the process of rapid growth and industrialization resulted in the development of two industrial sectors with rather different profiles.

The industrialization of the 1960s and especially the 1970s also resulted in a dramatic shift in the composition of exports and in the nature of the product markets in which firms were competing. Table 2.3 shows the aggregate change across all industries, and indicates that the value of manufactured goods increased greatly while a decline occurred in the share of commodities such as cattle and food-products, which tended to be lower value-added products, in the total value of exports. But the expansion in manufacturing exports came disproportionately from the newer foreign-owned

TABLE 2.3. *Composition of Merchandise Exports, 1961 and 1983* (%)

	1961	1983
Live animals and food	61	25
Beverages and tobacco	4	3
Raw materials, fuel, oils	9	5
Manufactured goods (non-food)	18	62
Other	8	5
TOTAL	100	100

Source: Croughan, 1984: 35.

companies. Foreign-owned companies tended to export a high proportion of total production, averaging about 75% in 1979. Irish-owned industry, on the whole, exported about 30% of total production (National Planning Board, 1984: 6; NESC, 1982: 295). The latter figure conceals significant variations across Irish-owned companies, since these firms were spread across sectors experiencing very different competitive conditions, including those fully subject to international competition, those subject to low-wage competition, and non-traded businesses.

Thus the liberalization of trade and the reliance on foreign investment resulted in rapid changes in the pattern of industrial ownership, the structure of industrial employment, and the export orientation of Irish industry. It seems clear that in the course of the 1970s the competitive sector of Irish industry became quite diverse with respect to the market situations in which different businesses operated (see Stewart, 1976).

PAY POLICY AND THE SMALL OPEN ECONOMY

The 'small open economy' model won widespread acceptance among Irish professional economists and policy-makers in the course of the 1970s. There has been some debate concerning which assumptions in the 'pure' model may stand and which must be relaxed (see, for example, Honohan, 1982). Nevertheless, this model has been adopted as the most appropriate and most coherent account of the economy in the 1970s. The ratio of imports and exports to GNP was very high. Foreign trade was already quite important for Ireland during the protectionist period; during the period between 1949 and 1961 the average annual value of imported goods and services amounted to 40% of GNP, and that of exports to 37% of GNP (Kennedy and Dowling, 1975: 38). By 1976 the ratios of imports and exports to GNP were respectively 55% and 47%, and these ratios stood at 67% and 53% respectively in 1980 (National Income and Expenditure data, 1984). These were higher ratios than in any country outside the small city-states of the developing world (Colm McCarthy, 1979: 201).

Irish manufacturing was, on the whole, highly exposed to international trading conditions on the domestic market as well as on foreign markets. The great majority of Irish manufactured goods were price takers rather than price setters on the world market, although as we have seen in the preceding paragraphs the nature of the competitive conditions varied across companies and across sectors. On the other hand, non-traded goods and various services were 'sheltered' from the trading conditions experienced by those businesses in the 'exposed', competitive sector. The Irish economy in the 1970s has, on these grounds, been termed 'one of the closest real-world approximations to the textbook "small, open economy" ' (Colm McCarthy, 1979: 202).

Ireland therefore experienced strong pressures to adopt a politically mediated form of wage determination. Industrial competitiveness may be seen to be vital for the economic adjustment of such economies to the rigours of international trade. Wage costs were central to the competitiveness of large sections of Irish industry, particularly the labour-intensive industries. But even in the capital-intensive, export-orientated sector the rate of increase of money wages, and the incidence of industrial action, were of no little importance for overall competitiveness. Moreover, because of the central role of industrial policy in economic development and the heavy reliance on attracting foreign investment, public policy was directed towards minimizing strikes and restraining the rate of pay increases. Even if potential investors were high-wage employers, it was held that a poor record in industrial relations and manifestly high rates of wage inflation would be a deterrent to their investment decisions.

There were other features of the Irish economy which led to pay policy being made central to government efforts at economic management. The close links with the British economy limited the range of policy instruments available to government to stimulate growth and increase employment. A fixed exchange rate kept the Irish pound at parity with sterling, until 1979 when Ireland joined the European Monetary System (EMS) but Britain did not. Monetary policy was therefore closely tied to that of Britain. The structural limitations to government's policy instruments will be discussed further in Chapter 4. But, most importantly in the present context, they had the consequence of heightening the relevance of pay policy for efforts to contain the effects of distributive conflict on economic performance. The logic of this analysis and its relevance for industrial competitiveness may be seen most clearly in two instances: first, the control of inflation, and second, employment expansion.

The 'importation' of the British rate of inflation under the regime of exchange rate parity between the two countries meant that the Irish rate of inflation could not diverge significantly from the British in the long run (McDowell, 1975; Geary, 1976; see OECD *Economic Survey*, 1981: 37). The British rate of inflation was transmitted through increased import costs, both of raw materials and of finished goods, and through the free mobility of factors of production between the two countries.[6]

Compensatory cost-push inflationary movement in Ireland, however, had to encounter an upper limit because price levels were on the whole established on the world market and imported substitutes were readily available. Competitiveness is determined by a complex of related factors. But it could be expected that unrestrained wage-cost increases would result in reduction of manufacturing capacity and eventually in employment losses. Furthermore, wage pressures in the sheltered sector, so much of which was accounted for by public sector employment, would place severe burdens on the Exchequer and limit the discretionary role of fiscal policy.

Academic opinion has tended to concur that available policy instruments, under a fixed exchange-rate policy, could make little worthwhile impact in the long run on the rate of inflation. However, the manner of adjustment of inflationary pressures could have important consequences for the level of employment:[7] 'In the long run, with a fixed exchange rate, there is a trade-off between

[6] Austria, another small open economy, has the 'good fortune' to have Germany as a neighbour, enabling it to 'import price stability by tying the value of the schilling to that of the deutsche mark' (Katzenstein, 1984: 23). In theory, since the break in parity between the Irish currency and sterling occasioned by Ireland joining the European Monetary System (EMS) while Britain remained outside, independent control of inflationary trends is possible. In practice, however, domestic cost pressures, fuelled by higher tax levels, were high in the early 1980s, while British inflation rates declined. The appreciation of sterling against EMS currencies transmitted the costs of exchange rate adjustments throughout the Irish economy. (Bacon, Durken, and O'Leary, 1982: 36; OECD *Economic Survey*, 1982: 19).

[7] In many respects this view parallels the analysis of 'local instability of the wage and price formation process' in the small open economy put forward by Lindbeck (1979: 21–3): 'Whereas in closed economies, Keynesian-type unemployment, due to deficient aggregate demand, may be the most important type of unemployment, in highly open economies "classical" unemployment, reflecting too high real wage rates, may be more important'. However, the low wage rates and underemployment which prevailed in the 1950s and 1960s, and the structural changes which the economy experienced over the 1960s and 1970s, would caution against uncritical acceptance of the relevance of this analysis to the Irish case.

the rate of growth of the real incomes of employees and the rate of growth of employment, regardless of the rate of inflation [in Ireland] and in the rest of Europe' (McDowell, 1975: 10; see also ESRI *Quarterly Economic Commentary*, June 1977: 7). If government was constrained in the degree of direct control it had over the rate of inflation, it was similarly limited in the direct measures it could take to increase employment levels, and once again a pay policy was seen to play a very important role. Budgetary constraints would place a limit to the expansion of direct public sector employment (although experiments in this direction were made in the 1970s). Demand management policies are of limited value in the small open economy. A high marginal propensity to import means that the domestic multiplier effect is small. A boost in demand is more likely to worsen the balance of payments position than to expand employment in domestic industry.

A realistic policy for increasing levels of employment was therefore seen to depend crucially on the performance of private industry; job losses could best be countered by improving industrial competitiveness, and wage costs were held to be an important variable component of any measure of competitiveness. Some foreign industries had been attracted to Ireland by the prospect of low labour costs. More generally, 'orderliness' in industrial relations and predictability in the rate of increase of money wages were held to be important for the success of the IDA's endeavours.

Consequently, because of the openness of the Irish economy and the scale of the adaptive challenge that the country faced in the 1960s and 1970s, government came to attach considerable importance to processes of wage formation, and to the general pattern of industrial relations.

Collective Bargaining as a Focus of Policy Interest

CRISIS IN THE SYSTEM OF COLLECTIVE BARGAINING

During the 1960s the average annual rate of economic growth in Ireland was over 4%, a marked contrast with the 1950s. But the 1960s also saw the intensification of distributive conflict and a sharp upturn in the incidence of industrial conflict. A striking feature of collective bargaining over the course of the decade was the wage competition between bargaining groups; this gave a strong upward thrust to wage claims (see McCarthy, O'Brien, and

O'Dowd, 1975). Protection of relativities and differentials was deeply entrenched in the collective bargaining practices of the post-war period. During the depressed years of the 1950s wage round negotiations displayed a certain 'orderliness'. But by the end of the 1960s the prevailing system of collective bargaining was widely acknowledged to have reached a point of crisis.

Collective bargaining after 1946 was characterized by wage rounds negotiated at fairly regular intervals. Most wage rounds over the period 1946–69 were decentralized, but some took the form of loosely centralized agreements between the peak federations of unions and employers. These centralized agreements, however, were quite rudimentary and unsophisticated.[8] (See O'Mahony, 1964; Charles McCarthy, 1973; McCarthy et al., 1975). Agreements were open-ended until the latter part of the 1960s, when fixed-term agreements became standard. The flat-rate cash increases of the main wage rounds had the effect of depressing the wage structure. Supplementary bargaining, undertaken between the main wage round movements, tended to restore to some extent differentials between groups of workers.

During the 1960s a relatively small number of bargaining groups came to assume a leading role in establishing headline agreements. Among the foremost 'wage leaders' were a number of craft groups. The craft sector was traditionally highly protective of its relativities with other groups. The scope for 'wage inflation' was widened by the prevalence of multi-unionism in the craft sector. Efforts to

---

[8] See Charles McCarthy's (1977a) argument that the war years and afterwards saw the beginnings of a consistent government interest in promoting 'social and economic partnership', chiefly due to the sustained influence of Seán Lemass, a leading Fianna Fáil politician, Taoiseach from 1959 to 1966. Proposed changes in trade union and industrial relations legislation were subject to the primary objective of 'winning the support of trade unions for government policies' (p. 527). The second post-war wage round was to have been the first stage of a prices and incomes policy under the auspices of the Labour Court, but, apart from the difficulties this plan might be expected to encounter with the trade union movement, the momentum was lost when Fianna Fáil lost office in 1948. Some measure of Lemass's thinking on the subject may be had from the following quotation: 'In a democratic state, the trade union movement must play an increasingly important part in the national life, not merely as a guardian of the workers' interests, but as an essential part of the machinery of industrial organisation, accepting the responsibilities which relate to its real power, and proceeding from the stage of negotiating particular agreements with private employers to the stage of formulating and carrying into effect a general policy for the furtherance of the long-term interests of the workers as a class'. (Seán Lemass to the Annual Conference of the Irish Trade Union Congress, 1945, cited in McCarthy, 1977a: 572.)

establish national-level, multi-employer agreements covering craft workers were central to some of the most-publicized disputes and most sizeable wage increases of the decade. (See the Fogarty Report (1965) on industrial relations in the ESB, and the Murphy Report (1969) on the dispute between FUE and maintenance craft unions).

Efforts at modification of the system of wage rounds failed to restore the admittedly tenuous orderliness of earlier collective bargaining practices. In 1964 the ninth post-war wage round took the form of a centralized National Wage Agreement (NWA), termed at the time a 'Recommendation on Wage and Salary Adjustments'. But this agreement was far less sophisticated than those which came to prevail during the 1970s, and it foundered on the issue of the admissibility of non-wage claims, chiefly that of the 40-hour week, which was raised by a building workers' strike later that year. Introduction of fixed-term agreements did not alleviate competitive pay pressures across main and supplementary bargaining periods. Attempts by employers to forestall additional claims by some sections of craft workers had the contrary effect to that intended. Differentials between groups of craft workers, and between craft and general workers, became all the more a focus for grievance as craft pressures intensified to 'level up' ensuing pay settlements.

The culmination of these trends in competitive wage bargaining was the maintenance craftsmen's strike in early 1969, which lasted for six weeks (see the Murphy Report, 1969; Charles McCarthy, 1973; McCarthy et al., 1975). It was the source of unprecedented bitterness: deep divisions were apparent both on the unions' and on the employers' side. This strike appeared to many to signal the development of unrestrained 'free-for-all' bargaining. In the light of the unhappy experience of this strike, free-for-all bargaining was something which the majority of unions were anxious to avoid.[9]

---

[9] ICTU's own report on the strike singled out for special criticism 'the almost casual attitude adopted on the picketing of firms', a feature of the dispute which had been particularly disruptive for the general unions (ICTU *Annual Report*, 1970: 263). This dissatisfaction was expressed much more trenchantly by Jimmy Dunne, General Secretary of the MPGWU, one of the general unions seriously affected by the dispute, who was also President of ICTU at this time. In his presidential address to the ICTU ADC he said: 'We have a "do it yourself" brand of trade unionism which treats with contempt all the institutions, practices and procedures that our trade union movement has created in this country over the last sixty years . . . I have come through a year in which I have seen my own Union smashed to the ground and bereft of everything except its fighting spirit. Smashed in

The employers, too, were alarmed by the implications of the strike and its aftermath. There seemed to be no way back to earlier bargaining practices. But the way forward remained unclear.

THE SEARCH FOR A SOLUTION

These issues had been a major concern of government for some time. From early in the 1960s efforts had been made to influence the level of pay settlements, for reasons of the sort discussed earlier in this chapter. As competitive wage bargaining intensified during the 1960s, fuelled by the 'coercive comparisons' of differentials and relativities, the government developed a keener interest in tackling what it saw as the root of the problem, that is, the structure of trade union organization, with its overlapping representation, multi-union workplace organization, and relatively weak centralization of authority in ICTU. In 1966 the draft heads of a Trade Union Bill were circulated to unions and employers for discussion. This bill contained a number of measures designed to induce a rationalization of unions' conduct of collective bargaining and to curtail the autonomy of bargaining groups other than those constituted according to the new rules. The bill was circulated along with the Industrial Relations Bill, 1966, which proposed far-reaching changes in the functions and powers of the Labour Court, the principal third-party body which had responsibility for resolving disputes on a voluntary basis. Predictably, there was trade union resistance to these proposals, and the political will to proceed with these bills in their original form was dissipated in the course of lengthy consultations with the trade unions. The eventual Industrial Relations Act of 1969 was a highly modified version of the original proposals. The Trade Union Bill lapsed, and was not revived after the general election of 1969; the question of structural reform of the trade union movement was left to the voluntary efforts of trade unions themselves (see Hardiman 1983a).

The option of effecting structural reform of trade unions so as to alter their collective bargaining practices was thus effectively closed

a way that no employer or combination of employers could achieve in the thirty-seven years of militant and uphill trade unionism that is the history of my Union. I would be a liar and a hypocrite if I came to this rostrum and left aside my feelings of hurt at the senseless and almost completely unnecessary damage done, not alone to my Union, but to other of our affiliated Organisations' (ICTU *Annual Report*, 1970: 327–8).

to government. From the early 1960s on government tried to influence the course and conduct of collective bargaining. But neither exhortation to match wage increases to the growth in national productivity (in the White Paper *Closing the Gap*, February 1963) nor direct intervention (which secured the 1964 NWA but ended with all sides dissatisfied) was found to be satisfactory, and deflationary fiscal policy was thought to be a poor substitute for voluntary employer–labour restraint as a means of curbing inflationary wage pressures (Kennedy and Dowling, 1975).

Thus the National Industrial and Economic Council (NIEC) was established in 1963 expressly as a consensus-building body, comprising representatives of the trade union movement and of employer and industry organizations and some senior civil servants and academics. It was to give its views: 'on the principles which ought to be applied for the development of the national economy and the realisation and maintenance of full employment at adequate wages with reasonable price stability and reasonable long-term equilibrium in the balance of external payments' (NIEC terms of reference). The NIEC produced some twenty-eight reports between 1963 and 1970, drafted in the main by the small General Purposes sub-committee in which the leading members of each organization participated. The NIEC's reports were consensual documents, agreed to by all members. In the opinion of key participants a very valuable feature of the NIEC was the opportunity it afforded unions and employers for mutual education and exchange of views on the functioning of the economy.[10]

From the mid-1960s successive NIEC reports argued that the main tasks to be addressed were control of domestic inflation, improvement of industrial competitiveness, and reduction of the balance of payments deficit. Increasingly the Council came to focus on distributive conflict as the source of much economic instability

[10] The chairman of the NIEC, T. K. Whitaker, doyen of economic programming, subsequently recollected that a new psychological mood existed at the time of the Second Programme, review of which was the first task of the NIEC: a 'common will and sense of interdependence' was in evidence (interview with T. K. Whitaker). A prominent trade union leader confirmed this early impression, likening the debates at the NIEC to a 'graduate seminar in economics' in which each side explained its position and learned from the other (interview with Donal Nevin). Several erstwhile members have commented on the political sensitivity in drafting reports displayed by the chairman of the General Purposes Committee, Professor Louden Ryan (interviews with Ruaidhri Roberts, Donal Nevin, T. K. Whitaker). On the significance of the NIEC, see Lalor, 1983; Hardiman 1984a; W. K. Roche, 1982.

(NIEC No. 11, November 1965: 6; No. 18, January 1967: 57). The Council had a number of specific recommendations on the measures government might usefully undertake to improve the economic climate in which wage bargaining took place. But it also stressed the importance of addressing directly the phenomenon of distributive conflict. Initially the NIEC saw this as primarily a task for employer–labour debate, perhaps facilitated by some outside agency. What was required was:

widespread appreciation of the importance of the relationship [between wage increases and competitiveness] and a commitment to economic expansion and full employment, to make individuals and social and economic groups disposed to subordinate immediate private gain to future benefit; [also] consensus on the manner in which increases in national output should be shared between persons and different categories of income. (NIEC No. 18, January 1967: 80.)

The NIEC presented the case in several of its reports for orderly wage increases within the context of an incomes policy of some sort. The need to address rapid wage and price inflation was urgently stated in the latter years of the 1960s:

Throughout the 1960s, money incomes have consistently outstripped the rise in national production . . . Since the devaluation [of sterling] in 1967, the rise in money incomes relative to national production has been greater here than in Britain. The increases in money incomes have not been constrained within any framework of measures that could be termed an 'incomes policy'. *The Council is convinced that the stage has now been reached at which future growth, which must fundamentally depend on growth of exports, may be in serious jeopardy.* (No. 25, March 1969, emphasis in original; see also No. 28, 1970.)

By 1969, in view of the high level of wage settlements which followed the maintenance craftsmen's strike and the high incidence of industrial action during that year, the shortcomings of the existing mode of collective bargaining were apparent to all sides. At the government's invitation, the NIEC prepared its 'Report on Incomes and Prices Policy' (No. 27, April 1970), proposing new structures of collective bargaining. The detailed recommendations of this report were never implemented. But the report received the assent of both the union and the employer representatives on the NIEC, and it coloured the context in which the centralized

National Wage Agreement (NWA), the first of the series in the 1970s, was negotiated.

The proposed new mode of wage determination involved some institutional innovations. Guidelines on pay increases would be formulated in broad terms by the NIEC itself. A new national joint employer–labour body would refine the guidelines into more specific terms. The functions of this body, as outlined in the report, were far more limited than those which the Employer–Labour Conference of the 1970s actually carried out. The main reason for this was that the NIEC report placed greater emphasis on another new body, an Incomes and Prices Committee, which would take a leading role in monitoring pay developments and setting out the terms on which particular cases ought to be investigated. The Incomes and Prices Committee would be a tripartite body. But the NIEC report did not propose to burden it with a whole range of new powers all at once: it was hoped that, over time, it would develop as an authoritative and influential body (p. 40). For this reason it was not designed as a body analogous to the British National Board for Prices and Incomes, responsible for deciding on the justifiability of departures from the guidelines and acting as the arbiter of the public interest. The tasks of assessing and evaluating such cases would be spread among other bodies, although these would be fully briefed by the Incomes and Prices Committee. The Labour Court would take a part in evaluating cases. So, too, particularly where price increases were involved, would the Department of Industry and Commerce.

But the Incomes and Prices Committee was never established, and the NIEC itself, the usefulness of which now seemed to be at an end, was allowed to lapse in the discussions on what sort of body should replace it. The problems which proved fatal for the recommendations of the NIEC's report arose at ICTU's Annual Delegate Conference in July 1970. In a development which was surprising to many trade union leaders, in view of the support for the idea of a voluntary, government-backed prices and incomes policy at the previous year's ADC, and the agreement among ICTU's Executive Council to the proposals advanced in the NIEC report, influential sections of the trade union movement expressed various reservations about the details of the proposed new arrangements, and a string of apparently contradictory motions on the NIEC report was put forward. A complicated series of votes was taken on this subject. The outcome of the voting left open the possibility of some form of wage regulation policy, but one in which the norm would be less subject to direct determination and evaluation by government and civil servants.[11] The tripartite element in establishing the norm, and the evaluating role of government departments, were rejected by the conference. But the way was opened for the negotiation of the bipartite National Wage Agreement (NWA) in 1970, the first of what was to become a series of centralized agreements spanning the decade of the 1970s.

Before the NIEC's proposals had been definitively rejected, the bipartite Employer–Labour Conference (ELC) was established in May 1970. This was the only one of the institutional innovations proposed by the NIEC which was given effect. It would be more correct to say that the ELC was re-established, because a bipartite ELC had met earlier in the 1960s, from the spring of 1962 until its demise in the controversy over the White Paper 'Closing the Gap', early in 1963. The reconstituted ELC of the 1970s comprised forty-two members at first: twenty-one ICTU representatives (the members of the Executive Council and its senior full-time officers), and the same number of employers' representatives. Twelve of these were drawn from the employers' umbrella group, the Irish Employers' Confederation (IEC), five were senior civil servants representing government as employer, and four were representatives of state-sponsored bodies. Professor Basil Chubb acted as independent chairman. Membership was expanded to twenty-five from each side in 1972 when the Executive Council of ICTU was enlarged.

The terms of reference of the ELC were broad. In addition to providing 'a forum for the discussion and review of developments and problems in money incomes, prices and industrial relations', its brief extended to eleven other areas of industrial relations.[12] But

[11] ICTU *Annual Report*, 1970, section B5: 99–104. The General Secretary of ICTU at the time, Ruaidhri Roberts, rejects the view that the motions passed were confused and contradictory. Rather, he points out that a consistent course was carefully steered through them. The result was to reject the now controversial NIEC proposals while leaving the way open to a voluntary prices policy. The government's proposal to legislate unless a voluntary agreement was secured had some influence on the course of the voting (interview with Ruaidhri Roberts). There is further discussion of these events in Chapter 3.

[12] Terms of reference of the ELC, as stated in press release, courtesy of the Dept. of Labour; see also *IT* 23 May 1970. The other areas which fell within the ELC's competence were the scope of national, industrial, and plant-level agreements;

most of the work of the ELC during the 1970s centred on the negotiation of the centralized pay agreements.

So by the end of the 1960s there was general agreement that industrial relations had reached a nadir. The high level of industrial conflict during 1969 and 1970 was widely perceived as representing a crisis in collective bargaining practices. Trade union leaders were concerned to overcome the consequences of unbridled inter-union rivalry. The maintenance craftsmen's dispute had jolted them into a willingness to put collective bargaining on a new and more organized footing. The employers, too, recognized the need to develop a more co-ordinated approach. The NIEC report could not be implemented as it stood, but it provided the catalyst for the restructuring of employer–labour negotiations. The scene was set for a new approach to collective bargaining.

wages, prices, and productivity; pensions and other non-wage benefits; negotiating procedures; codes of fair employment and dismissal procedures; Rights Commissioners; grievance procedures; shop stewards' training and day release; decimal currency; functions and powers of shop stewards; local information meetings.

3

The Politicization of Collective Bargaining

The Centralized Agreements 1970–1980: An Outline

This chapter surveys some of the main developments in centralized collective bargaining during the 1970s, paying particular attention to the changing role of government in these agreements. The general features of the agreements will first be outlined briefly, and the remainder of the chapter will set out in more detail some of the important moments in the developing relationship between collective bargaining and government's broader economic objectives.[1] (For a detailed analysis of the centralized agreements see O'Brien, 1981).

Between 1970 and 1978 seven National Wage Agreements (NWAs) were negotiated between unions and employers; and in 1979 and 1980 two National Understandings (NUs) were agreed, each of which involved two elements, a union–employer pay agreement and an agreement between the unions and the government on 'non-pay' items, that is, government undertakings on a wide range of issues. All the centralized pay agreements, and the pay policy part of the second NU, were negotiated through the Employer–Labour Conference (ELC). As Chapter 2 noted, the centralization of bargaining through the ELC came about in response to what was widely perceived as a crisis in the prevailing mode of collective bargaining, and in reaction to proposals for a more formalized prices and incomes policy. In the early 1970s the NWAs were bipartite employer–labour agreements in which the government was represented solely in its capacity as employer. But over the decade government came to contribute more directly to the

---

[1] This chapter draws upon a variety of source material and therefore notes and references are only given when they seem to be particularly needed. Details of sources used are given in the bibliography at the end of the book. They include *Annual Reports* of ICTU, FUE, and CII, FUE *Bulletin*, CII *Newsletter*, Central Bank *Quarterly Bulletin*, ESRI *Quarterly Economic Commentary*, *Dáil Debates*, press statements from Government Information Services, ICTU, and FUE, texts of NWAs and NUs, ELC reports, personal interviews, and *Irish Times* and other newspapers.

negotiation of agreements, in order that the outcome might be more congruent with other objectives of economic performance.

The government's growing involvement in the course and conduct of centralized bargaining centred on the use of budgetary policy (see O'Brien, 1981: 82, 231; Colm McCarthy, 1979: 204). Three phases in this development may be distinguished. Between 1970 and 1974 the three NWAs were fairly straightforward employer–labour agreements, though they became more sophisticated over time. The second phase spans the period between 1975 and 1977, when government made a more explicit, though still indirect, input into the terms on which agreements were concluded. The culmination of the 'concertative intent' of governments, noted in Chapter 2, was the two NUs of 1979 and 1980. These marked a qualitative break with the bipartite NWAs, because the pay and 'non-pay' elements of these agreements were negotiated simultaneously as interdependent parts of the NUs.

MAIN FEATURES OF THE CENTRALIZED AGREEMENTS

All the pay agreements negotiated during the 1970s shared a similar format. The central element of each agreement was the clause governing the basic norm for pay increases, the amount payable, and the phasing of its implementation. Each agreement also provided for the conditions under which cost-increasing claims 'above the norm' (ATN) could justifiably be sought, generally covering anomalous or inequitable pay rates, productivity agreements, and improvements in conditions of employment. From 1972 a clause allowing for employers to plead inability to pay, that is a 'below the norm' (BTN) clause, was also included in each agreement. All of the pay agreements prohibited recourse to industrial action in pursuit of ATN claims 'pure and simple', anomalies in wages and conditions, and productivity claims. An exception was the 1978 NWA, which permitted industrial action on some issues, subject to specified conditions. The agreements set out, in varying levels of detail, the procedures which should be followed in advancing admissible ATN claims. (For details of NWAs, see O'Brien, 1981; Charles McCarthy, 1974a, 1977b).

The Steering Committee of the ELC (involving five members from each side of the Conference and the chairman), and the Interpretation Committee (established in 1970 to clarify the meaning of terms of the agreements in cases of dispute) and Adjudication Committee (established in June 1974 to rule on actions or proposed actions which might be in breach of the NWAs, when such cases were referred to it by the Steering Committee), played an important part in resolving conflicts about the terms of the agreements. The Steering Committee dealt in the first place with problems and difficulties as they arose, referring them if necessary to the Adjudication Committee or the Interpretation Committee. In practice, however, a substantial number of cases were dealt with by the Steering Committee itself. Under the National Understandings of 1979 and 1980 the Steering Committee alone had responsibility for dealing with such problems. (See the *Report of the Commission of Inquiry on Industrial Relations*, 1981: 193). But the centralized agreements allocated to the Labour Court the principal role of evaluating and deciding upon the admissibility of claims involving workers in the private sector and the commercial state bodies and manual workers in the civil service and local authorities. The Court is a voluntary, non-binding institution which was established under the provisions of the Industrial Relations Acts of 1946. In addition to providing a conciliation service, the Court may hold full hearings of disputes before its divisions, each of which comprises an employer member, a union member, and an independent chairman/ woman. All disputes on issues covered by the agreements which were not settled at conciliation level were obliged to be jointly referred to the Labour Court. Public service employees were obliged to process claims through the various Conciliation and Arbitration (C&A) schemes which served different parts of the public service. (On the disputes machinery see O'Mahony, 1964; McGinley, 1976; Department of the Public Service, 1978; McCarthy and Prondzynski, 1981; Kelly and Roche, 1983.)

The format of the first NWA in 1970, although devised in a somewhat *ad hoc* manner (the headings were 'jotted on the back of an envelope', according to the Chairman of the ELC), served as the model for subsequent agreements. The substantive terms altered from one agreement to the next. The basic pay increase was, of course, subject to the greatest variation; it generally featured a tapered percentage increase with cash thresholds. Some experiments with indexation were undertaken, especially in 1974 and 1975. The BTN and ATN clauses also varied a good deal; for example, the 1977 NWA included a reference for the first time to the possibility of public sector 'inability to pay' if the claim were to involve 'serious financial or budgetary consequences', though this clause did not reappear in later agreements. The 1978 NWA experimented with a 2 per cent allowance for local-level 'kitty bargaining'. It also broadened the criteria to be considered by the Labour Court in assessing ATN claims. Most of the restrictions prohibiting recourse to industrial action remained unchanged, but a unique provision was made in this NWA explicitly permitting industrial action on legitimate ATN claims, subject to specified procedural and temporal constraints.

The pay agreements of the NUs were similar in format to the preceding NWAs. The 'non-pay' section of the 1979 NU included employee tax rebates and improved social welfare provisions, and other government undertakings on job creation, institutional innovation to improve public sector enterprise, industrial planning, review of the tax structure, a job-creation scheme funded by a payroll levy on employers, and an employer–labour commitment to improving industrial relations. The 'non-pay' provisions of the 1980 NU were also wide-ranging. They included an increase in employee tax allowances and extra one-off welfare payments, further government commitments regarding job creation, a statutory maternity leave scheme, and other declarations of government intent on issues such as education and training, employment of the disabled, and worker participation.

Centralized Agreements and Government's Input

The preceding section identified three periods in the development of centralized collective bargaining during the 1970s, according to the role played by government in facilitating the negotiation of employer–labour pay agreements: the period of straightforward bipartite collective agreements, 1970–4; the period of somewhat greater implication of budgetary commitments in collective agreements, in mid-decade; and the more explicit connections between government commitments and pay agreements in the NUs at the end of the decade.

In this section four events in the development of the centralized agreements will be looked at in greater detail. These are the negotiation of the first NWA in 1970 and three episodes which represent turning-points in centralized bargaining: the renegotiation of the 1975 NWA, the NWA of 1977, and the first NU of 1979. The second NU of 1980 is briefly discussed towards the end of this section, and the events leading to the eventual breakdown of centralized collective bargaining are also considered.

THE NATIONAL WAGE AGREEMENT OF 1970

The first NWA of the 1970s established the model for later agreements. But it was not easily negotiated. ICTU's Annual Delegate Conference in July 1970 produced an agreement in principle to negotiate an employer–labour pay agreement, as Chapter 2 noted. But the very factors which made necessary a new system of pay determination seemed likely to prevent the success of the pay talks which opened in the ELC in September 1970. ICTU was seen to have suffered some loss of prestige in the preceding period of industrial conflict. The ending-dates of current agreements were widely dispersed. The agreements of some of the wage leaders were due to expire at the end of the year, and in spite of government warnings about the need for pay restraint workers' expectations were high. It seemed likely that sectionalist pressures could precipitate another decentralized wage round.

The ELC talks broke down in October. At this point the government intervened to avoid a return to free-for-all bargaining, proposing, among other measures, to introduce statutory controls on wages and salaries until the end of the year. A Prices and Incomes Bill was introduced in the Dáil. Trade union reaction was immediate and highly critical. The public sector unions, who would have been affected more than other groups by the government's proposed measures, were particularly critical. But in negotiations with ICTU the government indicated that it was prepared to modify its intentions if wage talks resumed. The ELC reconvened, and in December an agreement was reached. The government withdrew its Prices and Incomes Bill at the same time.

The government's intervention broke the impasse which talks at the ELC had entered, and this proof of its concern for the state of the economy may have 'introduced a new realism into negotiations, a consciousness of the current economic perils' (Charles McCarthy, 1973: 181). But the unions were strongly opposed to statutory wage legislation. Over the decade of the 1970s governments intermittently proposed to legislate unless agreement was forthcoming, but with the exception of limited measures directed against the employers in the country's associated banks[2] no statutory wage controls were implemented. The evident preference of government for an agreed pay policy, even on higher terms than those proposed for the statutory restraints, calls into some question the seriousness of government's intention to legislate. (This point is taken up again in Chapter 7.) But in 1970 the credibility of the government's plan to pass the proposed legislation seems not to have been in doubt among the parties to centralized bargaining.

Once the NWA had been established the prospects for relatively smooth implementation of the agreement seemed reasonable. The establishment of the ELC on a permanent basis offered the pay agreement greater stability than the ill-fated NWA of 1964. The relative success of the NWA contributed to improving the standing and the influence of the peak federations on either side after the difficult years, from their point of view, of 1969–70. Although there was no formal or statutory commitment that this NWA would be followed by another, both sides voluntarily chose to re-enter into agreements in 1972 and 1974. These NWAs followed largely the same pattern as the first, and in 1974 an agreement of some complexity greatly rationalized the terminal dates of agreements (Charles McCarthy, 1974a; O'Brien, 1981). The first three NWAs contained a partial retrospective index-linked element. The onset of the oil-price-led recession during 1974 meant that expectations regarding inflation were central to the negotiation of the 1975 NWA. The employers agreed to a one-year agreement involving quarterly phased increases linked to the Consumer Price Index (CPI). The principle of indexation was also endorsed by the government White Paper *A National Partnership* (November 1974). The final index-linked phase of the 1974 NWA, although it only applied over a high threshold, proved costly because inflation during the relevant period was higher than foreseen. But initially

[2] These were the Regulation of Banks (Remuneration and Conditions of Appointment) (Temporary Provisions) Acts, 1973 and 1975, which restrained the bank employers from paying agreed increases to their employees, even though neither side was party to the NWAs. See *IT* 22 June 1973, 11–15 Dec. 1975, 24 June 1976; also R. Keatinge and P. Tansey's review article, 'Principal Issues in Bank Dispute Still Unresolved', *IT* 30 Aug. 1976. However, it was generally accepted that these measures were not likely to be extended to other employments (see Charles McCarthy, 1973). Moreover, the possibility that the bank officials' pay claims could undermine the NWAs made them unpopular within ICTU—the Irish Bank Officials' Association (IBOA) was not affiliated to ICTU.

both this phase and the proposed index-linked terms of the 1975 NWA were acceptable to employers as a means of containing inflationary expectations of employees. To this end, this NWA also placed a low ceiling on the value of ATN increases which could be sought for the duration of the agreement.

THE RENEGOTIATION OF THE 1975 NATIONAL WAGE AGREEMENT

Shortly after the ratification of the 1975 NWA an unexpected surge of 'imported' inflation caused concern for government and employers. It became clear that the inflationary consequences of the agreement would be much greater than initially anticipated, because full indexation would rapidly transmit the higher cost of imported goods and materials thoughout the economy. Not only would this be damaging to employers' cost-structure, but the cost of public service pay to the Exchequer would also be significant. Full indexation would add considerably to public service pay costs in 1975, at a time when the carry-over effects of the 1974 NWA and the cost of the many 'anomaly' claims being advanced through the public service C&A schemes were already the focus of considerable government concern. In response to this, government took the unprecedented step of providing various measures to offset the increase in the cost of living in a supplementary Budget, introduced in June 1975, on condition that the terms of the NWA were revised in a downward direction to a satisfactory level. The cost of absorbing perhaps four percentage points on the Consumer Price Index (from some 24% to 20%) would be met by recourse to additional public sector borrowing. This was the first time that budgetary provisions were explicitly used to offset the terms of a centralized wage agreement. It was a one-off measure which, far from being negotiated as an integral element of a 'comprehensive' pay agreement, presented the parties to collective bargaining with something of an ultimatum. However, this innovation in the relationship between fiscal policy and collective bargaining opened the way for similar agreements, which would be more than emergency measures, to be negotiated in the future.

Governments in the 1970s were able to conceive of a more ambitious strategy concerning wage formation because of the change of direction in fiscal policy which occurred in the early years of the 1970s. The development policies of the 1960s had initiated state activism in infrastructural development and consequently the value of capital spending for productive purposes was recognized. But influential policy-makers in the Department of Finance and the Central Bank had traditionally had deep reservations about the wisdom of running a deficit on the public current account (Ryan, 1972; Moynihan, 1975; Dowling, 1978; Fanning, 1978; Whitaker, 1983c). However, in 1972 the Fianna Fáil government increased current spending without raising taxes, 'opting for growth rather than stability',[3] with the objective of pursuing more vigorous counter-cyclical policies. This was the first time that a deficit had been permitted in the current account. The Coalition government followed this trend in 1973, and in 1974 and 1975 sharply increased Exchequer borrowing and expenditure to sustain demand and protect employment levels to some degree, in response to the 'exogenous shock' of inflation. By 1975 current borrowing levels stood at about 16% of GNP (as against 7.5% in Britain at that time). Trends in the volume of public expenditure and in borrowing levels are examined in more detail in Chapter 4.

The Budgets of 1972, 1974, and January 1975 were each supposed to have an indirect effect on the level of pay settlements reached in the NWAs. The extra spending was intended to modify the severity of the impact of the recession, and some adjustments to employee tax allowances were intended to alter expectations regarding disposable income.[4] These Budgets repeatedly stressed the imperative need to curb the domestic pressures exacerbating inflation, as a condition of improving competitiveness and employment levels; in this governments echoed similar exhortations by the Central Bank.[5]

During these years the FUE grew interested in the possibilities presented by a direct government input into agreements, in the form of tax relief and, perhaps, welfare and employment commitments. This would relieve employers of the full cash burden of each agreement and would contribute, in their view, to a slackening in employee pressures for cash increases to compensate for fiscal drag. The Central Bank, too, began to advocate the merits of a 'social

[3] *Dáil Debates* 19 Apr. 1972, vol. 260, cols. 560, 578.
[4] *Dáil Debates* 19 Apr. 1972, vol. 260, col. 578; 16 May 1973, vol. 265, col. 1242; 3 Apr. 1974, vol. 271, col. 1426.
[5] See Central Bank *Quarterly Bulletin*, e.g. Spring 1973, Spring 1974, Spring 1975, Winter 1975.

Social contract [handwritten margin note]

contract' (the term then current in Britain), in which pay, tax, and welfare would be integrated.[6]

Over the same period, the incidence of employee taxation was emerging as an important new issue for ICTU. The tax structure had an unusually narrow base in Ireland because of the corporate tax concessions which were an integral part of state industrial policy, and because of the low rates of tax paid by the agricultural sector, the greater part of which had traditionally been depressed but large sections of which quickly—and conspicuously—prospered under EEC farm price policies. More employees had experienced fiscal drag: rapid increases in money wages in the late 1960s and early 1970s had pushed into the tax net a great many employees who had previously been exempt, since revision of tax bands had not kept pace with inflation. Further information on this subject is presented in Chapter 4.

ICTU began to include tax questions in its direct representations to government, independently of pay talks, for example in its pre-Budget submissions. Direct negotiations on tax issues had played no part in securing NWAs in the first half of the 1970s. But in 1974 the government was clearly interested in influencing the course of wage negotiations, however diffusely, through its use of the Budget. The NWA of that year was ratified before the Budget; although there was no agreement linking pay and tax, trade unions were now more alert than previously to the implications of fiscal policy for the issues which concerned them. In the words of one trade unionist, members were now looking to 'the vague promise by the Minister for Finance that he would reform the tax code. If his actions do not come up to his promise, our commitment to the National Wage Agreement will have to be reconsidered notwithstanding any decisions that are made here today'.[7]

By 1975 both unions and employers wished to see a more active role for government on issues related to the process of wage formation, but the emphasis of each party differed on how this should be related to wage bargaining. These differences became evident when the government presented its supplementary Budget in June 1975.[8] The benefits contained were attractive, and included

---

[6] See Central Bank, ibid. The FUE expressed interest in a 'social contract' as early as 1972–3; see FUE *Bulletin*, Feb. 1973.

[7] Brian Doyle (IPOEU), ICTU *Annual Report*, 1974: 283.

[8] *Dáil Debates* 26 June 1975, vol. 282, cols. 1940–72.

subsidies on food and gas, removal of value added tax (VAT) from other fuels, clothing, and footwear, and additional incentives to employers to increase employment. They were given immediate effect, but they were conditional upon acceptance of the other elements of the package as well. To counter the common assumption that, once conceded, these measures would not be revoked, the government stressed on several occasions that they really were conditional.[9] Chief among the conditions was the obligation to renegotiate the 1975 NWA, dropping the third-phase increase altogether and modifying the increase due under the fourth and last phase. In addition the government announced an embargo on concession of all ATN claims in the public sector. Public sector pay already accounted for a sizeable proportion of current expenditure (see Chapter 4), and the rate of 'special' increases was adding an unexpectedly large amount to the annual public sector wage bill. The Minister also stressed in his Budget speech that the measures he was introducing represented only the start of a process of adjustment intended to curb inflation, and that the large current deficit was not sustainable in the long term.[10]

The Budget of June 1975 was based on a plan developed, at the government's invitation, by the National Economic and Social Council (NESC). This was a consultative body established by the Coalition government in 1973 to replace the NIEC. But it functioned quite differently from its predecessor. In particular, reports were no longer necessarily unanimously agreed.[11] NESC's

[9] It was agreed between the Ministers for Labour and Finance that the former, a Labour Party minister, should impress this point upon ICTU. Although his intervention created something of a stir within the Labour Party, it was believed by government ministers to have been decisive in altering the climate of trade union opinion. (Interviews with Michael O'Leary and Richie Ryan).

[10] Budget (No. 2), *Dáil Debates* 26 June 1975, vol. 282, col. 1942. See also the CII's 'Strategy for Tackling Inflation', submitted to the Minister for Finance, *IT* 24 June 1975.

[11] NESC included representatives of ICTU, employers' organizations, and farming interests, with public servant and academic members also. It was larger than NIEC, comprising almost fifty members, and differed in function from the earlier body. Its reports were intended to be informative policy-oriented documents rather than consensus-building exercises, and dissenting views were frequently appended to its reports. The government also convened an Economic Task Force in May 1975 with representatives of ICTU, industry, and agriculture, but this made no progress in discussing economic problems. The core of this group was also on NESC. The task of making policy proposals was therefore referred to NESC. The ICTU members did not agree with the pay pause recommendation in the final NESC report. See ICTU *Annual Report* 1975, sec. D.3; NESC No. 9 (1975): 66; also the speech by the Taoiseach, Liam Cosgrave, at the CII Annual Lunch, *IT* 15 May 1975.

Report on Inflation (No. 9, May 1975) was controversial from the start. The Irish Employers' Confederation (IEC) included an addendum proposing, among other matters, that the government should postpone introduction of legislation, then under consideration, guaranteeing equal pay for equal work to men and women, 'until such time as there is a significant improvement in the economy'. ICTU added a reservation rejecting outright the desirability of modifying the 1975 NWA in any way. On the basis of these dissenting views, acceptance of the government's proposals seemed unlikely. The two sides were in conflict over the risks of a downward revision and over the acceptability of deferring equal pay.

The NESC report contained no specific reference to an embargo on 'special' increases in the public sector. But the inclusion of this measure in the Budget added to ICTU's objections. The Public Services Committee of ICTU referred the case to the ELC for investigation as a unilateral breach of the terms of the 1975 NWA. In July 1975, in a measured report by the Adjudication Committee (Report No. 8), the government's statement of intent was found to be in breach of the agreement; but since no employer was obliged to make an offer in relation to any particular claim, ICTU could not be guaranteed that ATN claims would in fact be conceded. This conclusion did not dispose of ICTU's objection to the government's clear intention to limit ATN increases in the public sector.

The government played an active role in ensuring acceptance of the Budget–NWA package. The embargo on special pay increases in the public service was not removed, but on several occasions the government held meetings with ICTU to 'clarify its intentions', indicating that it was prepared to be flexible in the way in which the embargo was implemented. The conditions for employer–labour agreement were finally reached in mid-September. In fact neither side had to compromise its position on renegotiation. The rate of increase of the CPI in the three months to August fell by 0.8%, the first such drop in twelve years. The issue of dropping a phase of the NWA was no longer a matter of contention between unions and employers. The conflict over threshold and ceiling in the final phase of the agreement was irrelevant if inflation was going to be low in this period anyway.

The renegotiation of the 1975 NWA was initiated in conditions of mounting economic difficulty and was concluded without establishing the principle of a direct trade-off between pay and public policy commitments. But it created a degree of expectation that NWAs and Budgets might be closely linked again in future.

THE NATIONAL WAGE AGREEMENT OF 1977

The NWA of 1977 was the first in which a pay agreement was explicitly negotiated with reference to budgetary provisions, that is, where government offset an employer–labour agreement on pay and conditions with commitments on tax, employment creation, and social welfare improvements. The antecedents to this agreement may be traced to the renegotiation of the 1975 NWA and its aftermath. However, the progression to a Budget-linked NWA in 1977 was not a smooth one. Before the innovative 1977 NWA was conceived, it seemed likely that centralized bargaining would break down altogether.

In the wake of the renegotiated 1975 NWA, employers still hoped for a total 'pay pause' during 1976, or, if this was not possible, then for a small pay increase spread over a relatively long duration. Because of the continuing depressed economic conditions and some dissatisfaction with NWAs, many employers were believed to be more reluctant than before to enter into a centralized agreement. This reflected a view that decentralized bargaining would result in relatively low increases and would be more sensitive to variations in local conditions than a centralized agreement could be. The employers' position at the ELC when talks opened in 1976 was therefore more determined than previously. In this they were backed by the government's reiteration of the need for a pay freeze to carry through the 'adjustment' measures outlined in the Budget of June 1975 and subsequent policy statements.[12]

ICTU was aware that economic conditions were not favourable either to sizeable pay increases through centralized bargaining or to a reversion to a 'free-for-all'. In the proposals emerging for a 1976 NWA it was primarily the stringency of the clauses governing productivity and other ATN bargaining, advanced by the employers,

---

[12] The Taoiseach, Liam Cosgrave, gave a television broadcast on 10 Dec. 1975 to issue a public appeal for a wage freeze, and the same message was conveyed to ICTU and FUE. The ELC was to be convened to respond to this initiative. ICTU's General Secretary responded immediately and unfavourably in a letter to the Taoiseach; cf. FUE's press statement, *IT* 31 Dec. 1975.

which the unions found unacceptable, and a proposed agreement was narrowly defeated, by only nine votes, at an ICTU SDC in June 1976. Pay negotiations had reached a stasis, and it was not clear how they might be reactivated.

By mid-1976 trade unions and employers were coming increasingly to hold that whether or not there would be a pay agreement in 1976 would depend mainly on the government. Furthermore, the government's policy of firm control over public sector pay was one of the obstacles to an agreement which caused problems for the senior civil servants representing government at the ELC.

The deadlock in the pay talks at the ELC was broken by the employers' offer of an interim pay settlement, conditional upon agreement subsequently to negotiate the sort of 'social contract' which they had long favoured. Talks on a pay policy for 1977–8 would have to take place as part of a broader, tripartite strategy for economic development. This plan would necessarily include a much more direct involvement by government in collective bargaining than ever before, because it would cover job creation, taxation, welfare, and general economic development.

The Minister for Labour responded favourably to the employers' initiative. As a gesture of good faith to ICTU, he promised that if the tripartite package proved capable of being negotiated, greater flexibility in public sector pay policy would be considered as part of an economic and social policy. Evidently the government's preference was for greater restraint in public sector pay policy, but this objective seemed not to be compatible with obtaining a national agreement. The government was faced with a choice, and it chose in favour of securing a negotiated centralized agreement.[13] The proposals for an Interim Agreement were accepted at an ICTU SDC in September 1976 by an unusually large majority.

The prospect of a Budget-linked pay agreement secured significant support from both employers and trade unions, most firmly and unequivocally from the employers. The FUE later commented that the tripartite talks 'were the breakthrough sought by FUE in

---

[13] Cosgrave had earlier indicated the government's intention to introduce statutory wage controls if no agreement was reached in March (see *IT* 17–18 Mar. 1976). On the significance of government's change of tack, see the opinions of W. P. Smith, one of government's civil servant representatives on the ELC, reported in *IT* 27 May 1976; also Patrick Nolan, 'The Private and the Public Sector', *IT* 31 May 1976.

working towards the determination of total pay costs'.[14] At the
June ADC of the largest trade union, the Irish Transport and
General Workers' Union (ITGWU), which organized almost one-
third of all union members, Senator Fintan Kennedy, the President
of the trade union and an ICTU official of long standing, argued
that one of the lessons of these NWA negotiations was that it was
'no longer feasible to examine rates of pay separately from the
government's intentions on taxation and investment'.[15] The union's
General Secretary, John Carroll, also expressed the view that some
form of social contract covering a broad span of policies was
desirable because: 'Whether we like it or not we are now at an
evolution on our economic scene. We cannot divorce political and
industrial action.'[16] An ICTU study group advanced the view that:

Reliance on wage-bargaining alone cannot resolve our continuing problems
. . . We cannot see National Wage Agreements as a resting-period between
one free-for-all and the next. We see them as a necessary transitional phase,
a step in the direction of a greater and more powerful role in the life of the
nation for the trade union movement. It is our view that a National Social
and Economic Plan should be a negotiated document . . . *an extension of
collective bargaining* to a higher level . . . negotiating with both employers
and government.[17]

All parties were agreed in principle that the Tripartite Conference
convened in October 1976 should discuss pay developments in
1977 in the context of economic performance more generally. But
between this date and January–February 1977, when the Budget
was introduced and the NWA was ratified, various disagreements
emerged to trouble the course of the tripartite talks.

The first concerned the agenda for discussion. The government
regarded this as an opportune time to reintroduce an element of
economic planning, deferred during the years of instability due
to very high and unpredictable levels of inflation. It therefore
published a Green Paper, *Economic and Social Development
1976–80* (September 1976), immediately prior to the opening of
the talks. The Green Paper drew criticism for what some held to be

---

[14] FUE *Annual Report*, 1976, also FUE *Bulletin*, July 1976.
[15] ADC Report, ITGWU *Annual Report*, 1976; see also F. Kennedy, 1981.
[16] Speech at the SDC, 22 Feb. 1977, in ICTU *Annual Report*, 1977: 222.
[17] ICTU Summer School on Economic and Social Planning, 1976, Final Group
Report No. 1, in ICTU *Annual Report*, 1976: 161 (emphasis in original).

its too hasty preparation and unrealistic projections.[18] But in addition to this criticism the ICTU delegates maintained that they had their own mandate for these talks, which antedated the Green Paper and which primarily concerned the nature of government input to the new pay agreement.

ICTU representatives had reservations on another, related matter. They professed to be unhappy about the low priority which the government appeared to give the talks, the Green Paper's ambitious terms of reference notwithstanding. The government representation at these talks was usually limited to the Minister for Labour, Michael O'Leary.[19]

Finally, the IEC was concerned about the content of the government's input to the proposed agreement. The employers were anxious not to advance too great a pay offer at the concurrent ELC discussions, lest the government should withdraw its fiscal commitments on the grounds that the cash increase was too large. They were also concerned that the volume of the government's commitment to tax concessions and employment creation expenditure should be large enough to secure trade union assent.

Contemporary observers noted that the emerging pay pact 'hinged on the tax changes', and that pre-Budget meetings between members of the government and the unions and employers, previously considered a formality, were now 'deeply political'.[20] Some days before the Budget in January 1977 the government approved the terms then being finalized at the ELC. This Budget, then, was explicitly designed as part of an incomes policy. The Minister for Finance, Richie Ryan, cited the OECD report on the Irish economy which stated that 'by far the most urgent task confronting the (Irish) authorities is the need to reduce substantially the increase in nominal incomes. This is a prerequisite for

---

[18] *IT* editorial, 27 Sept. 1976: 'To say that the Green Paper ... is a disappointment would be an understatement of truly heroic proportions.' The NESC report 'A Prelude to Planning' (Oct. 1976) was more rigorous in its analysis of economic options and was implicitly critical of the government approach. NESC's ICTU members, however, did not endorse this report.

[19] In the Minister's view, the Tripartite Conference 'was not taken very seriously by the trade unions ... but it did become the model for later developments' (interview with Michael O'Leary). But see reports of the unions' dissatisfaction, *IT* 29 Sept. 1976. Some of those who participated recall that sessions were conducted in some haste, 'with the engine of the Minister's Mercedes running outside the door' (personal communication).

[20] See comments in *IT* 24 Dec. 1976 and 18 Jan. 1977.

improving competitiveness, setting the conditions for export growth in the medium term, and bringing about a significant reduction in unemployment.'[21] Among other measures, the Budget made available £50m. in 'reductions in personal tax rates to give worthwhile improvements in take-home pay'. The increase in disposable income which resulted from these changes was estimated at about 3% to 4% on average. The Budget also provided an equivalent sum for public sector employment creation programmes. On the basis of these budgetary concessions the NWA was ratified by an ICTU SDC in February 1977.

Thus, in spite of the difficulties in the course of negotiations and, it might be suggested, the somewhat uncertain status of the tripartite discussions conducted in parallel with the ELC negotiations, the first Budget-linked NWA was concluded in 1977. Nowhere in the text of the 1977 NWA was there any reference to the budgetary input. But it was generally recognized that the pay agreement alone did not compensate for the increase in the rate of inflation, and that the budget input had been an important consideration in ICTU's acceptance of the package. A contemporary observer noted: 'Most union leaders see that at present levels of taxation and inflation, wages can no longer be meaningfully discussed in isolation from general economic and social planning.'[22] The Economic and Social Research Institute's *Quarterly Economic Commentary* commented: 'The terms of the agreement mark a remarkable downward shift in the size of negotiated income increases. At the root of employee acceptance was the belief that an agreement of this sort was necessary for employment purposes through direct government action in the budget provisions and through increased profits in firms'.[23] A later, equally approving assessment was presented by the OECD in its annual *Economic Survey*: 'On the basis of the movements in real earnings, and the progress made towards reconstitution of the profit share in 1976 and 1977, the pay agreements in these two years made a significant contribution to improving the employment and inflation performance.'[24]

For individual employees, moreover, a senior ICTU figure noted

[21] *Dáil Debates* 26 Jan. 1977, vol. 296, col. 239; see also cols. 246, 250, 281.
[22] 'Behind the Tripartite Conference', *Business and Finance*, 7 Oct. 1976.
[23] ESRI *QEC*, June 1977: 19.
[24] OECD *Economic Survey*, 1978: 29.

that the combination of pay increases and tax concessions yielded an increase in real disposable income which was generally regarded as satisfactory.[25] If ICTU and the executive councils of individual unions seemed slow to publicize its merits prior to the SDC vote in February, this was mainly in order to 'avoid provoking a counter-reaction' from unions suspicious of dealing directly with government.[26] Furthermore, it was commonly held that the government was anxious to avoid the risk of failure in the projected pay–tax–jobs deal, because a general election was anticipated later in the year. Thus, for example, the government noticeably avoided references to the possibility that it might withdraw its commitment to the proposed bargain, in contrast with its previous threats of non-payment. Indeed some trade union leaders formed the opinion, immediately before the Budget, that the government would not insist on making the budgetary measures dependent upon any particular level of pay settlement.[27]

However, if the 1977 NWA was intended to help the government's re-election effort, it proved to be of little direct use. Its public image was tarnished, among other factors, by its association with the period of recession and its unpopular image as a government excessively concerned with 'law and order'. The economic upturn in 1977 only became apparent after the election. Most importantly, Fianna Fáil conducted a vigorous election campaign which had greater popular appeal and which involved a medium-term economic strategy more attractive to the electors than that of the Coalition. Moreover, its election manifesto promised specific benefits on a wide range of issues. The election was said to have been decided by the issues of 'prices, jobs and taxes';[28] Fianna Fáil was returned to government with the largest majority ever won in an Irish election. The significance of these developments is discussed further in Chapter 7.

THE NATIONAL UNDERSTANDING OF 1979

The first NU involved a qualitative extension of the role of government in securing the terms of a centralized employer–labour

[25] Interview with Ruaidhri Roberts.
[26] 'Day of Decision', *Business and Finance*, 3 Feb. 1977.
[27] Ibid.; also personal communications.
[28] Irish Marketing Surveys Ltd. opinion poll; published in *IT* 31 May 1977. Fianna Fail's campaign slogans were 'Get the Country Moving' and 'Let's Back Jack' (Jack Lynch, party leader).

agreement. In an obvious sense, therefore, it represented a development of the possibilities first suggested by the 1977 NWA. But there was no direct progression from the Budget-linked NWA of 1977 to the 'integrated' NU of 1979. This was, rather, a discontinuous development. The links between the Budget and the NWA in 1978 were somewhat looser than in the previous year, but the expenditure commitments and tax concessions contained in the Fianna Fáil government's first Budget in February 1978 were introduced on condition that an acceptable pay agreement was negotiated. It was in response to the grievances of both unions and employers in the course of this agreement, and the apparently imminent collapse of centralized bargaining on the expiry of the 1978 NWA, that the NU was conceived by the government.

It was noted above that the Coalition government perceived a Budget-related pay agreement as an important element in the restabilization of the public finances. Similarly, the Fianna Fáil government hoped for a pay agreement linked to the Budget (a Budget in which many of the manifesto commitments were given effect) because its development policies required an 'orderly' means of determining pay increases.

The emergence of the NU must therefore be understood in the context of Fianna Fáil's development strategy. The party's election manifesto and consequent White Paper *National Development 1977–80* (January 1978) proposed greatly to increase the level of foreign borrowing in the short term in order to boost employment and stimulate growth which would then become self-sustaining. These measures were intended to yield rapid economic growth, projected by the new government at 7% per annum in 1977–8; inflation was anticipated to be about 7.5%. An essential part of the expansionary strategy was that the rate of increase of money wages should be limited to 5% in 1978. The large increase in foreign borrowing and public sector spending was then to be tailed off sharply within a few years. This would require further political and economic adjustments which could only be achieved through ensuring that the overall strategy was complemented by collective bargaining. The task of co-ordinating these objectives in a coherent plan was allocated to a new Department of Economic Planning and Development.

In order to facilitate the negotiations of the 1978 NWA, which had reached deadlock by the time of the Budget in February, the government withdrew the strict limit of 5% on pay increases. This enabled employers to improve their money offer to the unions without risking a clawback of the manifesto-based budgetary concessions (the 'initial stages' of the government's strategy of creating 'the conditions under which the private sector can move ahead and take over as a prime generator of economic growth and employment', according to the Minister for Finance, George Colley[29]). The softening of the government's approach was widely interpreted as signalling its commitment to maintaining a centralized agreement. It was also seen as evidence of the symbolic importance attached by this government to proving that, like the Coalition government, it too could secure co-operation with the unions.[30]

The 1978 NWA was agreed in March, and involved a basic norm of about 8%. This agreement contained two unusual features worthy of note at this point. First, it allowed for negotiation of an additional sum of up to 2% at local level, subject to prevailing firm- or industry-level conditions, without prejudice to other admissible cost-increasing claims. This element of 'kitty bargaining' was proposed by the employers, who were increasingly unhappy about the relationship between centralized bargaining and local-level ATN bargaining. Second, this NWA included closer specification of the grounds on which ATN claims could be sought. In some respects this meant that the ATN clauses were stricter than before, but in others provisions for ATN bargaining were seen to be liberalized. The agreement explicitly permitted industrial action once certain procedures had been gone through, a Labour Court recommendation had been obtained, and specified temporal restraints had been observed. Furthermore, the upper limit was removed from the value of ATN claims which the Labour Court could normally recommend. The employers were particularly concerned to curtail the extent of supplementary bargaining in this

---

[29] *Dáil Debates* 1 Feb. 1978, vol. 303, col. 375. The need for pay restraint had been stressed in the Taoiseach's Adjournment Debate speech, 14 Dec. 1977, vol. 302, cols. 1358–76. See also ESRI *QEC*, Jan. 1978.

[30] The Taoiseach, Jack Lynch, told ICTU leaders that the basic objectives of ICTU and of the government were 'close and perhaps identical'; see *IT* 24 Sept. 1977. The Opposition Fine Gael and Labour deputies made much of the government's relaxation of its 5% target and of its new-found commitment to 'discipline' in the period prior to EMS entry. See e.g. the question on pay guidelines, *Dáil Debates* 23 Nov. 1977, vol. 301, cols. 1555–66; Jim Tully (Labour), 16 Feb. 1978, vol. 303, cols. 1457–78; questions on the economy, 16 Dec. 1978, vol. 325, cols. 1167–78.

agreement, and they hoped that by the provision of greater explicit opportunities for ATN bargaining the volume of additional drift could be restrained.

The majority at the ICTU SDC in March 1978 in favour of the proposed agreement was very slender, and considerable dissatisfaction was expressed at what many unions perceived as a restriction on ATN bargaining at a time when most sectors were experiencing growth. The employers had hoped to relieve some employee frustrations by explicitly allowing inclusion of permission to strike subject to certain conditions. But many trade union delegates did not regard this as a particularly valuable concession because the strike level was already quite high at this time (see Chapter 4). The FUE had attempted to counter trade union antipathy to the proposed terms by appealing directly to employees over the heads of the union leaders. Thus the reservations of such a sizeable proportion of trade union members—including, for the first time, several important public sector unions (see Chapter 5)—presaged difficulties in the implementation of the agreement and an uncertain future for the series of centralized agreements.

The ITGWU was among the most vociferous critics of the 1978 NWA. Its stated reason for opposing this NWA was that its terms imposed excessively strict limitations on trade union action without providing enough in return; only in the context of a more inclusive social and economic plan, with adequate guarantees for employment creation, would another pay agreement be acceptable. Similar themes were aired at the ICTU ADC in July.[31] But it was not until the ICTU SDC in November, convened to decide on opening talks for a new centralized agreement in 1979, that the implications of the impasse became clear. ITGWU adopted a series of economic and social demands which it proposed should form the backdrop for any discussion with the employers for a new NWA. At the ICTU SDC a majority of delegates, including those of the ITGWU, voted against opening talks for a new pay pact, for the first time since 1970.

However, there were several reasons why the government was particularly anxious to maintain centralized bargaining in existence

---

[31] ITGWU Executive Council statement, *Liberty*, Mar. 1978; see also May and June issues. See especially the growing trade union pressure for increased state enterprise, e.g. ICTU *Annual Report*, 1978: 186–91, and debates on motions 27 and 28 at the ADC.

and to avoid the disruption and uncertainty which would accompany a decentralized wage round in 1979. For the first time Ireland was about to break the parity of its currency link with sterling, by joining the European Monetary System in March 1979, since Britain had opted not to join. Irish inflation rates, and the government's monetary and exchange-rate policies, would no longer be as heavily influenced by Britain. This would increase the responsibility of the Irish government for control over domestic inflationary pressures. If this could successfully be achieved, it would also improve the chances of realization of the governments job-creation targets. Although public sector employment had provided a boost to these targets, the government's development strategy was based on assisting the recovery of private industry. Thus if industrial competitiveness was essential for job creation, a pay policy would be essential, to ensure competitiveness (see Chapter 2).[32] In a Green Paper, *Development for Full Employment* (June 1978), it was claimed that with co-operation and discipline from the 'social partners', and the steady reduction of public spending commitments, full employment could be achieved in five years. Although this document found little favour anywhere, in the view of the Minister for Economic Planning and Development, Martin O'Donoghue, it signalled that the government was in earnest about its development strategy.[33] However, the development strategy as initially outlined in 1977–8 required a rapid scaling-down of public spending during 1979 and 1980 in order to reduce the volume of public sector borrowing, especially foreign borrowing. This would entail curbs in public spending, especially in the area of public sector pay, which would be very difficult to achieve in the absence of a pay policy.

The OECD, in its annual *Economic Survey* in 1978, was sharply critical of government policy, arguing that increased public spending for growth would not result in the expansion of employment unless competitive conditions were improved. It urged government to involve trade unions and employers in a more extended, tripartite

---

[32] See *Dáil Debates* 17 Oct. 1978, vol. 308, cols. 404 ff., 419 ff.; 30 Nov. 1978, vol. 310, cols. 410 f. Also FUE *Bulletin*, Feb. 1979.

[33] NESC, in its *Comments on* Development for Full Employment (Dec. 1978), urged government not to deflate as rapidly as projected—unnecessary advice, as it turned out. But in the view of the Minister, the Green Paper 'put full employment firmly on the political agenda' and presented a challenge to the unions to take the prospect seriously (interview with Martin O'Donoghue).

exercise combining discussion of economic policy and of wage formation.[34]

This was the course on which the government now embarked. With another White Paper in its series of 'rolling plans' in January and the Budget in February, the government tried to lay the foundations for another employer–labour pay agreement, this time to be negotiated in a more inclusive policy framework. Pay policy featured significantly in the White Paper as 'central to the success of policies in growth, inflation and employment'. ICTU had no further mandate to engage in pay negotiations at the ELC, because of the SDC's rejection of proposals to open discussions with the employers. But the White Paper stated that: 'Within the context of a ceiling on pay increases and a major effort to secure industrial peace, the government would welcome an understanding with employers and unions on targets for the creation of employment, and possibly, change in working conditions and policies in relation to non-wage incomes . . . 1978 cannot be repeated.'[35] In the Budget in February some move was made to meet ICTU's demands on equity in taxation, and extra public spending was committed to job creation in the public service—in contrast with the earlier conception of government strategy which had anticipated a scaling-down of public sector projects by this time.[36] On the basis of these fiscal plans government invited the trade unions to discuss a broad range of policies including tax, welfare, and employment expansion, in exchange for co-operation on wage determination when the NWA came to an end the following month. This would be 'a national agreement for national development'.

ICTU agreed to convene an SDC in March to discuss the proposal. This SDC also provided the occasion for ICTU to discuss a comprehensive policy document of its own, which was influenced by the debates which had previously been taking place within the ITGWU and at ICTU delegate conferences.[37] These policy proposals, dealing with taxation, employment creation, and welfare provisions, among other issues, were accepted as a basis for negotiation with

[34] OECD *Economic Survey*, 1978: 36; see also FUE *Bulletin*, Dec. 1978.

[35] White Paper *Programme for National Development 1978–81*, Jan. 1979: 105. Cf. ICTU *Annual Report*, 1979: 163–5.

[36] *Dáil Debates* 7 Feb. 1979, vol. 311, cols. 632–82. The Taoiseach reiterated the primary objective of employment maximization in the context of an economic plan: see 8 Feb. 1979, vol. 311, cols. 799–817.

[37] See the report of the SDC of 9 Mar. 1979 in ICTU *Annual Report*, 1979.

government. Taxation was by now an issue of particular urgency for employees. Notwithstanding the changes made in the tax structure over the preceding few years, employees' frustration with the continuing inequitable distribution of direct taxation and its heavy reliance on the pay-as-you-earn (PAYE) sector was now widespread. A campaign of demonstrations was initiated by the Dublin Trades Council and supported by the ITGWU. Although the Executive Council of ICTU was critical of action overtly directed against an aspect of government policy,[38] it recognized the strength of popular feeling on this issue. Mass protest stoppages were organized under ICTU's leadership in response to these grass-roots feelings. These were generally regarded as strengthening ICTU's negotiating position with government.

Two sets of negotiations thus got underway in March 1979, which together were to culminate in the agreement known as the National Understanding. Trade union representatives met with civil servants and government ministers in working parties on various subjects. Simultaneously, trade union and employer representatives engaged in pay negotiations. These employer–labour meetings were in fact composed of the members of the ELC negotiating committee, with the exception of the chairman of the ELC.

To general surprise, the first package of pay and non-pay proposals was rejected at an ICTU SDC.[39] Since it appeared likely that no renegotiation would be possible, given the employers' reluctance to concede more and the dissatisfaction of the unions with the agreement as it stood, the government proposed to introduce pay guidelines for an interim period, observance of which would determine whether or not the proposed fiscal concessions would be made. However, rather than risk union–government confrontation on pay policy, the FUE initiated a new pay offer, which was endorsed by the Taoiseach Jack Lynch and the economic

[38] Harold O'Sullivan, ICTU President, at the Association of Higher Civil Servants' dinner, cautioned that 'taxation is fundamentally a job for parliament and government', and that no answer would be found in 'the mass democracy of the streets' (reported in *IT* 2 Apr. 1979, also cited in Whitaker, 1979: 292). See also Ruaidhri Roberts, ICTU *Annual Report*, 1979: 272–4.

[39] See report of the SDC of 23 May 1979 in ICTU *Annual Report*, 1979; appendix 7. The Executive Council of the ITGWU decided to vote against these proposals at the SDC, claiming that the arrangements for longer-term tripartite consultation were not far-reaching enough. This decision was regarded as surprising by the other NU negotiators (see *IT* 2 May 1979). Various explanations have been suggested, such as the internal politics of the union or the volatile nature of the union's leadership (interviews with Ruaidhri Roberts and Donal Nevin).

ministers.[40] At an ICTU SDC in July this package was accepted.

The NU was regarded by most unions (incuding the ITGWU[41]) as a major breakthrough in collective bargaining, particularly in the central place given to the issue of employment: it stated that 'the central policy objective of economic and social policy is, and must continue to be, the creation of more employment' (NU 1979: 3). The unions were particularly pleased with the guarantee that further government action would be taken to increase levels of employment by direct means. One such measure was an employment scheme funded by employers' contributions and administered by a Tripartite Standing Committee on Employment. Another was the creation of a new agency, a 'National Enterprise Agency'. The function of this agency would be to initiate new state enterprises in areas not being exploited by the private sector and to invest state funds in new, commercially viable businesses (see the White Paper *Investment and National Development, 1979–83*, January 1980). The idea of establishing a body of this sort had been in existence for some time—it had featured, for example, in the Coalition government's Green Paper *Economic and Social Development 1976–80* (September 1976)—but nothing had previously come of the idea.

The pay element of the NU was higher than either government or employers had at first intended. But after the years of rapid growth induced by the government's expansionary policies workers' expectations, on the whole, were running high. Neither government nor employers were prepared to risk the failure of the negotiations at a late stage in the talks, particularly when it was known that some unions were prepared to press quite large pay claims in a decentralized wage round, and also because many bargaining groups would inevitably take the final terms of the rejected pay agreement as the floor for their own claims. Some high-profile public sector strikes had already dented the government's image somewhat, particularly the prolonged Post Office strike which lasted from February to July 1979, during which time there was no postal or telephone-exchange service. These contributed to the unexpectedly poor showings for Fianna Fáil in the first direct elections to the European Parliament in June 1979. It may therefore be suggested that government attached importance to the successful

---

[40] FUE was anxious to avert a free-for-all at a time when another oil crisis seemed imminent (FUE *Bulletin*, May–June 1979).

[41] See *Liberty*, July 1979.

negotiation of the first NU for political reasons, as well as in connection with economic management.

THE NATIONAL UNDERSTANDING OF 1980 AND THE COLLAPSE OF CENTRALIZED BARGAINING IN 1981

Another NU was negotiated in 1980. The second NU, like the first, involved a pay and a non-pay element. The institutional channels through which negotiations were conducted were different this time: the pay talks were negotiated through the ELC and the non-pay elements were negotiated directly with the Taoiseach and senior ministers (the Department of Economic Planning and Development had been abolished early in 1980).

By 1980, however, the private sector employers had grown dissatisfied with the performance of the centralized agreements.[42] The balance between the centrally agreed norm and supplementary local bargaining, in their view, was unsatisfactory; they were unhappy about the high level of days lost due to strikes in spite of the commitment to improving industrial relations contained in the 1979 NU (para. 12); and they were increasingly critical of the cost of the government's non-pay commitments to the agreements. Nevertheless, they were prevailed upon to conclude a pay agreement with ICTU as part of a second National Understanding.

Not only were employers dubious about the economic advantage to them of entering into further centralized agreements on the terms available, but there was also mounting criticism of the government from the opposition parties on account of the cost of supporting the agreements. But although high levels of current expenditure produced a budgetary over-run in 1979 and 1980, the government continued with expansionary policies in 1980 and 1981. Two reasons may be adduced for the government's stance at this time.

First, there were economic constraints on reducing the level of public borrowing as earlier projected by the development strategy. International economic conditions began to worsen with the onset of the second oil-price crisis, and this contributed to renewed inflationary expectations among Irish workers. Recession in the Irish economy had adverse implications for the government's job

---

[42] See e.g. FUE *Bulletin*, Apr. 1980; FUE *Annual Report*, 1980. The circumstances under which the second NU was negotiated led the employers to reappraise their approach to a pay policy; see Fogarty, Egan, and Ryan, 1981.

creation commitments; maintenance of high levels of public spending provided temporary support for employment levels.

Second, a change of leadership in Fianna Fáil and consequently a change of Taoiseach took place at the end of 1979, when Jack Lynch announced his resignation. The party was divided by the leadership contest between old adversaries Charles Haughey, Minister for Health, and George Colley, Minister for Finance. Haughey, as the new Taoiseach, needed to prove his authority with an electoral victory during 1981. This contributed to the government's reluctance to adopt unpopular economic measures, and appeared to colour the approach it adopted to trade union pressures on pay and other issues.

A strong challenge was advanced in 1980–1 by a renewed Fine Gael–Labour coalition, arguing that 'correct' management of the public finances, particularly restraint of the foreign borrowing requirement, was an essential condition of competitiveness, growth, and employment protection. A period of political instability followed between June 1981 and November 1982, with a change of government at each of the three general elections held. But by mid-1982 all parties were committed to the need to curb public spending. This objective was not compatible with underwriting collective agreements on the sorts of terms which had characterized the two NUs.

When the second National Understanding expired in 1981 no further centralized agreement proved possible. Although talks opened towards negotiating a new agreement, an impasse was soon reached on pay terms between employers and unions, and the newly elected Coalition government was unwilling to intervene to avert a breakdown of the discussions. From mid-1981 onwards wage rounds were decentralized, dampened by worsening economic conditions (see Cox, 1983). The course of collective bargaining during the 1980s is discussed further in Chapter 8.

Three turning-points in the development of centralized bargaining during the 1970s have been looked at in this chapter, each of which involved a progressively closer interrelation between budgetary policy and pay negotiation. These were the renegotiation of the 1975 NWA, the negotiation of the 1977 NWA, and the development of the 1979 NU. Each came about in the context of economic difficulties which made some form of planned wage agreement desirable, but which made compensatory commitments from government necessary if collective bargaining outcomes were to be congruent with government's other economic objectives.

In 1977 and 1979 continued union involvement in centralized bargaining seemed uncertain; on each occasion government commitments to support the employer–labour agreement were increased. This trend may perhaps be recognized as a manifestation of the 'learning curve' of trade unions, whereby progressively greater government inputs are sought as the quid pro quo of union participation in wage regulation agreements (Goldthorpe, 1983; W. K. Roche, 1982: 66).

However, the 'concertative intent' of governments persisted until the early 1980s, and both unions and employers, despite their various misgivings, continued to participate in centralized collective bargaining throughout the 1970s. The following chapter therefore looks at aspects of economic performance over the 1970s, to see what the consequences were of a decade of centralized and progressively 'politicized' collective bargaining.

4

Evaluating the Centralized Pay Agreements

THE centralized pay agreements of the 1970s had two main objectives which were shared by both employers and government. First, they were intended to provide the framework for the 'orderly' adjustment of employee incomes by establishing the norm for pay increases and identifying the conditions under which additional claims could be advanced. Second, they were intended to minimize the incidence of industrial conflict by dealing with all wage round increases in a single agreement and by placing firm restrictions on resort to industrial action in pursuit of additional pay and other cost-increasing claims.

The objectives of trade union participation in centralized pay agreements were several.[1] Protection of the living standards of trade union members was of central importance to the unions. Therefore ICTU sought protection of real income against erosion by inflation; increasingly, also, the issue of taxation, particularly the adjustment of tax allowances and tax bands in line with inflation, became more central to the unions' objectives in centralized wage bargaining. In addition to protection of real wages, the trade union movement looked for a centrally negotiated share in the growth in national productivity. Centralized agreements were also intended to improve the relative position of low-paid workers through provision of a floor for pay increases and tapering increases for the higher-paid, and the early agreements also made provision for negotiating equal pay for women. Furthermore, the trade union movement attached great importance to the objective of growth in employment, and as the 1970s progressed it saw greater opportunities for advancing its interest in this objective through centralized bargaining. But whereas government took the

[1] For statements of ICTU objectives see e.g. O'Brien, 1981: 279; ICTU *Annual Report*, 1971: section B5 on Prices and Incomes Policy 1970, also section B6 on Employer–Labour Conference Working Committee, Sept.–Oct. 1970; *Annual Report*, 1974: 227, General Secretary's address to SDC in Sept. 1973 on opening new NWA talks; *Annual Report*, 1975: appendix 1, 'Trade Union Priorities', discussed at ADC in Nov. 1974.

view that increased employment would come about through the contribution of wage regulation to industrial competitiveness (see Chapter 2), the trade unions were anxious to obtain government commitment to direct employment creation. ICTU's position on each of these issues, and its view of the relationship between its various policy objectives, will be discussed further in Chapter 5.

By the early 1980s, however, employers and unions each expressed frustration with their experience of centralized bargaining, and government could no longer intervene to reconcile their differences as it had previously. The success of centralized bargaining in stabilizing economic performance was very much open to question, and one commentary concluded that 'perhaps the greatest prospect offered by central pay bargaining, the opportunity to achieve positive adjustment to external imbalance in the context of achieving national economic objectives, did not materialise' (Bacon *et al.*, 1982: 77). Inflation continued at a high rate after severance of the link with sterling. Unemployment levels continued to increase in spite of government commitments to make full employment a priority objective, and the onset of another international recession offered a prospect of worsening conditions. Public sector borrowing was running at historically high levels, but it was far from clear how the adjustment to more sustainable deficits was to be made. Both employers and unions maintained that their interests had suffered through involvement in centralized bargaining, not least because of inadequacies in the role which government had played in relation to pay policy.

In this chapter, then, the reasons for dissatisfaction with the centralized agreements on the part of all parties are considered. We shall look first at the issues which were of greatest concern to the employers, and to government insofar as it shared similar objectives: pay developments, their implications for competitiveness, and trends in industrial action. We shall then consider the trade unions' experience of centralized agreements in the light of their objectives, looking at developments in real disposable income, and at changes in the rates of employment and unemployment. Finally, we shall argue that government, despite its wish to contribute to the negotiation of employer–labour agreements, did not successfully play a concertative role. Other policy objectives, and structural and fiscal constraints on government action, made it difficult for government effectively to mediate between employers and unions.

Performance in Areas of Employer Interest

PAY TRENDS

By the time the second NU drew to an end in 1981 the employers were openly dissatisfied with the performance of the centralized agreements. They had expressed the view intermittently during the 1970s that the centralized agreements made possible too great an increase in money wages. But they had been willing to sustain these increases on the grounds that 'the inflationary consequences of national agreements have to be judged against the unknown or hypothetical outcome of uncoordinated rounds of pay increases' (FUE *Annual Report*, 1975: 5). In 1981, however, the FUE's critique of the way centralized agreements had functioned was formalized in the report they commissioned from an expert review group, *Pay Policy for the 1980s* (Fogarty *et al.*, 1981). In this report a theme which had recurred in the course of ELC negotiations was reiterated: the view taken was that 'a wrong balance' had long been in existence between central- and local-level bargaining (Fogarty *et al.*, 1981: 15). The employers considered that excessive use had been made of the provisions for above-the-norm bargaining. A degree of wage drift might be expected even in the most successful wage regulation policies (see e.g. Hart and Otter, 1976), and there must be scope available for some degree of flexibility in pay agreements. But the volume of additional wage gains was, in the employers' view, undesirably large. The extent to which ATN increases were obtained may be gauged by comparing the hypothetical outcomes if only the basic terms of the agreements had been conceded with actual pay developments. The basic provisions of each agreement contained measures designed to improve the relative position of low-paid workers; if these terms alone had been implemented, a marked compression of the wage structure would have ensued. In fact, though, this did not occur. If anything, a greater compression of differentials had taken place during the period of decentralized bargaining during the 1960s (O'Brien, 1981: 174; Mooney, 1978: 245). Table 4.1 documents the extent to which actual wage increases outstripped the projected levels in transportable goods industries.[2]

[2] See also Durkan and McCarthy, 1981; Fogarty *et al.*, 1981: 22–3, 16–17; *Trade Union Information*, Autumn 1979: 8; Winter 1980–1: 16, 22; Mooney, 1978: 245–7.

TABLE 4.1. *Increase in Hourly Earnings in Transportable Goods Industries (%)*

	NWA Basic	Actual	
	(1970–7)	(1977)	(1979)
Men			
High paying industries	142	216	370
Middle paying industries	152	210	359
Low paying industries	163	212	363
Women			
High paying industries	222	252	420
Middle paying industries	249	258	445
Low paying industries	263	268	446

Source: Mooney, 1978: 245–7, also cited in Fogarty *et al.*, 1981: 16.

Developments in civil service pay show a somewhat different picture. Table 4.2 shows that the grades which were negotiated through the Conciliation and Arbitration scheme, the first three in this table, also obtained increases in excess of those projected if the norm alone had been paid. But the upward trend is much less marked than that in Table 4.1. The period 1970–7, in particular, shows a slower upward trend. The relatively low level of ATN increases apparent for most grades over this period reflects the effect of public sector pay curbs, especially the restrictions placed on payment of 'special' increases between 1975 and 1977. Civil service pay was more tightly controlled than pay in the broader public sector (Fogarty *et al.*, 1981: 21–2). But these employees rapidly made up for the previous restraint in the later 1970s and early 1980s. The salaries of the higher grades, the latter two in Table 4.2, were set by a special Review Body which could be authorized by government to investigate salary levels. The Review Body recommended increases in 1972; by 1979, when it made further recommendations, gains by other grades and developments in the salary structure of comparable external employments led it to award sizeable increases which substantially restored differentials.

The private sector employers held that the criteria according to which ATN claims were evaluated for both private and public sector workers were inherently ambiguous and unsatisfactory, particularly the two most common grounds for claims, contribution to productivity and anomalies in rates of pay or in scales which

TABLE 4.2. *Increase in Civil Service Salaries, 1971–1979*
(Pre-Phase 1 1970 = 100)

	1971–7		1971–9	
	NWA Basic	Actual	NWA Basic	Actual
Clerical Officer	220	220	290	325
Exec. Officer	207	216	271	332
Higher Exec. Officer	198	207	259	312
Asst. Secretary	180	184	233	323
Secretary	179	189	232	340

Source: Fogarty *et al.*, 1981: 17, based on DPS information (see also O'Brien, 1981: 173).

had fallen 'seriously out of line' with genuinely comparable employments. As was noted in Chapter 2, relativities were deeply entrenched in the Irish system of industrial relations, and very prominently so in the public service, and the third-party bodies were reluctant to begin pronouncing on questions of equity. On the issue of productivity, the agreements contained various provisions for reporting agreements and having claims assessed. But it was also recognized that employers were often willing to concede what might be regarded as 'spurious productivity agreements' for 'industrial relations reasons' (Charles McCarthy, 1982). Awareness of this made it difficult for the Labour Court to develop a strict monitoring role in this matter. A further complication could arise when productivity increases were consolidated into basic pay, as often happened, and this provided the basis for a relativity claim from another group of employees. The opportunities for local-level bargaining to escalate in this way made some employers wonder whether these matters were properly the subject of collective bargaining at all, and whether much more extensive use ought not to be made of job evaluation and inter-union, plant-level involvement in productivity bargaining (for example, Patterson, 1981: 20).

COMPETITIVENESS

The private sector employers, supported in the main by government, contended that the rate of overall wage increases over the period of the centralized agreements impaired industrial competitiveness, because the norm was negotiated with reference to increases in the cost of living and growth of national productivity, but employees tended to take the norm for granted as 'an award from Heaven or Dublin' (Fogarty *et al.*, 1981: 19) and to seek additional ATN increases. Already, in the employers' view, the norm provided larger increases than some sectors could really afford, but the volume of additional ATN bargaining was seen by them as inimical to competitiveness and profitability and hence to employment-creating investment.

Competitiveness is governed by many factors besides labour costs, such as managerial efficiency, technical innovation, product differentiation, energy costs, raw material costs, and marketing,[3] but there is little dispute that unit labour costs are an important element none the less. Their precise significance will differ from sector to sector, or even from company to company. Wages are not the exclusive determinant of unit labour costs, but they are obviously a very significant element. The average annual increase in hourly earnings in Ireland during the 1970s was estimated at just over 18%, which was the highest in the EEC outside of Italy.

Two factors offset the impact of this level of earnings on industrial competitiveness: fluctuations in exchange rates and growth in productivity. External changes in exchange rates had implications for Irish competitiveness, even though Ireland did not have an independent exchange rate policy, and even though after 1979 it endeavoured to maintain a stable exchange rate policy *vis-à-vis* the EMS countries. During the 1970s, when the Irish pound was held at parity with sterling, Ireland's industrial competitiveness improved somewhat relative to other EEC countries, but worsened relative to the US. The period following EMS entry was one in which unit labour costs increased rapidly. The competitive advantage of currency depreciation relative to EEC countries was no longer available. However, the appreciation of sterling meant an effective competitive gain in relation to British goods (see *Report of the Committee on Costs and Competitiveness*, 1981: 47–50; Bristow, 1982).

The indicators of competitiveness are summarized in Figure 4.1, which portrays the competitive gains of the early- to mid-1970s diminishing in the early 1980s relative to all currencies besides sterling. An assessment of these trends by the OECD during the period in which Ireland was responsible for its own exchange rate

---

[3] See Jobs and Wages, 1983; Bristow, 1982; the proceedings of the Irish Management Institute Annual Conference, 1982, on the theme of 'Competitiveness'.

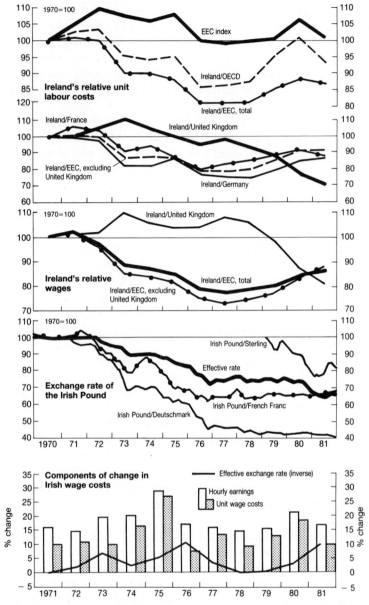

FIG. 4.1. Competitiveness Indicators: Annual Changes in Manufacturing

Source: OECD *Economic Survey*, 1982: 22.

policy concluded that 'had it not been for the relative appreciation of sterling since 1979, which provided a major offset to the worsening on other fronts, it is possible that the rapid rise of nominal wage costs would have resulted in a net loss of competitiveness over the longer period' (OECD *Economic Survey*, 1982: 22).

An important determinant of unit labour costs and hence overall competitiveness is the productivity rate, that is, GNP per person employed adjusted for overall profitability. The evidence would appear to suggest that a real wage–productivity gap opened in the first half of the 1970s (OECD *Economic Survey*, 1979: 34). This trend was reversed in 1976–7, but marked increases in productivity appear to have contributed more than adjustments in the real wage. The rate of increase of real earnings quickened between 1977 and 1980, during which period productivity also grew, though without a significant increase in the numbers employed. These trends and their implications for factor shares may be seen from Figure 4.2 (see also Conniffe and Kennedy, 1984: 91).

But although the two factors of external movements in the exchange rate and growth in productivity offset the loss of competitiveness which might otherwise have occurred, they each had other implications of a less favourable kind, indicative of the failure to adapt domestic wage formation processes to international pressures in the course of the 1970s. Moreover, aggregate data tend to obscure the differential responses of Irish industry to changing competitive conditions.

The competitiveness of Irish goods on the British market was improved by the Irish pound's relative weakness following the appreciation of sterling in 1979–80. But many close links persisted between the Irish and British economies, particularly in relation to purchase of production components, thus contributing to the persistence of 'imported' inflationary costs.

National productivity trends tend to give a misleading picture of what was happening in different sectors of the economy, for the average trends cover a great diversity of experience in manufacturing industry. First, the high productivity rates of many of the new projects started up during the 1970s were attributable in large measure to their capital intensity and technological sophistication. Second, overall productivity figures are artificially enhanced by the closure of many of the older firms in 'traditional' industries during

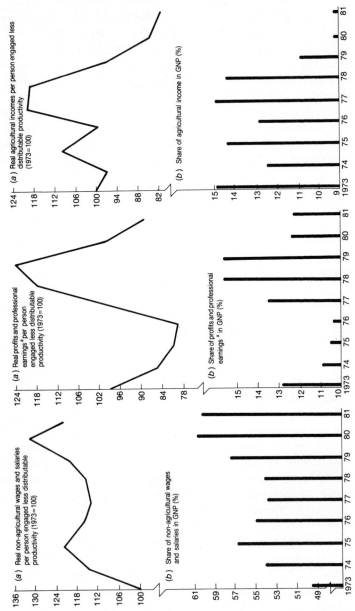

FIG. 4.2. Real Income, Productivity, and Factor Shares, 1973–1981

Source: Bacon *et al.*, 1982: 72.

the 1970s, which tended to be highly labour-intensive and to have a relatively low level of productivity per worker employed (see NESC No. 67, 1983). Aggregate productivity was improved at the cost of considerable labour-shedding in Irish industry, and even at that, as Chapter 2 showed, there were still wide divergences in the performance capabilities of different sectors of Irish industry.

The divergent performances of different sectors resulted in different responses to the constraints of centralized bargaining. In some cases profitable firms were prepared to accept or even encourage higher rates of pay than those provided for under the permissible increases of the pay agreements, which gave rise to the sort of difficulty noted above in relation to ATN claims.[4] In other cases the basic norm itself exceeded what employers in low-productivity firms or particularly vulnerable market-positions believed could be sustained. Yet it appears that, apart from in the very worst years of recession (1975–6), relatively few claims of inability to pay were made by private sector employers at company level. It has been suggested that the main reason for this is that

the right to plead inability-to-pay was so demanding in regard to the level of information to be disclosed, so unpredictable as to the questions that might be asked about management's performance, so uncertain as to its prospect of success, so transient as to the advantage which success might confer and so uncertain as to the prospect of peace in the event of success, that few individual employers, and no industrial or trade group of employers were prepared to pursue this course until the recession of the mid-seventies reached an advanced stage. (O'Brien, 1981: 195.)

Private sector employers came to wonder whether these matters were best dealt with under what they had come to see as the relatively inflexible mechanism of centralized pay agreements.

Government also observed these problems in the early 1980s, and experimented briefly with an exercise in pay determination in the light of economists' evaluation. Thus in August 1981 the incoming Coalition government appointed a three-man Committee on Costs and Competitiveness in order to 'make recommendations on the appropriate rate of domestic cost increases during a stipulated period consistent with sustaining the competitiveness of

---

[4] Interview with John Horgan.

the economy at home and abroad' (terms of reference, *Report of the Committee on Costs and Competitiveness*, 1981). But the report of the Committee did not become the basis for an agreed employer–labour approach to pay increases, as government had hoped. ICTU was highly critical of the initiative, suspecting that it would be used as a means of enforcing real income cuts on employees who were already aggrieved at trends in their income levels.[5] Furthermore, the authority of the Committee's report was thrown open to question when, shortly after publication of the report advocating a pay increase such that 'average 1982 costs should be no more than 11% above the average level in 1981' (p. 15), the Committee issued a press statement revising this figure downwards to 'no more than 8%', in the light of recent adverse movements in the exchange rate. Two factors cast doubt on the Committee's deliberations in the unions' view. First, the value of the exercise was questioned, if the volatility of exchange rates was such as to require a rapid revision of its recommendations at short notice. Second, it was widely held that the revised figure in fact owed not a little to political influence by a government anxious lest the higher figure should be treated as a 'floor' increase, as the norm evidently had been during the lifetime of the centralized wage agreements. The experiment in 'expert' wage recommendation was not repeated, and its failure is indicative of the conflicting perspectives of employers and unions on economic performance, a theme which will be further explored in this chapter and in the following two chapters.

In addition to their concern over the rate of growth of employee wage levels, employers became increasingly concerned about government's own contribution to total labour costs and hence to problems of competitiveness. Employers' social insurance contribution, payroll taxes, and other non-wage labour costs were relatively low during the 1970s. In Ireland, as in Britain, wages and salaries accounted for over three-quarters of total labour costs during the 1970s, a share which was among the highest in EEC

---

[5] ICTU's Executive Council called the exercise in 'expert' determination of a pay norm 'an academic fig-leaf' for government's interest in containing real wage increases. Brian Anderson (AUEW) probably expressed the sentiments of many trade unionists when he called the Committee a 'three-man razor gang' at an ICTU SDC on 29 Sept. 1981, convened to decide upon participation in new centralized pay talks.

countries.[6] Towards the late 1970s, however, the non-wage component of total labour costs increased markedly. Further increases in employers' costs, including a sharp increase in employers' pay-related social insurance (PRSI) contribution for employees, and a rescheduling of value added tax (VAT) on imports, were to be imposed in 1982 as a result of government's urgent need to increase tax revenue. But more pressingly for employers, a widening gap opened during the 1970s between employers' total labour costs and employees' disposable income, and the government's tax take accounted for the difference. This trend provided the stimulus for employers to seek a greater government input to wage bargaining. They hoped that government tax concessions would be won to alleviate employee pressure for money wage increases. While their expectations were initially met to some extent, government's rapidly increasing need for tax revenue led to sizeable increases in the personal tax burden, particularly in the early 1980s. This theme will be taken up again in the following section, when we consider the unions' criticisms of the outcomes of centralized bargaining, and in the last section, in our discussion of the constraints on government's concertative role.

INDUSTRIAL ACTION

Both employers and government were concerned about what were in their view adverse developments in employee wage costs. But their dissatisfaction with the centralized agreements which produced these outcomes might have been less marked if the agreements had at least ensured industrial peace. However, centralized collective bargaining did not bring any sustained reduction in the incidence of strikes or of days lost due to industrial action. The evidence of the strike statistics shows that although the NWAs appear to have had some initial success in this regard between 1971 and 1973, the total numbers of strikes and days lost resumed an upward trend over the decade, and the total number of days lost in 1979 (although this was a somewhat exceptional year due to a major and protracted strike in the Department of Posts and Telegraphs) exceeded even

[6] *Trade Union Information*, Autumn 1979: 14 (on labour costs in manufacturing in the EEC, 1975); Winter 1980–1: 20 (on hourly labour costs in manufacturing in 16 nations in 1979).

TABLE 4.3. *Annual Statement of Strike Frequency, Days Lost, Workers Involved, and Average Days Lost per Worker, 1960–1979*

	Strikes	Total days lost	Workers involved	Average days lost per worker
1960	49	80,349	5,865	13.70
1961	96	377,264	27,437	13.75
1962	60	104,024	9,197	11.31
1963	70	233,617	16,067	14.54
1964	87	545,384	24,245	21.60
1965	89	556,475	39,745	14.00
1966	112	783,635	52,238	15.00
1967	79	182,645	20,925	8.73
1968	126	405,686	38,880	10.43
1969	134	935,900	61,760	15.15
1970	134	1,007,714	28,752	35.05
1971	133	273,770	43,783	6.25
1972	131	206,955	22,274	9.29
1973	182	206,725	31,761	6.51
1974	219	551,833	43,459	12.70
1975	151	295,716	29,124	10.15
1976	134	776,949	42,281	18.38
1977	175	442,145	33,805	13.08
1978	152	624,266	32,558	19.17
1979	140	1,464,952	49,621	29.52

Source: Irish Statistical Bulletin; also in Report of the Commission of Inquiry on Industrial Relations, 1981: 328.

the record levels reached during 1969 and 1970. Table 4.3 sets out the year-by-year statistics over the 1960s and 1970s.

This upward trend is not simply attributable to the increase in the size of the workforce over the decade; the statistics on strikes per 100,000 employees still show a considerable increase for the 1970s, as Table 4.4 reveals. Days lost per 100,000 employees were down on the 1960s level in the first half of the 1970s, but well in excess of it in the second half of the decade. We shall argue that this trend may be explained by changes in the pattern of industrial conflict arising from the centralized agreements. Under the centralized agreements claims for ATN increases 'pure and simple' were proscribed and industrial action on these matters was barred. Claims in pursuit of matters covered by the flexibility clauses were obliged to follow the prescribed conflict-avoidance procedures, and only under the 1978 NWA was explicit sanction given for industrial action on these issues, once the prescribed temporal and

TABLE 4.4. *Five-Yearly Statement of Annual Average Strike Frequency, Days Lost, and Workers Involved, 1960–1979 (per 100,000 workers)*

	Strikes	Days lost	Workers involved
1960–64	6.8	25,271,2	1,579.8
1964–69	10.1	53,713.0	3,994.7
1970–74	14.9	41,999.9	3,178.1
1975–79	14.0	66,989.4	3,483.1

Source: Kelly and Brannick, 1983: 68.

procedural conditions had been fulfilled. But it would appear that although there was a marked reduction in the incidence of strikes on pay-related matters at the start of the 1970s their number grew as the decade progressed.

Data on the reported reasons for undertaking strike action are notoriously unreliable (see Shalev, 1978). The meaning attached by respondents to the limited choice of categories available is uncertain, wage claims may well be the vehicle for other, less easily expressible grievances, and the categorization of strikes is not weighted to allow for variations in the size of strikes. But the trend over time of strikes attributable to 'wages', as revealed in *Irish Statistical Bulletin* data, may nevertheless be significant.

During the years of decentralized bargaining in the 1960s pay and pay-related issues such as hours were key issues in industrial conflict. 'Wages' were cited as the main reason for striking in about 40% of instances of strike action in the second half of the 1960s. The great bulk of man-days lost, frequently in excess of 90%, were attributable to strikes over wages and hours. With the advent of centralized bargaining under the NWAs and NUs, wage round increases for all bargaining groups were negotiated simultaneously, and restrictions were placed on the conduct of supplementary bargaining. There was an obvious expectation that industrial conflict on pay matters should diminish greatly. But despite an initial drop in wage-related disputes this expectation was not borne out. Between 1970 and 1974 the proportion dropped to about 30% of all strikes. In 1971 the proportion of days lost attributable to strikes over wages and hours dropped to less than one-fifth, and remained relatively low in relation to earlier levels in the following couple of years (O'Brien, 1981: 228). But increasingly strikes over wages came to account for a greater proportion of all strikes and of all days lost; and the figures themselves showed an upward trend in absolute terms. From 1974 on, 'wages' was once again cited as the main reason for striking in about two-fifths of cases, and in over one-half of all strikes in 1979. Wages alone accounted for about one-half of all days lost in 1975, four-fifths in 1976, and two-thirds in 1978 and 1980; in 1979 96% of days lost were attributed to this issue.

However, the NWAs unquestionably shaped the pattern taken by strike activity. The strike breadth, or number of workers involved per strike, was never as high during the 1970s as the average figure for the 1960s.[7] The reason for this seems evident: because of the centralization of bargaining in the 1970s, the disputes which occurred were more likely to be confided to individual workplaces and sectional claims and grievances. In addition, ICTU opened a debate on picketing policy in the wake of the 1969 maintenance-men's dispute, and as a consequence adopted a 'two-tier' picketing policy designed to confine the impact of individual unions' pickets to their members alone unless an 'all-out' picket was specifically granted by ICTU (see the debate in ICTU *Annual Report*, 1970). The average duration of strikes remained fairly constant over the 1960s and 1970s, but this statistic masks a good deal of variation in the pattern of strike activity during the 1970s.

During the 1960s, in each year a small number of strikes accounted for a high proportion of total days lost. This phenomenon was evident during the 1970s as well, but the few major strikes, while often lasting a long time, involved on average a smaller number of workers than in the 1960s. For instance, on the basis of Central Statistics Office data, almost half the total days lost in 1974 were attributable to four major strikes; in 1976 a bank strike alone accounted for two-thirds of all days lost, and another six strikes accounted for a further 20%; in 1979, as already mentioned, the Post Office strike, which lasted for eighteen weeks and was the most protracted major strike ever to occur in the public sector,

[7] The principal official statistical source on industrial stoppages is the Central Statistical Office: its strike statistics are compiled according to ILO criteria and published in the *Irish Statistical Bulletin*. But there are certain shortcomings in these data (Brannick and Kelly, 1983). The Department of Industrial Relations at University College, Dublin, embarked in 1981 upon a comprehensive analysis of strike activity between 1960 and 1979, using an amended data-base. The present study therefore relies heavily on the early results of this project.

accounted for almost 80% of days lost due to strikes in that year. Large or lengthy strikes must also be seen as a function of employer resistance: this aspect of the question is discussed further in Chapter 6.

Strikes making a major contribution to total days lost are generally strikes in large employments, and among these may be found many public sector enterprises. Disputes in the public sector came to account for a greater proportion of strike activity over the course of the decade, accounting for 18% of all strikes between 1970 and 1979, but for 33% of all workers involved. The trend was especially marked in the second half of the 1970s. According to the results of recent research on strike data 'the outstanding characteristic in the trend of public sector strike activity is one of an increasing number of longer strikes with the larger proportion of days lost being derived . . . from more sustained and longer drawn out strike campaigns by comparatively smaller groups of workers than in the past' (Kelly and Brannick, 1983: 74; see also id., 1985). These data also accord with the growth, noted in Chapter 3, of restiveness among some public sector unions, not previously prone to strike activity, over the tight controls placed on public sector pay by the Coalition government and the perceived restrictiveness of the later NWAs.

Public sector strike activity tended to be concentrated in three industrial areas: 'turf extraction and mining, energy and power conversion, and communications, storage and transport' (Kelly and Brannick, 1985: 21). These were highly 'visible' strikes, capable of causing widespread disruption, not least to private sector business. Strikes by workers in key services and utilities in the private sector, such as banking or petrol and fuel distribution, also tended to have a high public profile. The disputes involved tended therefore to be politically sensitive; the implications of this observation are discussed further in Chapter 7.

Unofficial strikes appeared to show no secular decline in the 1970s compared with the 1960s, when they were a source of considerable employer concern. An estimation of the proportion of the total number of disputes accounted for by unofficial disputes, based on Labour Court data, suggested that in the late 1960s between one-half and two-thirds of disputes were unofficial, as were approximately 70% from 1970 to 1973, and roughly two-thirds throughout the rest of the decade (*Report of the Commission of Inquiry on Industrial Relations*, 1981: 312, 72). They accounted for about one-fifth of all days lost over the 1970s, and for almost one-half of all workers involved (Hillery, 1985). Not surprisingly, therefore, the average duration was relatively short by Irish standards: eight days, or about one-third of the average for official strikes. Unofficial strikes usually involve a breach of workplace disputes procedures (Prondzynski, 1982), and a certain proportion undoubtedly arose over grievances for which recognized disputes procedures were regarded as inadequate or unwieldy.[8] For instance, the Monitoring Unit of the Department of Labour estimated the porportion of unofficial strikes accounted for by suspensions and dismissals in 1977–8 at about 25%;[9] however, it also cited 'pay and conditions' as the reason for two-fifths of all unofficial disputes in 1977 and 1978, and about one-half of all unofficial strikes in 1979. In an ICTU discussion document on unofficial industrial action, which was the subject of trade union debate in 1980, a number of 'proximate reasons' for unofficial disputes were cited. Among these were shortcomings in workplace procedures, employer inaction, and delays in gaining service from conciliation bodies; but in addition specific reference was made to 'reaction against the restrictive clauses of the NWAs'. One of the long-term measures proposed to eliminate the causes of unofficial action was the recommendation that 'unions must provide speedy and effective service to members'.[10] These remarks are indicative of the pressures unions experienced during the period of centralized bargaining, and reflect a view that, far from serving to reduce the incidence of industrial action, centralized agreements themselves may have been a significant cause of unofficial strikes. This issue is explored further in Chapter 5.

In addition to the small number of large strikes and the persistence of small-scale, unofficial strikes, the private sector also exhibited a pattern of strikes of 'medium' duration, with a

---

[8] The government hoped that the passage of the Unfair Dismissals Act in 1977 would reduce the incidence of both official and unofficial strikes attributable to suspensions and dismissals, by obliging employers to follow reasonable procedures; see *Dáil Debates* 2 Mar. 1977, vol. 297, col. 667; also O'Brien (1981): 225. The Act seems to have had some success in this regard: see Murphy (1985).

[9] R. Hayes McCoy, in 'Strike Record Threatens Growth', *IT* 24 Aug. 1978, estimated that up to 40% of unofficial strikes in these years were due to suspensions and dismissals.

[10] ICTU *Annual Report*, 1980: 250 (appendix 4: Discussion Document on Unofficial Industrial Action).

'medium' number of workers involved (see Kelly and Brannick, 1983). It is likely that the incidence of such strikes varied across industrial sectors, depending on the profitability of the industry, union wage militancy, and employer resistance (the variability in profitability and in the type or market competition experienced by firms was noted in Chapter 2). It is also likely that the incidence of strikes varied in relation to other aspects of workplace industrial relations. The formalization of disputes procedure is not incompatible with an intensification of bargaining activity (Goldthorpe, 1974; Batstone, 1984; also Hardiman, 1982). But where enterprise-level procedures and managerial performance were poor, a higher level of industrial conflict might be expected. Recent research would suggest that Irish-owned firms, on the whole, combine a less well developed managerial approach to workplace industrial relations with a greater incidence of industrial action than foreign-owned firms (IDA, 1984; Wallace, 1982; Murphy, 1982a).

The pattern of overall workplace industrial militancy increases sharply if industrial action short of a stoppage such as go-slow, work-to-rule, overtime ban, and other forms of industrial action short of a strike are taken into account. Research indicates that the incidence of industrial action short of a strike exceeded that of actual stoppages by quite a margin. Wallace (1982: 107) found that the ratio of other forms of industrial action to stoppages was about five to one. An IDA study found a ratio of between two-and-a-half and three to one (1984: 42). Fogarty et al. (1981: 25) noted that in 1977 at RTE (the state-sponsored radio and television company), out of thirty-two cases where industrial action occurred or was threatened, there was an actual stoppage in only eight. It would appear that Irish-owned companies experienced higher levels of these forms of industrial action. One survey found twice as many incidents of this sort among such establishments, resulting in a cumulative total of employee working days lost through disputes which was seven times greater than the time lost in the international plants (IDA, 1984).

A full account of the reasons for strikes in the 1970s is likely to require multifactoral explanation (Durcan, McCarthy, and Redman, 1983; Edwards, 1983). Nevertheless, the impact of the large strikes and the prevalence of medium-sized strikes, in addition to the extensiveness of unofficial or wild-cat action and of industrial action short of a strike, suggests that Irish employees were very far from reducing their reliance on their market power.

It may be concluded that this trend is not consistent with the 'under-utilization of market power' which would be necessary, as Chapters 1 and 2 argued, if the centralized agreements were to function as a vital complement to economic management.

Performance in Areas of Trade Union Interest

During the 1970s the employers frequently criticized the upward trend in earnings. They argued that for employees to seek full money compensation for inflation would be self-defeating because it would have further inflationary consequences for future pay trends. They took the view that employees should not press for wages increases to compensate for effective tax increases, whether direct or indirect. Both employers and government insisted upon the need for wage restraint as a condition for the success of public policies directed towards employment expansion.

But employees became increasingly aggrieved over the performance of the centralized agreements. Although nominal earnings were increasing, their view was that they were benefiting to a far lesser extent than was apparent. The strategy adopted by ICTU in negotiations at the ELC and with government is analysed in greater detail in the following chapter. In this section we shall survey developments in the two main issues which were important to ICTU's commitments to centralized wage bargaining: first, protection of real disposable income and of workers' share in rising GNP, and second, improvement in employment levels and reduction of unemployment.

REAL DISPOSABLE INCOME

The divergence between employers' and employees' views on pay trends was marked during the 1970s. The employers saw in the upward trend a continuing problem for competitiveness; this was also of serious concern to government, which as an employer was also greatly worried by the implications for current expenditure levels. But whatever the view of government and employers about the developments in nominal wages shown in Tables 4.1 and 4.2, unions argued that real earnings, i.e. earnings net of the effects of inflation, showed a far less dramatic increase. The trend in real income in different sectors is graphed in Figure. 4.3.

But employees' real *disposable* income did not follow these trends: the fiscal gap between real pre-tax employee income and real net income widened in the course of the 1970s. Real disposable income was maintained in the early years of the NWAs. But whereas real pre-tax incomes rose in the years of high inflation, 1974 and 1975, the combined effect of pay curbs and fiscal drag depressed real disposable income between 1975 and 1977. In the years of the Fianna Fáil growth-oriented policies, real gross income increased quite sharply, but the rising incidence of taxation resulted in a growing gap between real pre-tax income and real disposable income. These developments are graphed in Figure 4.4. Even more marked, in this graph, is the dramatic widening of the gap between employers' total labour costs, the increase in which was noted in the last section, and employees' real disposable income. While employers could with justice complain that total labour costs were rising steeply, employees could also with justice complain that the net value of their earnings had increased but little over the period of centralized bargaining.

Government tax revenue from all sources grew rapidly during the 1970s, in line with the sharp increase in the level of public expenditure, which will be considered further in the next section. In the early 1960s government tax revenue amounted to 17% of GNP,

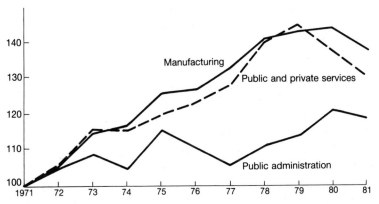

FIG. 4.3. Real Income per Employee by Sector, 1971–1981 (1971 = 100)

Source: *Report of the Committee on Costs and Competitiveness*, 1981: 38.

and by 1969–70 this had grown to 24%. By 1975, however, total tax revenue came to about 33% of GNP, by 1981 to 41%, and by 1983 to over 45%.[11]

But the trade union movement came increasingly to resent the fact that governments relied to a disproportionately large degree on employee income tax as a source of tax revenue, and the tax burden on all employees increased during the 1970s. Changes over two decades in the distribution of tax revenue by categories of taxation may be seen from Table 4.5. (see also OECD *Economic Survey*, 1982: 40; Raftery, 1982).

TABLE 4.5. *Distribution of Tax Revenue by Type of Taxation, 1960–1980 (%)*

	1960	1965	1970	1975	1980
Personal income	14.8	16.7	18.3	25.2	32.0
Capital gains	—	—	—	0.0	0.2
Corporate income	6.6	9.1	8.8	4.8	4.6
Social security					
Employees'	2.3	3.2	3.8	5.6	5.1
Employers'	2.6	3.3	4.5	8.2	9.1
Rates	15.7	12.2	10.1	7.3	3.4
Wealth	—	—	—	0.3	—
Estate, inheritance	2.2	1.9	1.2	1.1	0.3
Stamp duty	1.7	1.0	0.8	0.9	1.4
Goods and services	54.2	52.7	52.4	46.5	43.5
Other	0.1	0.0	0.1	0.0	0.3
Total tax revenue (£m.)	143.6	249.5	506.0	1195.5	3180.4

Source: Rottman and O'Connell, 1982a (based on OECD data).

A heavy though declining reliance on indirect taxation persisted. All categories besides personal income tax and the social security contributions both of employers and employees show a relative decline. This is evidence of the increase in overall labour costs combined with the decline in employee disposable income graphed in Figure 4.4. To some extent, this is explicable by changes in tax policy on other items.[12] But it is also attributable to real increases in

[11] *Dáil Debates* 22 April 1970, vol. 245, col. 1765 (supplement to the Financial Statement); *National Income and Expenditure* data to 1981 and ESRI estimates for 1983, in Conniffe and Kennedy, 1984: 77.
[12] For example, wealth tax and domestic rates were abolished in 1977; the upper rate of taxation in 1974 was 80% and by 1980 this was lowered to 60%; the June

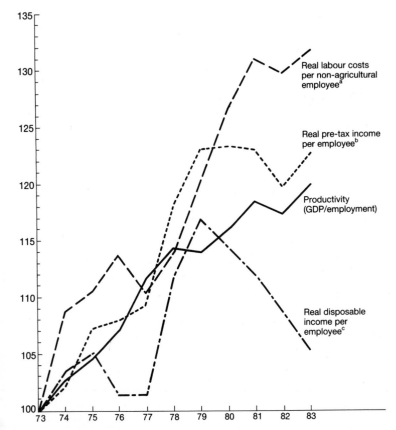

FIG. 4.4. Productivity, Labour Costs, and Real Income, 1973–1983 (1973 = 100)

Source: Adapted from National Planning Board, 1984: 160.

the incidence of direct taxation, and especially of personal income tax and social security contributions. From 1960, these two revenue sources grew at an average annual rate of nearly 20%, compared with an average rate of growth in nominal GDP of about 13.5% per annum (OECD *Economic Survey*, 1982: 39).

The income tax base, however, was very narrow. Substantial exemptions were available for manufacturing companies, as an

Budget reduced indirect taxation by removing VAT from some items and subsidizing others.

integral part of industrial policy, and for the agricultural sector, in spite of the existence of a prosperous stratum of large farmers and the more general improvement in farm incomes following entry to the EEC (see Rottman, Hannan, Hardiman, and Wiley, 1982; Rottman and Hannan, 1982). By the late 1970s almost 90% of income taxation came from employees' PAYE income tax. But no substantial alteration was made to the structure of the tax system.

The number of employees paying income tax increased rapidly from the late 1960s, due to the rise in money incomes, high inflation, and tax bands and allowances which were little modified between 1962 and 1974.[13] Although more frequent adjustments were made after this latter date, revenue buoyancy remained high.

The proportion of personal tax to personal income was about 7% in the mid-1960s; this rose to almost 12% in 1974 and to over 15% in 1976. The tax-related Budget of 1977 reduced this figure somewhat, and some real benefits occurred in connection with the National Understandings. Thereafter, however, fiscal drag reappeared; the average rate of personal income tax was estimated at 20% in 1983 (Conniffe and Kennedy, 1984: 78; Dowling, 1981). Figure 4.5 shows the extent to which marginal tax rates became more burdensome in real terms over time. In sum:

The direct tax burden of all households increased by approximately one-third over the decade. Direct taxation (income tax plus pay related social insurance) amounted in 1972–73 to 23% of the average industrial wage for single men, 19% for a childless couple, and 6.7% for a married couple with three children aged under eleven. The percentages in 1978–79 were 23.6, 23.0 and 13.7. respectively. The general growing burden is attributable primarily to the erosion in the value of tax allowances and the speed with which most (employee) income earners now exhaust their allowances and move into higher tax rates. (Rottman et al., 1982: 180.)

Thus not only did government involvement in pay–tax bargaining evidently make relatively little contribution to the overall process of wage determination, but it appears to have had the opposite effect throughout this period. In the words of one economist, 'the government has actually, through the way it uses the fiscal system, militated against pay restraint . . . Except for a short period around 1979–81, the inadequate revision of allowances and rate-bands in the face of inflation has caused the effective rate of income tax

[13] OECD Economic Survey, 1974: 24–6; NESC No. 37 (1978); First Report of the Commission on Taxation, 1982.

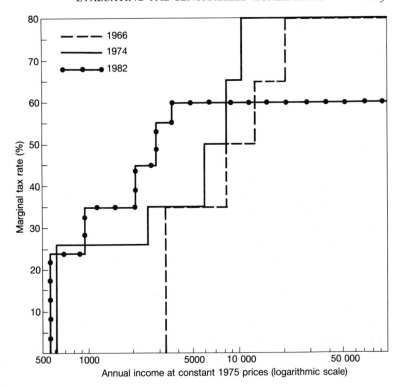

FIG. 4.5. Marginal Tax Rates for Comparable Levels of Real Income, 1966, 1974, 1982

Source: OECD *Economic Survey*, 1982: 39.

applicable to any given level of wages to rise steadily over many years.' (Bristow, 1982.)

EMPLOYMENT AND UNEMPLOYMENT

The trade union movement was committed to a number of more general objectives in the area of public policy pertaining to the collective interests of employees and the realization of social justice. Among these, of course, attainment of high levels of employment was particularly important. But other issues such as the extent of welfare provisions were also matters of concern. In this section we shall survey developments in some of these other areas, but a full discussion of the issues raised would require a separate study; they cannot be dealt with in detail within the confines of the present book.

The government and the employers insisted that wage restraint was essential to curb the domestic contribution to the inflationary cycle, thus improving competitiveness and providing the conditions for increased employment. The trade unions disputed the employer and government claim that employee incomes were rising too rapidly. They held that by participating in the centralized agreements they were forgoing opportunities to increase real wages. But growth in levels of employment was an objective in which the trade unions had an obvious interest; and if the employers' and government's analysis was well-founded, the trade unions would have expected to see an improvement in employment levels and a decline in unemployment. However, no significant decline in unemployment levels was apparent. Some decline occurred in the second half of the decade, due to the international economic upturn and the Fianna Fáil government's fiscal boost, but 1976 had been a peak year for unemployment, and subsequent unemployment levels remained consistently higher than they had been in the first half of the decade. Trends in employment and unemployment during the 1970s may be seen in Table 4.6.

TABLE 4.6. *Persons At Work and Unemployed 1969–1982 ('000s)*

Year	At Work	Unemployed	Labour force	Unemployed as % of labour force
1969	1032.6	43.4	1076.0	4.0
1970	1023.7	52.4	1076.1	4.9
1971	1030.4	49.4	1079.9	4.6
1972	1039.4	56.6	1096.0	5.2
1973	1059.8	52.4	1112.2	4.7
1974	1077.5	52.5	1130.0	4.6
1975	1073.0	73.0	1146.0	6.4
1976	1064.0	90.0	1154.0	7.8
1977	1083.3	88.6	1171.9	7.6
1978	1110.0	85.0	1195.0	7.1
1979	1145.0	74.0	1219.0	6.1
1980	1163.0	76.0	1239.0	6.1
1981	1151.0	113.0	1264.0	8.9
1982	1146.0	137.0	1283.0	10.7

Source: Conniffe and Kennedy, 1984: 22.

Moreover, the trade union movement was sceptical about the relationship between control of the rate of pay increases and increase in the level of employment. From the trade unions' point of view, there was relatively little assurance that wage restraint would not simply result in increased profits without entailing any need for reinvestment. The suspicion was all the greater in the case of foreign-owned firms, many of which were highly profitable. Many employees were of the belief that such companies had little long-term commitment to the Irish economy in any case, and that whereas in view of the scale of their operations they could easily tolerate extra wage costs, wage restraint would not necessarily have any bearing on their reinvestment decisions. Towards the mid-1980s evidence on the extent of profit repatriation by foreign-owned firms during the 1970s (which accounted for most of the 'black hole' of capital outflows from the country during this period) provided greater substance for these earlier suspicions.[14]

One policy commentator noted in 1977 that the relative cost gains of NWAs could only be maintained if tensions arising from this uncertainty were eliminated. The remedy should be: 'a form of participation in decisions affecting capacity utilisation and investment where these are being financed by wage restraint and an institutional framework to ensure that wage restraint is reflected in increased output and employment' (ESRI QEC, December 1977). No such provisions were ever made. In fact, guarantees of this sort were held to be politically undesirable because they would cut across the main thrust of industrial policy. Open-ended reliance on the job-creating potential of private industry continued to be the mainstay of employment policy, supplemented though it might be from time to time by government job-creating measures. The Minister for Economic Planning and Development, Martin O'Donoghue, in a speech in the Dáil in November 1977, acknowledged that government could provide no guarantees in this matter, but insisted that wage restraint was necessary all the same: 'I take the point that pay restraint of itself does not necessarily lead to increased employment, but on the other hand in the absence of pay restraint it may not be possible to bring about additional

[14] In 1984 the OECD reported that total profit repatriation and royalty payments abroad amounted to an estimated IR£900m., 10% of the value of all exports in that year (OECD *Economic Survey*, 1984–5: 47).

employment or increased investment.'[15] But for the trade unions a vague commitment of this sort was less than wholly satisfactory.

SOCIAL EXPENDITURE

The logic of a government strategy directed towards effecting a concertative integration of collective bargaining with other policies, as outlined in Chapter 1, would imply a preferential orientation of social policy towards the working class. But this was far from being in evidence in Ireland.

The rate of increase of social spending in Ireland was high in the 1960s and 1970s, as welfare provisions expanded in line with the transformation of Irish society (McCashin, 1982). Social expenditure, comprising expenditure on health, education, housing, social security, and welfare, grew from 15.9% of GDP in 1951 to 19.8% in 1970 and 26.5% in 1979, accounting for over half the increase in the GDP share of social expenditure in this period (Maguire, 1984: 75). During the 1970s transfer payments constituted the second largest component of current expenditure (after public sector pay). Much of the increase under this heading was accounted for by both structural and cyclical factors which increased the number of those entitled to receive benefits. The real value of welfare benefits also improved, however, especially towards the end of the decade (*Report of the Committee on Costs and Competitiveness*, 1981: 32; National Planning Board, 1984: 50). Some of the improvement in the real value of social spending, including health care entitlements, may be attributed to the extension of the scope of collective bargaining in the form of the National Understandings (see Coughlan, 1984).

But although all categories of social spending saw significant increase in the course of the 1970s, looked at in conjunction with state taxation policies the overall redistributive effect was very restricted.

Working class categories, despite high average receipts of state transfers, were net contributors to state revenue. Only unskilled manual workers and marginal farmers were on average consistently net recipients from the

---

[15] *Dáil Debates* 23 Nov. 1977, vol. 301, col. 1563. The Minister hoped that the trade union movement would regard Fianna Fáil's high level of spending on direct job creation as the government's earnest of good intent, even though no guarantees could be given on job creation (interview with Martin O'Donoghue).

direct tax and transfer system; white collar households were the only consistent net contributors. (Rottman *et al.*, 1982: 175.)

The taxation system favoured the ownership and inheritance of capital and property (whether in agriculture, manufacturing, or distribution). State intervention in income distribution thus tended to strengthen the boundaries of already existing class advantage (see OECD, 1976). The highly inegalitarian character of state funding for education, and the extent of the net benefits accruing to the already privileged, has been documented by Tussing (1978) and Barlow (1981). Research by Whelan and Whelan (1984) would seem to suggest that inequality of access to educational opportunities has an important bearing on patterns of social mobility. Some reservation must be entered with regard to their findings, because in their comparative work the Irish data were limited to the Dublin region whereas nationwide data were available for other countries. Nevertheless, their conclusions are of interest in the present context:

(i) The available evidence suggests that the association between social origins and educational achievements is stronger than in other countries.
(ii) Intragenerational or career mobility is comparatively restricted and educational qualifications are a particularly strong determinant of class position. (p. 187.)

It was argued in Chapter 1 that the basis for trade unions' commitment to bargained co-operation with government is the assurance that class-related social objectives are made central to public policy, with a reasonably reliable expectation that government would be able to fulfil its commitments. But it would appear that state social policy in Ireland offered relatively little reassurance to the working class and lower middle class.

The Role of Government

The disadvantages of abandoning the centralized system of collective bargaining were evident to both employers and unions: the calculations of each side relevant to their continued participation are discussed more fully in Chapters 5 and 6. But employers and unions both came increasingly to believe that the interests most important to them were not well served by the centralized agreements. As we have seen, part of the reason for each side's dissatisfaction had to do with the role of government. Both unions and employers were dissatisfied with its role in the wage formation process. The trade union movement was also critical of the lack of success of both the Coalition and the Fianna Fáil governments in improving employment levels. However, a number of constraints limited the effectiveness of government in its efforts to facilitate employer–labour agreements. First, there were structural limits to the control it could exert over employment levels and (a related issue) over investment decisions. Second, government discretion in the process of wage formation, particularly through taxation policy, was limited by problems which were developing in the public finances. Third, the effectiveness of government efforts to play a concertative role was limited by the diversity of the objectives each government chose to pursue.

LIMITS TO GOVERNMENT CONTROL OVER EMPLOYMENT LEVELS

During the 1960s and 1970s the Irish economy was undergoing profound structural transformation, the main features of which were set out in Chapter 2. It was noted in that chapter that direct foreign investment was seen as the motor of industrial development and economic growth. Industrial policy was therefore central to government policies on economic management. But the priorities of industrial policy were, in some respects, at odds with government commitments to protect and increase employment levels.

Ireland's industrial policy was based on provision of capital subsidies and export tax relief. Further grants were available for retraining and other labour-related costs. The number of job-approvals sanctioned in a year was an important measure of its success for the IDA, but there was no guarantee that any given level of investment would result in an increase in job opportunities.

One set of consequences of Ireland's industrial policy was to reduce the average age of industrial plant, to facilitate the attraction of 'best-practice' technology, and thus to contribute to the increase in productivity per person employed. However, the capital subsidies provided may also have distorted the relative costs of capital and labour to users in a manner inimical to the stated priority of employment expansion. Recent research suggests that up to the mid-1970s the real cost of capital declined more rapidly in Ireland than in selected other countries (UK, USA, Canada, and West

Germany), and even though this trend was reversed in all countries in the second half of the 1970s due to the rise in real interest rates, it was only in the early 1980s that the costs of using fixed capital in Ireland began to compare unfavourably with other countries (research cited in National Planning Board, 1984: 158). Thus while government policies had the effect of increasing real labour costs, they simultaneously contributed to reducing capital costs. The result was a widening divergence in the course of the 1970s between the relative costs of capital and labour to producers; this trend is graphed in Figure 4.6.

Provision of capital incentives remained the mainstay of industrial policy. Governments anticipated that economic growth would eventually generate demand for labour and thus an increased level of employment. However, growth does not necessarily, of itself, result in a significant increase in employment. The consequences for employment levels of the Fianna Fáil growth strategy adopted in 1977 were thus somewhat disappointing. The boost in public spending strengthened the effect of the recovery then under way, and economic growth and industrial output both picked up rapidly. Employment levels also rose, but not to the same degree. The reasons for this were several. Productivity gains may have reduced the demand for additional labour; some firms may have 'hoarded' labour during recession; others may have undertaken capital restructuring prompted by the trends in relative costs documented in Figure 4.6. (OECD *Economic Survey*, 1979: 34). Econometric modelling of economic performance is often controversial; but in 1975 it was suggested that in order to bring about an annual rate of increase in levels of employment of 1.5% to 2%, a sustained annual increase in the rate of growth of GNP of the order of 6% would be required—a level of performance which was never attained in Ireland (Kennedy and Dowling, 1975: 284–5).

Two major labour-force constraints further limited the capacity of government directly to influence the rates of employment. One was the highly elastic character of the supply of labour; the other was the demographic basis to the rapid growth in the employee workforce during the 1970s.

It has been shown that in Ireland during the 1970s an increase in demand for labour tended to expand the supply more rapidly than unemployment was diminished (Colm McCarthy, 1979; Walsh, 1978; Keenan, 1978). Heavy emigration to Britain occurred in

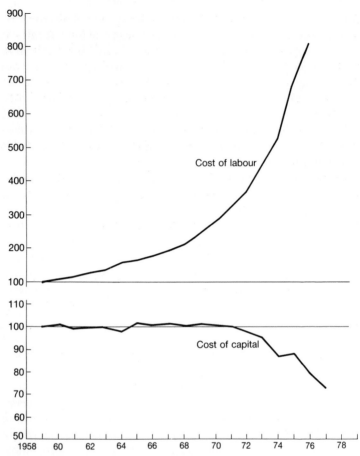

FIG. 4.6. Relative Costs of Capital and Labour (1973 = 100)

Source: OECD *Economic Survey*, 1979: 37.

earlier years and many of these people would choose to return to Ireland if suitable job opportunities were available. During some years in the 1970s there was a net inflow of migrants (Bacon *et al.*, 1982: 33–4). The participation rate fluctuated in relation to the availability of employment. New entrants into the labour market swelled the numbers of the unemployed (though many also sought outlets elsewhere, such as in higher education). The participation rate of married women was particularly variable (Walsh and O'Toole, 1973). The proportion of this group actively engaged in the workforce was low compared with other European countries, but participation increased rapidly during the 1970s, and many more married women were ready to take up employment if it became available.

In addition to the constraints presented by the elasticity of the labour supply, the total labour force increased very rapidly during the 1970s. A high birth-rate combined with a decline in emigration altered the demographic profile of the population. By the late 1970s the median age of the population was twenty-five, and the dependency ratio in Ireland was higher than in any West European country except Spain (National Planning Board, 1984: 257, based on OECD data). The number of new entrants to the labour force each year resulted in a level of demand for employment which far outstripped the opportunities available. Table 4.7. shows the changing age-structure of the labour force.

TABLE 4.7. *The Labour Force Classified by Age, 1961, 1971, 1977, 1981, (%)*

Age	1961	1971	1977	1981
15–24	24.7	27.1	27.3	27.7
25–44	36.6	35.5	40.1	42.8
45–64	31.6	31.3	28.1	25.4
65+	7.1	6.1	4.5	4.1
TOTAL	100	100	100	100
N ('000s)=	1060.2	1079.9	1172.0	1263.6

Source: Prof. J. J. Sexton, ESRI, Dublin.

In summary, then, although an 'orderly' adjustment of wage levels and restraint of the upward pressure on wage increases were essential to the public policy priorities of economic growth and expansion of employment, the likelihood that a pay policy would in fact bring about these objectives was very uncertain. Government was unable to guarantee that the projected consequences would be brought about. This was due in some part to the nature of its other policy commitments, principally those in the area of industrial policy; it was also due to the characteristics of an expanding labour force in a rapidly industrializing society. The nature of the relationship between the institutions of state and the economy was far from conducive to the development of full employment policies.

WAGE FORMATION AND PUBLIC FINANCES

It was earlier argued that high levels of employee taxation and growing levels of employer payroll taxes were inimical to the securing of effective wage regulation agreements. But government commitments to increased levels of public spending meant that extra revenue was needed. Although some of this need could be met

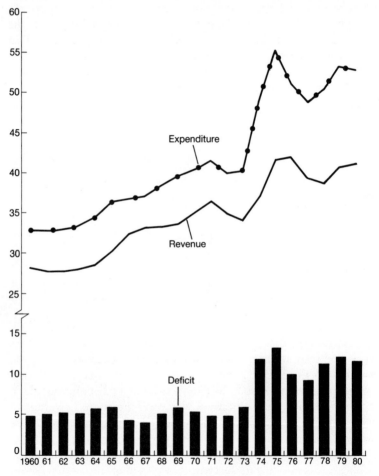

FIG. 4.7. Government Revenue, Expenditure, and Deficit, 1960–1980 (% of GDP)

Source: OECD *Economic Survey*, 1982: 38.

by increasing borrowing-levels, taxation obviously remained the key source of government revenue. Moreover, a large deficit on the public current account was intended to be a temporary expedient to boost economic performance, and both the Coalition and the Fianna Fáil governments intended their large deficits to give way to greater reliance on taxation revenue.

In the course of Chapter 3 it was shown that a cautious move to stimulate demand in 1972 and 1973 led to a break with the previous orthodoxy of a balanced budget. The Coalition government escalated the expansionary thrust in 1974 and especially in the worst year of the recession, 1975. Current government expenditure grew from about 25% of GNP in 1969 to 33.5% in 1971, and then increased to 41% in 1975. It levelled off at this point for a time, because the Coalition government followed a restrictive fiscal policy designed to curb the public component of total consumption and reduce reliance on borrowing. The Fianna Fáil government of 1977–81 (and that of February–November 1982) followed highly expansionary policies. Public spending continued to increase and current government expenditure reached a peak of 54.5% of GNP in 1982 (Conniffe and Kennedy, 1984: 71; see also K. A. Kennedy, 1981; Gould, 1981).

The increase in public spending during the 1970s presented governments with a mounting problem of financing the deficit thus incurred. The scale of this problem may be seen from Figure 4.7. Increasingly the government deficit was met by borrowing on foreign markets. Added together with the capital borrowing

TABLE 4.8. *Summary Data of Public Finances*

	1975	1976	1977	1978	1979	1980	1981	1982
PSBR								
£ m.	675	597	703	981	1230	1558	2205	2466
as % of								
GNP	18.1	13.1	12.9	15.6	16.8	18.0	21.5	21.0
External debt								
£ m.	688	1269	1269	1391	2032	2986	4812	6557
as % of								
official								
reserves	0.99	1.33	1.06	1.11	2.08	2.22	3.27	4.11

Source: Conniffe and Kennedy, 1984: 70; National Planning Board, 1984: 46. Drawn from Budgets; *National Income and Expenditure* (1981); *Economic Review and Outlook* (1983); ESRI *QEC* (various); Central Bank *Quarterly Bulletin* (various).

requirements of local authorities and state-sponsored bodies, total borrowing requirements were high in the mid-1970s and grew again from 1977 onwards. The growth in the size of the external debt may be seen in Table 4.8.

A rising proportion of tax revenue was therefore needed to service the public debt. During the decade to 1974 this was generally about 18%. In 1975 it was 19%, and the figure rose over the last years of the 1970s to 30% in 1983 (see Conniffe and Kennedy, 1984: 76; Dowling, 1978). The scope for reducing the employee tax burden was limited, to some degree, by government spending and borrowing commitments.

THE DIVERSITY OF GOVERNMENT OBJECTIVES

However, government's role in the wage formation process is not fully explained by the constraints imposed by the need for tax revenue. The need to increase tax revenue is clear. But it should also be recognized that by relying so heavily on the employee sector for this revenue, government cut across its objectives on pay policy. Moreover, government spending commitments themselves were not always well integrated with pay policy objectives. Both the Coalition and the Fianna Fáil governments were committed to protecting a variety of political and economic interests, and these did not necessarily complement government's interest in facilitating employer–labour wage agreements. Four issues concerning revenue and expenditure decisions will be looked at to illustrate this point: taxation, budget deficit and demand management, public sector pay, and capital spending, before we return to some concluding remarks about centralized pay agreements.

Taxation

A partial explanation for the heavy reliance on the employee sector as a source of revenue may be found in the fact that the tax structure of the 1970s was to a large extent 'passively' created. Fiscal drag provided a useful and reliable source of revenue. Extension of the tax net to include 'new' categories, such as farmers and self-employed, was likely to be politically controversial. For example, in 1974 the Coalition government modified its company tax plans, following representations from the CII, and in 1978 Fianna Fáil withdrew its plans to introduce an interim levy on farm profits (pending a fuller review of farmers' tax), because of the strong opposition to this plan expressed by agricultural interests. It may also be noted that the adjustments to tax allowances and bands obtained by employees in the late 1970s followed the manifestation of mass popular discontent. But by the early to mid-1980s, when such deficit-financed flexibility was no longer available to government, the employee tax burden was heavier than ever. Thus tax policy showed a certain inertia; rather than being actively shaped, it appeared to be the product of shifting vectors of political influence. The significance of this tendency is discussed further in Chapter 7.

Budget deficit and demand management

Both administrations during the 1970s were, on the whole, disposed to follow expansionary policies, even in years when the underlying growth was strong (Bacon et al., 1982), and when the consequence was to give a powerful boost to domestic inflation (Ryan, 1982). Growth in GNP was thus maintained at a high level, but not without creating other problems associated with chronic deficit by the early 1980s:

While this [expansionary approach] has facilitated employment growth which would not otherwise have taken place, the deterioration in the balance of payments with which these policies have been associated raises questions as to whether the positive results will be durable and whether fiscal policy should have had greater regard to its role of stabilisation which by now has become compromised by the present levels of borrowing. (Bacon et al., 1982: 60–1.)

A sceptical view of the value of this rapid growth in deficit-financed expenditure was expressed by T. K. Whitaker, formerly Secretary of the Department of Finance and Governor of the Central Bank. Calling it a 'flabby perversion of Keynesian theory' (Whitaker, 1983b: 105), he cautioned that: 'Once a large current deficit had been allowed to appear, the government would find it extremely hard on political grounds ever to close the gap again, even when this course was dictated by sound economic principles.'[16]

[16] Whitaker, 1983b: 99. Other comments advanced at this time were more unequivocally critical, for example: 'as of October 1980, the Republic of Ireland has no macroeconomic policy' (McCarthy, 1980); 'terms such as "policy", "strategy", or "rationale" would clearly be inapplicable so such a destabilisation of the public finances' (Whitaker, 1983b: 110); 'interest groups now press their claims

During the 1970s several economic commentators argued that decisions on public spending and on pay policy should be more closely integrated and policy objectives more closely specified. Some counselled adoption of a more 'technical' approach to these issues, through greater adherence to the planning framework of the 'rolling development plans' adopted by both administrations during the 1970s.[17] Others, such as the Central Bank, urged that the centralized agreements should have a more stable institutional framework, or that they should be negotiated for a longer span to make them really useful as instruments of planning (ESRI QEC, April 1979). Common to all these recommendations was the awareness that demand management policy and pay policy were not closely integrated in a coherent development policy.

It is commonly observed that demand management policies tend to be relatively more highly favoured by Social Democratic governments than by those of more conservative hue, and that this contrast is associated with an ideologically grounded difference in policy priorities. In Ireland, though, no explicit ideology prompted the initial adoption or perpetuation of these policies. Similarly, the 'adjustment' measures which the Coalition undertook in 1976 were developed in response to immediate pressures. Economic policy-making thus tended to have a certain *ad hoc* quality to it. In Chapter 7 the pressures which underlay the adoption of these policy priorities are explored further.

Public sector pay

Most of the increase in public spending during the 1970s was due to the increase in current expenditure, and the current budget deficit grew from virtually nothing in 1972 to approximately one-half of total borrowing a decade later. The largest single component of government current expenditure was public consumption, particularly the wage and salary bill of public employees, who constituted about one-fifth of the labour force and one-third of all

unrelentingly and successive governments—faced with lists of claims far in excess of current revenue—have conceded far too much for far too long so that we are now burdened with massive foreign debts' (Galvin, 1982).

[17] T. K. Whitaker, among others, regretted the dissociation of policy-making from the planning context; even though framework planning in the 1960s was not closely followed, it at least provided performance targets (interview with T. K. Whitaker).

employees in the late 1970s, absorbing about one-third of current Budget spending (Department of the Public Service, 1978). Public sector employment grew rapidly during the 1970s, as was seen in Chapter 2. As a consequence of the combination of a greater number of employees and the upward pressure on public sector 'special' wage increases, the public service pay bill increased rapidly, particularly in the second half of the decade. Between 1975 and 1981 the public service pay bill, including pensions, rose at an average annual rate of 25%. Average pay per person increased by 18.5% and numbers employed by 3.75% (Conniffe and Kennedy, 1984: 73).

Public sector pay was therefore a very important item in management of the government finances. However, the private sector employers criticized government policy in this area for causing 'confusion in the public sector' (Fogarty et al., 1981: 21). They argued that public sector pay was initially restricted too much, then allowed to catch up with other occupations at an inopportune time in the late 1970s in response to employee frustrations; and that the process whereby this occurred, through 'major disputes and a variety of special awards', was destabilizing. They also found fault with the fact that government's attempts to control the upward pressures on public sector pay were implemented at too late a stage in the process of public sector pay determination, for instance in the case of the embargo on 'special' increases in 1975–6. Although government in its capacity as employer might seem to be in a good position to shape public sector pay developments, there was relatively little evidence of a coherent public sector pay policy. The constraints which may have limited government options on this matter are considered briefly in Chapter 7.

Capital spending

Capital spending increased fairly steadily during the 1970s. It was mainly committed to infrastructural development, with expansion occurring over most of the government departmental programmes. Investment levels were thus maintained at times of declining private investment. As a proportion of GNP, the public capital programme rose from 12.6% in 1975 to over 16% by the early 1980s, a very high level by any standard (*Public Capital Programme* data, in Conniffe and Kennedy, 1984: 82).

But the rate of return on public capital expenditure became increasingly a matter of concern in the course of the 1970s (McDowell, 1982: 185–6). One of the issues over which debate developed was the potential for conflict between policy priorities, where withdrawal of commitment to a public enterprise project would have adverse consequences for employment, but continued commitment to it represented an increased liability on the public capital deficit. Governments found difficulty in determining acceptable guidelines in these matters, particularly when local electoral considerations leaned towards preservation of employment even at some cost to the state. The way in which these electoral pressures made themselves felt is discussed further in Chapter 7.

Chapter 3 showed that each government during the 1970s evinced a strong commitment to keeping the centralized agreements in existence, and that to do this the level of demand was sustained and employment levels were supported by increasing the government deficit. But in view of the discussion in this section it now appears that, with the partial exception of the 1977 NWA, government commitments served to absorb the costs of, rather than to 'mediate', the distributive conflict between unions and employers. Government's accommodating stance certainly achieved the objective of securing centralized agreements. But this approach also entailed costs which could not be deferred indefinitely. However, the Coalition's initiative to reverse this approach, in 1976–7, was undertaken in more favourable conditions than the adjustments which were seen to be unavoidable by 1981–2.

By contributing to the maintenance of centralized agreements governments helped to avert the outbreak of sectional distributive conflict, an objective shared for the most part by the private sector employers until the aftermath of the second NU. None the less, many employers were critical of the manner and timing of government intervention in collective bargaining, a criticism which was most unequivocally articulated in 1981, when it was argued that 'governments over the years have tended in national negotiations to do too little, too much, or sometimes both at once; that they have intervened either ineffectively or, if with effect, then with too much concern for short-term political needs and too little for the long-term welfare of the economy' (Fogarty *et al.*, 1981: 26). In particular, the FUE view was that governments lacked an adequate measure of the cost-effectiveness of their contributions to securing pay agreements, and that this was due to the absence of a coherent and effective long-term strategy in which pay policy and demand management policy complemented one another.

The evidence surveyed in this section would tend to bear out the opinion expressed by one commentary that 'the role of pay policy in relation to securing the broad objectives of demand management policy—growth and employment creation, subject to balance of payments, inflation and public finance constraints, was not articulated' (Bacon *et al.*, 1982: 77). This observation is not confined to the period in government of any particular party or parties. Each of the administrations of the 1970s betrays a similar lack of integration between the various elements of public policy. Government strategies tended not to be informed by a high degree of intellectual rigour, nor did governments experience any need to justify their 'policy mix' in terms of an ideologically coherent set of priorities. Surveying the upward trend in public expenditure since the 1960s, one economist advanced this opinion: 'The reasons for this have nothing whatsoever to do with the influence on government of imaginary Keynesian ideologues but with the infinitely more mundane pressures of *realpolitik* and vote-catching' (MacAleese, 1980). However, a more measured explanation of the consequences of a 'non-ideological' approach to economic management must wait until Chapter 7.

In summary, we have argued in the third section of this chapter that the contribution of government to securing centralized pay agreements was limited, and that the limitations had two sources. First, the capacity of government policies to shape economic performance was directly limited because the Irish economy was small, open, and undergoing structural transformation. Second, government policy objectives tended not to be closely integrated with one another. Industrial policy, based on promoting direct foreign investment, was seen as central to economic growth and development. But potential conflict between the objectives of industrial policy and those of pay policy was not clearly perceived. This resulted in some contradictory elements in the overall policy 'mix' of government, some of which supported the negotiation of wage regulation agreements, others of which were inimical to such agreements. These observations are not confined to either the Coalition or the Fianna Fáil government, but are common to both.

This chapter has surveyed the main aspects of economic performance which were intended to benefit from the negotiation of centralized wage agreements. It has shown that both employers and unions were dissatisfied because their respective objectives were not more successfully realized. Thus rather than engaging in a process of concertation and striving to bring about a 'politics of the virtuous circle' (Castles, 1978; Lange, 1984: 121 n. 1), employers and unions continued to experience a 'vicious circle'. Government was unable effectively to mediate their continuing conflicts of interest.

But the outcomes surveyed in this chapter were produced, at least in part, by the actions of each of the parties to the centralized agreements. There may have been structural limits to the possibility of producing effective wage regulation agreements underpinned by government commitment. But for a full explanation of the Irish experience we must also look at the internal organization and strategic commitments of the peak economic interests. The following two chapters therefore examine in turn the trade union movement and the employers' associations, to explain the distinctive contribution of each to the outcomes presented in this chapter.

Furthermore, we have suggested in this chapter that the non-ideological character of Irish governments, thought by many to facilitate the negotiation of an integrated prices and incomes policy (see Chapter 2), might itself have contributed to the failure of its concertative intervention. Chapter 7 therefore provides an explanation of the problems associated with attempting concertation in a political system in which class is not an important political cleavage and where ideological differentiation is not a significant feature of party competition.

5

The Trade Union Movement: Capacity for Strategy and Problems of Collective Action

THE trends in earnings and in levels of industrial action surveyed in the preceding chapter would seem to suggest that, notwithstanding the developments outlined in Chapter 3, economic performance was not consistent with the outcomes which might have been expected had all parties been committed to a strategy of 'political exchange'. This chapter examines the nature of ICTU engagement in the National Wage Agreements (NWAs) and National Understandings (NUs) in an effort to identify the actual priorities and strategies adopted by the trade union movement. Firstly, therefore, we shall consider ICTU's 'capacity for strategy' (Pizzorno, 1978), that is, the organizational and ideological conditions which govern its position of authority and leadership. We shall then look at the implications for ICTU's bargaining strategy at the Employer–Labour Conference (ELC) and the nature of its relationship with government. Finally, to complement the discussion of ICTU's centralized strategy, the last section explores some of the developments in local or decentralized collective bargaining during the 1970s.

Collective Identity and Collective Action

In Chapter 4 some of the reasons were outlined which would make political exchange, as discussed in Chapter 1, a risky strategy for the Irish trade union movement. But no discussion was entered into at that point concerning the nature of its strategic orientation. Before its actual priorities are examined further, it is important to discuss the sense in which ICTU may be seen as a strategic actor at all, and the kinds of constraints to which the leadership of the trade union movement had to pay heed in devising a strategy requiring collective commitment.

It was argued earlier that a trade union strategy of political exchange is implicitly a commitment to collective action involving a broad and inclusive conception of the shared interests of the membership. The organizational and ideological difficulties of securing commitment to collective action of this nature were noted, since it requires suspension of immediate sectional gains in favour of longer-term, 'public' benefits. The leadership of the trade union federation must articulate a 'new collective identity' in relation to which the focus of collective action is transferred from lower levels of trade union organization to the centre. This new collective identity must encompass the collective interests which are to be advanced through the strategy of political exchange. It was hypothesized in Chapter 1 that a conception of 'national interest' or of 'collective national identity' would be of limited value in this regard, since the conflicting economic interests need to be addressed directly. It was also argued that only where the trade union federation can explicitly articulate the collective interests which are central to the employees' side of employer–labour conflict would it be expected that it could engage effectively in a concertative or 'politicized' form of collective bargaining. A collective identity defining the interests of members as 'workers', or 'wage-earners', or in similar class-related terms, would appear to be the most conducive underpinning for rational commitment to concertative collective bargaining.

As Chapter 1 argued, the structural characteristics of the trade union movement have a major bearing on its capacity to forge such a class-wide conception of trade union strategy; industrial unionism was seen to have particular organizational advantages in this regard. Similarly, a close association with a political party with a complementary set of policy commitments may facilitate the adoption of a concertative strategy by the trade union federation. An allied party could serve as a kind of ideological 'pivot' in relation to which the trade unions' new collective identity would be strengthened and a new strategy of political exchange formulated.

The construction of a collective identity focused on class-related interests should be seen as a political programme requiring strategic calculation by the trade union movement. As Offe and Wiesenthal (1980), Mann (1973), and Elster (1985), among others, have argued, albeit from different perspectives, 'class mobilization' is far from being a direct product of social structural conditions. But the possibility of mobilization is shaped and constrained by the inheritance of previous strategies. The present structure and ideological orientation of the trade union movement must be understood in its historical context. Recent studies have suggested that the pattern of industrialization has a formative effect on the nature of trade union organization (e.g. Ingham, 1974; Wickham, 1980). Others have argued that the timing of the initial appearance of trade unions and of leftist parties is an important determinant of the relationship between the two. Where the development of the trade union organization 'runs ahead' of the political party, an imbalance in the 'political centre of gravity' is likely to ensue such that social contract policies will be difficult to secure (Maier, 1984).

The historical development of the Irish trade union movement was not very conducive to the development of a centralized, class-conscious trade union movement. Trade unionism in Ireland was powerfully influenced by British experiences (see Currie, 1979, on the intellectual roots of British trade unionism). British-based unions naturally sought to extend their membership in pre-independence Ireland, and the principal founders of Irish working-class organization have been termed 'ideological imports from Britain' (Mitchell, 1974: 286). Early indigenous craft associations evolved into branches of British-based unions. The growth of general unionism followed in the early decades of the twentieth century, based mainly on dock-workers, distributive and transport employees, and similar classes of workers. This pattern was later complicated somewhat by the acceptance of craftsmen who had not served their time in apprenticeships into some craft unions and by the emergence of non-craft occupationally-based unions.

Thus Ireland, both north and south, acquired trade union structures similar to the British. But the industrial structure of the two countries differed greatly. The north-east of Ireland was the only region with a developed industrial base. The remainder of the country came to have a developed trade union structure long before it had a developed industrial base or the demographic basis for a 'mature working class' (see Goldthorpe, 1978). Although various plans were advanced over the years for a major restructuring of trade union organization, this never came to pass (see Charles McCarthy, 1977b).

The development of the trade union movement and of the Labour Party were 'out of step' from an early date. The Irish Trade Union Congress (ITUC) founded the Labour Party in 1912 to advance the interests of its membership. The party was therefore likely from the start to suffer from the disadvantages of dependence on trade union membership. The limitations implicit in this had become obvious by 1930, when the joint organization was divided and the Labour Party was established as an independent party. 'The object was to free the Labour Party for political activity . . . the trade union type of organisation was frankly too limiting' (Charles McCarthy, 1974*b*: 357). The close association with the trade union movement which the Labour Party felt to be too restricting had already shaped the image of the Labour Party as a party exclusively concerned with a rather narrow range of trade union issues.

But the possibility of a close alliance between the Congress and the party was greatly diminished by the cross-cutting influence of nationalism; more will be said on this subject in Chapter 7. The trade union movement organized members on an all-Ireland basis, yet its members were divided on the national question. In order to preserve the unity of the labour movement, neither the ITUC nor the Labour Party took a position on these divisive issues during the formative period of electoral mobilization and state foundation. The unity was preserved at a cost, though: 'Because the Labour Party failed to claim the workers' political allegiance on the hustings from the beginning, the rule was established in Irish politics that a man could be a good trade unionist and yet cast his vote for a nationalist (or unionist) party.' (Mitchell, 1974: 292; see also Rumpf and Hepburn, 1977: 158.) The class cleavage acquired a secondary political importance, with no strong continuity between trade union membership and Labour Party voting: 'Loyalties born of the Civil War proved stronger than any class consciousness or any disposition to follow the political promptings of the trade union movement.' (Donal Nevin, Thomas Davis lecture, 1964, cited in Mitchell, 1974: 170.)

Nationalism also proved to be a divisive influence within the trade union movement. Unions which had their head offices in Britain continued to organize members alongside unions founded and based in what became the Republic. On the whole, the bulk of the members of the former were in Northern Ireland while the members of Irish-based unions were almost all in the south. But in addition to rivalries over membership, due to the frequent overlap or duplication of function, the coexistence of these unions of different national provenance was the focus of nationalist hostilities, compounded by conflicts of personality between influential union leaders. This was the proximate reason for the split in the trade union movement (and an associated but shorter-lived split in the Labour Party) in the 1940s and 1950s which was mentioned in Chapter 2. Charles McCarthy (1977*b*: 578–9; 1973: 51–5; also 1980*a*) has identified two traditions in the development of the trade union movement, associated respectively with the British-based and Irish-based unions, but which could interact in sometimes quite complex ways. The first he characterized as 'a powerful expression of a working-class tradition which persisted despite the political upheavals in the south, and the sectarian riots in the north . . . a common working-class tradition throughout these islands'. The second current within the trade union movement is that of 'chiliastic nationalism, and later . . . an expression of the catholic-nationalist subculture, from which the Commission on Vocational Organisation (1943) would have wished to extirpate any alternative working-class loyalties'. It must be allowed, however, that these depictions overstate the contrasting features of the British-based and Irish-based unions. There was, for instance, a signficant current of opinion of the first sort present within Irish-based unions. Furthermore, it must also be recognized that insofar as two traditions may indeed be identified, they were very much modified, particularly from the 1950s onwards, by a primary concern with the immediate and sectional interests of members. This point will be developed further in the course of the present chapter.

The reunification of the divided branches of the trade union movement in 1959 provided 'the basis of unity between two different conceptions of trade union organisation' (Jack Macgougan, a prominent northern union leader, cited in Charles McCarthy, 1977*b*: 350, 579). Inter-union conflict on nationalist grounds never recurred with the same intensity, even though it could not be said to have disappeared entirely.

The trade union movement developed, therefore, 'out of step' with the Labour Party, since class-consciousness did not provide the primary political identity of the great majority of workers in the formative years of the political system, and socioeconomic issues were overshadowed by the constitutional issue of independence. But the trade union movement could not take up an unequivocally nationalist position either, because its membership spanned the sectarian and nationalist divide in the north. The trade union movement, as a result, stood apart from the party political system.

The unions' anomalous relationship to the political system deprived them of an 'ideological pivot' for the development of a class-based analysis of inequalities or a class-wide conception of collective identity. Unions tend to be seen as the defenders and promoters of members' economic interests, and 'there is no doubt that the notion of class lies at the centre of the explanation' (Charles McCarthy, 1977b: 579). But for the most part members adopt a fairly instrumental approach to unions and to the benefits to be obtained through them.[1] Conflict over distributive outcomes does not necessarily entail a critique of the class basis of inequalities. Recent research has shown that although Irish employees, on the whole, have a reasonably accurate picture of socio-economic group inequalities, the range of criteria used in making justice evaluations is narrow and is not associated with a conception of conflict *between* socio-economic groups. This 'largely pragmatic if necessarily constrained evaluation of alternatives' (Whelan, 1980: 131) may be likened to Offe and Wiesenthal's (1980) notion of a 'monological' expression of workers' interests, which was briefly discussed in Chapter 1. As Whelan argues further:

An evaluation of [reward] criteria which could be described as class conscious would require a recognition that the existing criteria are such that there is an inevitable opposition of interest between certain groups . . . In fact, the available evidence provided no support for the existence among any of the socio-economic groups of such an understanding of the reward system. (Whelan, 1982: 82.)

The Structure of the Trade Union Movement

In Chapter 1 various organizational criteria were identified which tend to be conducive to the authoritative centralization of the trade union federation. The Irish trade union movement developed with relatively little political incentive to form a class-wide collective

---

[1] A poll conducted by *Business and Finance* in 1977 (8 Dec.) found that trade unions were not held in very high regard, even by trade union members. It found quite widespread popular acceptance of statutory restraint of unofficial strikes. However, it also found scepticism among respondents about the value of wage restraint as a means of increasing employment, and 2 : 1 opposition to any statutory control of pay. In contrast, polls in Germany found that the DGB (the general trade union federation) was quite successful in securing workers' identification and support during the 1970s (Dyson, 1977: 45–6).

identity. Its origins as an offshoot of British unionization also meant that its organizational structure bore little resemblance to the pattern of industrial unionism which has generally been held to be most conducive to overcoming sectional conflicts of interest. In this section the organizational basis of ICTU's leadership role will be examined, drawing on the conclusions of the earlier discussion, and the implications for union activity and for relations between and within unions will be outlined.

TRADE UNION DENSITY

Trade union membership grew rapidly during the 1960s, by about 18%, and even more rapidly between 1970 and 1979. It increased from 383,000 in 1970 to 499,000 in 1979, an increase of 19%. The employee workforce was itself increasing during this period, but since trade union membership expanded more rapidly the density of trade union membership, i.e. actual union membership expressed as a proportion of potential membership, also increased. Table 5.1 shows the increase in density between 1960 and 1983. It also shows that density declined between 1980 and 1983 even though trade union membership declined relatively little. This was mainly

TABLE 5.1. *Trade Union Density 1960–1983 (%)*

Year	Aggregate membership	Density[a]		
		A	B	C
1960	310,100	45.1	47.3[b]	44.7
1965	362,400	49.4	50.0	49.3
1970	416,300	53.6	54.0	53.2
1975	448,100	53.0	54.5	53.4
1980	524,600	55.1	56.7	55.0[c]
1983	512,500	50.4	52.3	–

[a] Three measures of union density are given. In each case the potential union membership is based on employees at work plus the unemployed, less Gárdaí (police) and the armed forces. The different estimates of union density are based on different statistical definitions and estimates of numbers unemployed.
Density A uses Live Register data on numbers unemployed.
Density B uses Labour Force Survey data on numbers unemployed.
Density C uses data on numbers unemployed in accordance with the definition of unemployment adopted in the population census.
[b] 1961 figure.
[c] 1978 figure.
Source: Roche and Larragy, 1987.

because of the rapid increase in the total labour force and a growth in the numbers of the unemployed during this period.

Irish trade union density is quite high compared with that of other European countries.[2] The increase in density was more marked in some sectors than in others. Trade union density was estimated at about 78% of the workforce in manufacturing industry during the 1970s.[3] It was traditionally high, and probably close to 100% during the 1970s, in the civil service (general grades), and it was also high in the larger state bodies, both commercial and non-commercial. White-collar occupations such as teaching, banking, and journalism were also highly unionized and sectors such as insurance and finance saw significant growth in the 1970s, similar to the trends also observed in Britain. Also resembling the British pattern, craft unions traditionally sought to establish 100% trade union membership. Trade union density also appears to be highly correlated with establishment size in public and private sectors (see Gorman, Hynes, McConnell, and Moynihan, 1975: 75, for Ireland; Brown, 1981: 53, for Britain).

TRADE UNION FRAGMENTATION

Trade union membership was however distributed across a very large number of unions. There were almost one hundred trade unions in the early 1960s, a number which had been rationalized to eighty-five by 1979 and seventy-eight by 1983. The extent of union multiplicity is evident from the fact that although the number of trade union members in Britain in 1980 was approximately thirteen million, or twenty-five times that of aggregate trade union membership in Ireland, the number of unions in Britain (438 in all in 1980) was only about five times as great (see, for example, Hyman, 1983: 38). Membership of the different categories of unions is shown in Table 5.2.

The expansion of white-collar unionization was one of the most remarkable features of trade union growth in Ireland, as in other countries, during the 1960s and 1970s. This trend continued into

[2] Eurostat, Social Indicators for the EEC, 1960–78, cited in Report of the Commission of Inquiry on Industrial Relations, 1982: 21. However, a mistake was made in the 1979 figures: see Hardiman, 1983b. For accounts of the data problems on membership see also Walsh, 1983; Hillery and Kelly, 1974; Trade Union Information, Nov.–Dec. 1975.

[3] Information from FUE, Research and Information Section.

TABLE 5.2. *Trade Union Membership by Union Type, 1960–1983 (%)*

Year	General	White-collar	Craft	Other manual	Aggregate membership
1960	57.2	20.9	13.2	8.7	310,100
1965	54.6	21.5	15.4	8.5	362,400
1970	51.8	24.4	15.5	8.3	416.300
1975	48.6	31.3	11.5	8.6	448,100
1980	49.4	33.7	11.8	5.1	524,600
1983	47.6	35.4	11.7	5.3	512,500

Source: Roche and Larragy, 1987.

the 1980s, becoming more pronounced as manufacturing employ-ment declined but employment in services continued to show some net increase (until 1985–6 at any rate).

Much of this white-collar union growth was in the public sector. There are no authoritative figures available on total union membership in the public sector, but it seems likely that by the early 1980s close to half the country's trade union members were public service employees, organized by exclusively public service unions and by white-collar and general unions. Public employees such as civil servants and teachers had their own unions, and half the country's unions had a membership confined wholly or almost wholly to the public sector. Moreover, there were estimated to be only fifteen or so unions which did not by the 1980s have at least some members in the public sector.[4] The Public Services Committee in ICTU played an increasingly important role in the late 1970s and early 1980s in co-ordinating the interests of public service employees in their dealings with central government and public sector employers.

Aggregate membership statistics reveal something of the fragmentation of trade union structures, but they do not reveal the very uneven distribution of trade union members in unions of different size. In 1981 the ITGWU, the largest single union, alone claimed to organize 178,048 employees in the Republic, about one-third of the total of 531,371 trade union members in the Republic of Ireland in that year.[5] The five largest unions accounted for about half of total membership. The two other large general unions were

[4] Information from the Dept. of Labour; see also Cox and Hughes, 1987.
[5] Thse data are drawn from Dept. of Labour research. See also *Trade Union Information*, Summer 1980; Winter 1980–1, for the (less reliable) ICTU affiliation figures.

the Federated Workers' Union of Ireland (FWUI), which had 46,358 members, and the Amalgamated Transport and General Workers' Union (ATGWU) which had 26,383. Other large unions included the Irish Union of Distributive Workers and Clerks (IUDWC) with 16,962 members; the Irish Bank Officials' Association (IBOA) with 16,911; the National Engineering and Electrical Trade Union (NEETU) with 14,950; and the Association of Scientific, Technical and Managerial Staffs (ASTMS) with 13,200 members. Besides these, the Union of Construction, Allied Trades and Technicians (UCATT) had 9,247 members, and the Electrical Trades Union (ETU) had 9,602. The largest public sector unions were the Irish National Teachers' Organisation (INTO) with 17,339 members; the Civil and Public Services' Staff Association (CPSSA) with about 14,000; the Local Government and Public Services Union (LGPSU) with 13,954; the Postal and Tele-communications Workers' Union (PTWU, previously the Post Office Workers' Union, POWU) with 13,552 members; and the Irish Post Office Engineering Union (IPOEU) with about 8,000 members. The smallest unions (with fewer than 2,000 members each), organizing about 6% of the workforce, still numbered forty by 1983. Table 5.3 indicates that some rationalization occurred over time, but relatively little.

The multiplicity and fragmentation of the trade union movement is further compounded by the frequent duplication of function by unions with their head offices in Ireland and unions with their head offices outside Ireland, i.e. British unions. The situation is complicated by the fact that both Irish-based and British-based unions organize employees both in Northern Ireland and in the Republic. However, the Irish-based unions have relatively few members in Northern Ireland. In 1983, for example, there were 101 unions organizing 283,000 members in Northern Ireland, but only five Irish-based unions had members in Northern Ireland, and these accounted for about 19,000 employees or about 6.7% of all union members in Northern Ireland. In contrast, there were 88 British-based unions, organizing 223,800 members or 79% of the total, and eight Northern Ireland unions organizing 40,600 members or 14.3% of the total (Black, 1984).

The branches of British unions organizing in the Republic of Ireland have considerable autonomy with regard to their activities and finances, under the terms of the Trade Union Acts 1941 and

TABLE 5.3. *Membership of Trade Unions by Union Size*

Union size	1966			1970			1979			1983		
	Trade unions	Member-ship	% all members	Trade unions	Member-ship	% all members	Trade unions	Member-ship	% all members	Trade unions	Member-ship	% all members
<1,500	60	26,100	7.2	54	24,500	6.3	43	23,400	4.7	35	19,966	3.9
1,500–3,000	16	33,200	9.1	17	35,000	9.0	16	34,400	6.8	16	35,838	7.1
3,000–5,000	6	24,700	6.8	10	40,300	10.4	6	23,600	4.7	7	26,680	5.3
5,000–7,500	8	46,500	12.8	9	60,600	15.7	5	31,900	6.4	3	17,626	3.5
7,500–10,000	2	19,100	5.2				3	26,700	5.4	4	35,896	7.1
10,000–15,000	1	13,000	3.6	3	45,000	11.6	9	121,600	24.4	7	86,863	17.1
15,000–20,000	2	31,200	8.6							3	49,992	9.8
>20,000	2	170,000	46.7	2	181,400	46.9	2	237,300	47.6	3	235,053	46.3
TOTAL	97	363,800	100	95	386,800	100	85	498,900	100	78	507,914	100

Note: These figures are based on somewhat different sources than Roche and Larragy (1987) (the latter do not provide a breakdown of union membership by size of union). See, however, Roche and Larragy, DUES Bulletin No. 2, on patterns of union merger and dissolution.

Source: Department of Labour records.

1975. Table 5.4 shows the numbers of Irish-based and British-based unions organizing in the Republic, and the proportion of total union membership accounted for by each.

Although ICTU organizes almost all trade union members, the tendency to trade union fissiparousness is increased by the small but significant minority of trade unions which do not affiliate to ICTU and which do not consider themselves bound by the policy decisions of ICTU. Their numbers are presented in Table 5.5.

CONSEQUENCES FOR TRADE UNION COMPETITION

The waste of resources involved in the duplication of services by trade unions has long been the subject of criticism in the trade union movement. As the then General Secretary of the country's second-largest union, the FWUI, noted in the early 1980s, 'the intellectual case for the rationalisation of the trade union movement is beyond dispute . . . and is contained, in some detail, in the many

TABLE 5.4. *Trade Unions with Head Offices Within and Outside Ireland*

Year	Number of Unions[a]		Year	% Members[b]	
	HO within	HO outside		HO within	HO outside
1966	70	27	1965	86.3	13.7
1970	71	24	1970	86.0	14.0
1976	73	16	1975	84.7	15.3
1979	68	17	1980	85.9	14.1
1983	64	14	1983	86.1	13.9

[a] Department of Labour.
[b] (Net membership excludes Northern Ireland residents who belong to unions based in the Republic.) Roche and Larragy, 1987.

TABLE 5.5. *Trade Union Affiliation to ICTU*

Year	Number of Unions[a]		Year	% Members[b]	
	Affiliated	Not affiliated		Affiliated	Not affiliated
1966	77	20	1965	93.6	6.4
1970	77	18	1970	93.4	6.6
1976	71	18	1975	91.1	8.9
1979	72	13	1980	91.0	9.0
1983	65	13	1983	89.0	11.0

[a] Department of Labour.
[b] Roche and Larragy, 1987.

reports of the Organisation and Structure Committee of the Irish Congress of Trade Unions' (Cardiff, 1982: 111). A major problem for the trade union movement which follows from the fragmentation and multiplicity of union organization is 'the way in which trade unions compete for membership, sometimes in a fashion that would make the most zealous laissez-faire entrepreneur of the nineteenth century, or indeed of the present day, seem inadequate' (ibid., 1982: 110). Competitive union recruitment policies were the subject of comment in ICTU's Annual Report in 1981, where it noted the 'lamentable narrowing in inter-union relations at all levels'.[6] Relations with some non-ICTU unions were also difficult, since ICTU's rules governing transfers of membership did not extend to the non-ICTU unions, with the added problem that disputes in these cases could not be referred to ICTU's Disputes Committee.

Inter-union competition was widely recognized to have far-reaching implications for trade unions' activities. Prominent trade unionists report that they are put under pressure to respond to rank-and-file members' demands and grievances if another union organizing a similar category of workers is seen to take a more militant approach. The organizational needs of each union may therefore be a powerful source of inter-union conflict. For example, a compelling reason for the largest trade union, the ITGWU, to refrain from increasing the level of its membership subscription is the lower level of subscription of its main rival, the ATGWU, a union whose head office is in Britain (the TGWU).[7] The ITGWU is the largest and most powerful union, but in the opinion of many the ATGWU has a reputation for greater wage militancy. Rank and file dissatisfaction with their existing union, and ICTU's tight rules regulating transfers (though ICTU amended its rules on the transfer of members in 1983), can lead to bitter disputes between unions over membership. On occasion these have led to public rows between unions. For example, in the course of a jurisdictional row between the Irish Union of Distributive Workers and Clerks and the ITGWU in 1982, the assertion was made that 'a section of membership was clearly enticed away to another organisation'.[8] This problem can be made more complex if the 'other union' does

---

[6] ICTU *Annual Report*, 1981: 55.
[7] Information from a senior ITGWU official.
[8] *The Distributive Worker* (journal of the IUDWC), Spring 1982: 10.

not subscribe to ICTU's rules: for example, third-level teachers in a Dublin College of Technology, formerly members of the Teachers' Union of Ireland (TUI), were recruited in the early 1980s by a small, non-ICTU general union, the Marine Port and General Workers' Union (MPGWU), whose traditional membership base had been among dockworkers. Pre-production agreements on recruitment and representation in new firms may be yet another source of inter-union strife; the main general unions, however, came to agreement on a 'code of conduct' on this matter in the early 1980s.[9]

Inter-union competition—and in particular, consciousness of traditional differentials—was identified as the single most important contributory factor in competitive wage bargaining, in a detailed study of wage bargaining in the post-war period in Ireland. But, the study points out, 'This is not to suggest that most union officials spend their time trying to poach another union's members; rather it is to argue that even the best-intentioned officials can be driven to extreme measures by those aspects of structural change that menace their traditional membership bases' (McCarthy *et al.*, 1975: 172).

IMPLICATIONS FOR TRADE UNION ACTIVITIES

Trade union officials thus experienced considerable pressure from the rank and file to attend to their immediate interests and grievances, with the possibility of unofficial action or of members' transfer to another union continually in the background, since inter-union competition tended to weaken members' attachment to a particular union. For the same reasons, pressure could sometimes be brought to bear on full-time trade union officials to make unofficial strikes official. The role of full-time officials had changed since the 1960s, when their main activity was the negotiation of wage-round increases. During the 1970s, when they were freed of this responsibility, it has been argued that, in contrast to the extensive autonomy of shop stewards in Britain discussed by Donovan (1968), 'One of the consequences of national pay bargaining [may have] been that whole-time officials have turned their attention to local bargaining, often at quite a low level in the structure of employment' (McCarthy, 1979: 308). The ratio of full-time union officials to members appears to have been much greater

[9] ICTU *Annual Report*, 1982: 96–9.

in Ireland than in Britain. Clegg (1979: 58) estimated that the ratio of officials to members in British unions, allowing for national officers and regional administrators, was on average about one 'field officer' to 5,000 members, although some unions had considerably more. In Ireland the overall ratio during the 1970s was fairly constant at 1 : 1,500, with fewer extreme variations than in Britain (Hardiman, 1982: 20–1, from ICTU data. Union officials may therefore have had more time than previously to become involved in workplace industrial relations and specifically in supplementary bargaining, and greater opportunity to do so than their British counterparts.

But the expanded role of trade union officials does not necessarily imply that they exercised greater control over workplace industrial relations. Rather, the growing importance of workplace representatives during the 1970s may have contributed to the pressures on unions to be attentive to rank-and-file members' grievances. Rapid growth and industrialization contributed to a 'drift of power to the shop-floor' in the 1960s and 1970s, a trend which was reinforced by the dispersion and fragmentation of trade union structure.[10] It would appear that, in general, there was more autonomy for workplace representatives in British-based than in Irish-based unions. It is likely that shop steward organization differed from the British pattern in being more integrated into trade union organization (see Hillery, Kelly, and Marsh, 1975: 30; Dwan, 1981). But the increasing importance of shop stewards is attested to by the expansion of ICTU and individual unions' training programmes over the course of the 1970s (as reported in their respective Annual Reports).[11]

There probably exists a strong correlation between enterprise size and the importance of shop steward organization. This supposition is lent weight by the observation that the mid-1983 rank-and-file PAYE protests in Dublin and Waterford tended to be

[10] See 'The Drift of Power to the Shop-Floor', *IRNR*, 20 (22 May 1981).

[11] ICTU appointed a Training Officer for the first time in 1970; the first training course had twelve participants. By 1979–80 the courses organized by ICTU either directly or indirectly (i.e. by other unions under ICTU's auspices) numbered 86, of which 24 were ICTU shop steward training courses and the remainder courses organized by other unions; the total number of participants was 1,410. The ITGWU also organizes its own training courses for shop stewards, and reports a similarly steady growth in the number of courses made available and in the number of shop stewards trained. In 1981 the ITGWU held first-stage courses for 636 shop stewards and second-stage courses for 200.

concentrated in large enterprises, whether in public sector employments such as CIE, Aer Lingus, ESB, and Dublin Corporation or in private industry, in companies such as Waterford Glass and Rowntree Mackintosh and among strongly autonomous groups of workers such as oil tanker drivers.[12]

Shop stewards became involved to a greater extent than before in plant-level industrial relations. Collection of union dues was traditionally a central, if not the central, function of trade union workplace representatives. But the use of the check-off (that is, the arrangement by which the employer deducts union dues from the pay of employees and pays them over to the trade union) spread very rapidly during the 1970s, following an agreed ELC recommendation in 1973 (see Hardiman, 1982: 34–6, based on FUE data). This may be seen as enhancing the security of union representation (Brown, 1981: 73). It may also have contributed to freeing workplace representatives for other functions. In his study of workplace industrial relations Wallace (1982: 206–8) found that over four-fifths of shop stewards regularly engaged in collective bargaining with management, and that they were actively involved in a variety of other industrial relations functions. Employers were as likely to deal with shop stewards as with full-time officers. On the whole, employers expressed some preference for dealing with shop stewards (see also FUE, 1981).

Thus considerable initiative lay with workplace representatives, but trade union officials were constrained to pay close attention to workplace grievances. Dr. Johannes Schregle, the ILO consultant commissioned in the mid-1970s to produce a report on Irish trade union structure, commented that: 'Compared with many unions on the European continent, the decision-making power within the trade union movement is stronger at the shop-floor level than at higher trade union levels. Irish trade union leadership must be very circumspect so as to make sure that it is followed by the rank and file membership.' (Shregle, 1975: 11.) In a similar vein Fogarty (1976: 12) spoke of 'a certain puddingish quality' in the work of Irish trade unions, involving 'a great deal of down to earth solidity' but very little innovative thinking beyond the bounds of conventional trade union concerns. Peillon (1982: 69–77) concluded that Irish trade unions are primarily oriented to 'wages and conditions', and McCarthy, O'Brien and Dowd contended that:

[12] See e.g. *IT* 16 May 1983.

the Irish industrial relations system is dominated by trade unions which are motivated by what Flanders has termed a philosophy of trade unionism pure and simple. This philosophy, which rejects revolutionary and reactionary interpretations of the union's role with equal vigour, has been summarised as follows: 'The first and overriding responsibility of all trade unions is to the welfare of their own members. That is their primary commitment; not to a firm, not to a industry, not to the nation . . .'. (W. E. J. McCarthy *et al.*, 1975: 56; see also Charles McCarthy, 1977*b*: 579.)

This was by no means the only current of opinion in the trade union movement, but its dominance in the area of collective bargaining, at the expense of any broader collective identity of commitment to more encompassing interests, is further borne out by, for example, Cardiff's comment that 'subjective sectional interest, as manifested in the present multiplicity of organisations, is directly contrary to the basic trade union principles of unity and solidarity' (Cardiff, 1982: 112); and by the remarks of the General Secretary of ICTU in 1968, on the failure to advance the organizational reform of the trade union movement:

If they in the trade union movement were not moved by the belief that they had an instrument in the hands of the workers which could be used to revolutionise society then possibly small sectional trade unions, or sections which demanded recognition by unions of their selfish acts, were the kind of unions which were most suited to their purpose . . . It may be therefore that the weakness of our interest in unified organisation reflects a weakness in the *sense of purpose* and direction within the Irish trade union movement.[13]

The difficulty in bringing about trade union structural reform is thus intimately bound up with the conception of trade union interests and collective identity with which the great majority of trade unionists operate. Yet even those trade union leaders who are drawn to a more explicit class-analysis of Irish society tend to see little prospect of altering established priorities and preferences. As one trade union leader said, speaking of the shortcomings of trade union organization:

Despite a wide acknowledgement of this archaic condition, very little can be done to achieve the progressive changes that are needed for the reason that trade union organisation is itself tied into the class structures of society and is made to respond more to the demands and expectations generated

[13] Ruaidhri Roberts, ICTU *Annual Report*, 1968: 246–7.

within that society than to secure the class solidarity of the workers themselves. (O'Sullivan, 1982.)

ICTU as a Strategic Actor

These features of trade union organization depart a good deal from the conditions which we would expect to be most conducive to the centralization of trade union authority. Without an adequate degree of centralization the trade union federation could not undertake strategic commitments in centralized bargaining on behalf of its affiliates. In Chapters 2 and 3 ICTU was implicitly treated as a strategic actor in this sense. But its authoritative capacity must be investigated more closely here. If, as the preceding section argued, individual affiliates were quite closely tied to the servicing of members' immediate priorities, ICTU's capacity to reformulate the general understanding of collective interests and collective identities was obviously severely limited. This leaves open the question of how preferences came to be shaped within ICTU. Having clarified this, we shall go on in the next section to discuss what sort of strategy ICTU pursued in ELC negotiations and in its relations with government, in the light of the increasingly concertative role government sought to play.

ICTU'S AUTHORITATIVE RESOURCES

The most commonly used indicators of the authoritative centralization, and hence capacity for strategy, of a trade union federation are on the one hand the powers it possesses of authoritative intervention into the affairs of affiliates, and on the other hand the financial and bureaucratic resources it commands (see Visser, 1984; Headey, 1970).

ICTU's constitution gives it no power to intervene in unions' conduct of collective bargaining or in their control or funding of industrial action. As we have already noted, the 'two-tier' picketing policy requires that a union wishing to place an 'all-out' picket must first secure ICTU authorization. But this still preserves the autonomy of individual unions. ICTU's only sanction against affiliates that infringe its rules is suspension and ultimately expulsion. This ultimate sanction was used on a few occasions during the 1970s. The MPGWU left ICTU following a conflict over its activities in 1973; the Automobile, General Engineering and Mechanical Operatives' Union (AGEMOU) was suspended and eventually expelled in 1978 for breaching the terms of the then current NWA; the Amalgamated Union of Engineering Workers (AUEW) was suspended for one year on similar grounds.

Constitutionally, the final authority of ICTU rests with the delegate conference and not with the Executive Council. In order to initiate centralized pay talks, or to ratify a proposed agreement, a vote has to be taken at a Special Delegate Conference. ICTU is a 'consensual' and not an 'authoritative' federation (see Charles McCarthy, 1980a). This means that extensive support for policies is required before they can become official ICTU policy. Given the number and diversity of interests represented in ICTU, policy- or decision-making can be problematical and protracted. It can also mean, however, that once ratified in this way, ICTU's rules and its policy commitments tend to be respected. ICTU may thus be said to enjoy considerable moral authority.

Problems of inter-union competition, or cases where ICTU's rules on transfer of members between unions are contested, are referred to ICTU's Disputes Committee.[14] The Demarcation Committee deals with inter-union conflicts over work organization. Individual members with grievances against their unions can have recourse to ICTU's Appeals Committee (see Sams, 1968). Furthermore, ICTU's officers are recognized to have played an important role as informal mediators in implementing centralized agreements and in settling disputes.[15]

However, ICTU's authority depended on the voluntary compliance of affiliates and no individual union was bound to accede to its authority. Unions which withdrew their affiliation, or were expelled for flouting its rules or disregarding the terms of agreements to which affiliates were collectively committed, were not bound by ICTU's rules. These unions could therefore have a

---

[14] During most of the 1960s disputes notified to ICTU in a year were in single figures, but they fluctuated in excess of twenty per year during the 1970s. See ICTU *Annual Reports*, Disputes Committee Reports. See also Hillery, 1973, on the work of ICTU in general.

[15] Interview with Séamus ÓConaill. The ELC was sometimes the forum in which disputes which could not go to the Labour Court were informally dealt with. For example, in April 1975 the Minister for Labour requested the ICTU and FUE Joint Secretaries of the ELC to 'do something' about an unofficial oil tanker drivers' strike. The case was shortly afterwards submitted to the Labour Court and settled within the terms of the NWA. See *IT* 18–28 Apr. 1975.

more significant 'disruptive' effect than their size would tend to indicate.

Although it commanded considerable moral authority, ICTU's financial and bureaucratic resources were quite meagre. Between the end of the 1950s and the 1970s the share of total union income taken by ICTU increased from 0.5% to 1%—and unions themselves accounted for less than 1% of workers' earnings overall.[16] The affiliation levy to ICTU is not index-linked and cannot be increased without a debate and vote at a delegate conference. Affiliates are often reluctant to incur the extra costs, particularly when they may be under financial pressure themselves. A direct government grant to ICTU is made, and accepted, exclusively towards its education and training services.

ICTU's full-time staff are few in number. In 1977/8, according to its *Annual Report*, it had four full-time officers and eight clerical staff in its headquarters; the other fourteen officials and eight clerical staff were occupied with the Education, Training and Advisory Services. This may be compared with its largest affiliate, the ITGWU. Among its full-time officials, in the same year, according to its *Annual Report*, the ITGWU had seven national group secretaries, and employed five people in its Development Services Division alone. While the ITGWU's revenue and expenditure from different accounts ran into the millions, ICTU's 1977 income was £173,026 and its expenditure £156,578. Thus ICTU tends to have neither the staff nor the time to do much devising of trade union strategy. The full-time staff are recognized always to be over-extended by the demands made upon their time and attention.

ICTU was generally seen by affiliates as more than merely a provider of services and a mediator of conflicts. It was also intended to act as the voice of the trade union movement, and also to have regard for the unemployed, the sick, and others dependent on welfare, in the representations it made to government. Irish trade unions recognized the need for an effective voice for the trade union movement in national politics (see Schregle, 1975). However, it did not follow that trade unions would work to build a strong

---

[16] In mid-1985 over 80% of workers were estimated to be paying trade union subscriptions of between IR£1.60 per week (Dept. of Labour survey), while average weekly earnings in transportable goods industries were estimated to be IR£172.66 (Dept. of Finance *Economic Review and Outlook*, 1986: table 15).

and effective centralized federation. The preservation of their autonomy usually took priority, leaving ICTU with few formal powers.

ALTERNATIVE AUTHORITATIVE RESOURCES

Although ICTU's formal powers were few, the leadership had certain other resources which helped it to play a somewhat stronger role in shaping policies at delegate conferences than its formal authority would tend to indicate. These were the resources accruing to leadership or, it might be suggested, the 'oligarchic' advantages available to leaders within a bureaucratic organization. Within the constitutional limits of the powers available to the Executive Council and to ICTU's full-time officers, and where opinion at delegate conferences was not too firmly set, it was possible for them to exercise an important degree of influence. One instance of this is the order of business at conferences and the management of outcomes. Issues of importance for trade union policy were generally referred back to the Executive Council for further investigation or for development of a further discussion document. The recommendation of the Executive Council, by virtue of its considerable moral authority, was also in itself an important influence on unions' voting behaviour.[17]

Of greater moment for the course of centralized bargaining was the composition of ICTU's negotiating committee at the ELC. This comprised a sub-committee of the Executive Council. Membership of this committee was informally but carefully selected. One important criterion was that the major blocs of interests and opinion (such as the craft unions, or the public sector unions) should be represented to maximize the consensual commitment to the terms negotiated. Another objective was to contain the influence of 'maverick' union leaders, and thus to maximize the chances that the views of the 'reasonable men' would prevail.[18]

But this observation leaves open the question of how ICTU leaders actually acquired a set of preferred outcomes—what considerations were held to be important and what constraints had to be taken into account in devising Congress strategy.

[17] See e.g. the resolutions on NIEC Report No. 27 on a Prices and Incomes Policy, ICTU *Annual Report*, 1971: 99–119.
[18] Interviews with senior trade union officials.

THE DETERMINANTS OF BARGAINING PRIORITIES

By now it will be clear that the negotiating committee of ICTU had little scope to engage in active promotion of a new collective identity or of collective interests that might run counter to members' immediate interests. The Executive Council comprised the general secretaries of the major unions and of a cross-section of the smaller unions, and the senior full-time officers of ICTU, and they were still obliged to consider the interests and preferences of their own members when they convened as a collective body. The opinions expressed at Special Delegate Conferences must therefore by surveyed, to give some idea of the views which influenced the Executive Council's negotiating position with the employers and with government.

The voting at ICTU SDCs is not recorded in detail, and the way individual unions cast their votes is not available from the records. This information can only be partially inferred from the speeches reproduced in the ICTU *Annual Report*: the following paragraphs are based on analysis of SDC debates and other information on the voting behaviour of individual unions.

Broadly speaking, two 'camps' of trade union opinion at SDCs may be identified: those who tended on the whole to favour centralized agreements, and those who tended to oppose them. For most unions, most of the time (and allowing that a diversity of opinion existed within unions, just as between them), centralized wage agreements had obvious organizational and other advantages. They provided an orderly means of securing wage increases and ensuring a higher increase for low-paid workers than they might otherwise have been able to achieve. In contrast with free-for-alls, they had advantages in terms of the demands made on financial and personnel resources. The ITGWU was generally (although not always) among the supporters of NWAs; others included the FWUI, IUDWC, and UCATT. The public service unions also tended to favour centralized agreements, since they were likely, in most years of the 1970s, to fare worse in decentralized bargaining.[19] The teachers' unions, the Civil Service Executives' Union (CSEU), and the LGPSU were generally in favour of NWAs. By and large, these were Irish-based unions, but whatever residue of nationalist sentiment may have been present among them, it was not relevant

[19] An exception among public sector unions was the CPSSA.

to the business of negotiating wage increases for members. On the whole, these unions took a pragmatic approach to centralized bargaining, and were generally prepared to endorse it, depending on the terms and conditions of the agreements proposed.

At each SDC, whether the opening of new pay talks or specific proposals were the subject of discussion, a minority comprising approximately one-third of all delegates could be expected to oppose the motion. Unions frequently to be found among opponents of NWAs at SDCs included the ATGWU, ASTMS, IPOEU, NEETU, the National Union of Journalists (NUJ), the Electrical, Electronic, Telecommunication and Plumbing Unions (EETPU), and the Amalgamated Union of Engineering Workers–Technical, Administrative and Supervisory Section (AUEW–TASS). These unions included many craft unions and some white-collar unions. Unions with a majority of members in high-paying or profitable sectors were likely to oppose the agreements on the grounds that they could do better otherwise; these were the groups which would be expected to pose the greatest problems for a wage agreement. A characteristic objection from the leader of one such union was expressed in 1976: 'As a representative of higher-paid workers, I have listened to the argument that we should restrain ourselves in the interests of the lower-paid. We have restrained ourselves for the last ten years, but I do not see any benefit accruing to the lower-paid.'[20]

The unions which opposed centralized bargaining frequently did so on ideological grounds; these unions tended to be the ones with head offices in Britain and with a more conscious adherence to the traditions of workplace autonomy than others.[21] They often took exception to the principle of centralized bargaining and to the growing involvement of government, because these phenomena were not consistent with their understanding of the proper role of

[20] Brian Anderson (AUEW–TASS), ICTU *Annual Report*, 1976: 426. See also Anderson, 1981; ASTMS pamphlet, 'Challenge and Irish Trade Unionism', 1973.

[21] Ruaidhri Roberts expressed the opinion that some of these unions may have sent delegates to SDCs in proportion to their total affiliation to ICTU rather than in proportion to their membership in the Republic, even though members in Northern Ireland would not be affected by the outcome of the debate. This would exaggerate the extent of opposition to NWAs and NUs in the Republic. ICTU officers were accustomed to discounting some element of the opposition, but they regarded the size of the opposing vote as a barometer of 'what would stick'—and also as a bargaining point with the employers at the ELC (see later in this chapter). (Interviews with Ruaidhri Roberts and Donal Nevin.)

trade unions (cf. Charles McCarthy, 1980a: 33, 36). One leader stated that: 'When people ask me why I am against NWAs, I simply tell them "because the employers are in favour of them".'[22] Most unions rejected out of hand government appeals to the national interest, in the name of which distributive conflict should be overcome; a not atypical critique from the same trade union leader, shaped by this tradition, was: 'In a class-structured society there is no equality on which partnership rests ... phrases like "social partners" and "working for the common good" ... have no validity for most working people' (Merrigan, 1976: 22). The priorities of 'trade unionism pure and simple' were articulated more flatly in 1977 by an official of a union suspended and eventually expelled from ICTU for overt violation of the terms of the 1978 NWA: he claimed that the controversial policies of his union (AGEMOU) were 'in pursuit of benefits for our members ... [which is] the whole point of trade unionism.'[23]

The rough distinction drawn above, between the two-thirds of SDC delegates who tended to favour and the one-third who tended to oppose centralized agreements, was by no means an unvarying proportion. The total number of delegates at SDCs ranged from about 350 to 400; on some occasions the vote was much closer than two to one, while on others a more decisive majority was recorded. Switching from one side to the other varied with individual unions' calculation of their own advantage. For example, the interim pay agreement of 1976, with its commitment to a tripartite conference, was accepted by an overwhelming majority (309 : 90) in September 1976, because many unions were aware that unless a centralized agreement were secured it would be very difficult to negotiate any wage increases, because of the persistence of the recession.

The side on which the large unions cast their votes influenced the way many others, particularly small unions, decided to vote. The vote which ratified the terms of the 1978 NWA provided an instance of this, with reference to ITGWU. Although it accounted for about one-third of trade unionists, it commanded 65 votes, or roughly one-fifth, at conference, while small unions were over-

---

[22] Matt Merrigan (ATGWU), ICTU *Annual Report*, 1974: 262.

[23] Charlie Mooney (AGEMOU), ICTU *Annual Report*, 1977: 222; see also 'Roadstone Cowboys', *IT* 25 Oct. 1978. On AGEMOU's suspension, see ICTU *Annual Report*, 1979: 132–3.

represented in relation to their size. Its support was commonly held to be crucial to the ratification of agreements. It was also generally recognized that among the unions which usually opposed NWAs were a number of small unions which nevertheless stood to gain from their ratification. The 1978 NWA was carried by a slender majority (240 : 215) even though on this occasion the ITGWU, among others, voted against the proposed terms. Various craft unions, including NEETU, ETU, and the National Graphical Association (NGA), more commonly to be found among the opponents of NWAs, voted for the proposals in preference to a costly free-for-all, particularly since the employers had made it clear that they were prepared to offer strong resistance to plant-level claims. The willingness of small unions to switch their usual practice of opposition in order to save the 1978 NWA also tends to bear out the hypothesis that their opposition was often more symbolic than real.

The public sector unions generally voted in favour of proposed terms. But in 1979, with mounting discontent among public sector unions, several of them, including the teachers' unions (the Irish National Teachers' Organisation, the Teachers' Union of Ireland, and the Association of Secondary Teachers of Ireland) and most of the civil service and Post Office unions, opposed the moves to open talks and ratify the first proposals for a National Understanding.

The reasons for favouring or opposing centralized agreements were varied, but central to them all was concern for the benefits accruing to the membership. It has already been shown that ICTU lacked the resources to construct a negotiating position based on encompassing class-interests. The constraints outlined here of catering for diverse trade union interests might be expected to have increased the difficulty of devising a coherent negotiating position in the increasingly 'politicized' process of centralized bargaining.

Implications For Trade Union Strategy

ECONOMIC ANALYSIS

ICTU had few resources to devote to research and analysis of economic issues. It therefore had little opportunity to develop a thoroughgoing conception of trade union strategy, and the evolution of collective bargaining during the 1970s took place in a somewhat *ad hoc* fashion. Nevertheless, ICTU was clear enough about what was, and more importantly what was not acceptable to the delegates at Special Delegate Conferences. The analysis of the economy which informed the strategic orientation of the Irish trade union movement conflicted with that of the employers at several points, chiefly on the benefits of wage restraint and the implications for competitiveness and levels of employment. ICTU's policy positions on these issues were also shaped by the intra-organizational constraints discussed above.

ICTU's objectives in wage bargaining included compensation for erosion of living standards, a share in any increase in national productivity, and protection for low-paid workers. But where these objectives might conflict, particularly on the question of what constituted an equitable pay structure, ICTU's objectives provided no ordered priorities. The scope and generality of its aims in centralized bargaining can be gauged from the following outline: 'to secure the highest possible wage increases for the greatest possible number of workers; the highest possible amount of money; the best possible protection against inflation; the quickest possible advance in conditions of employment and the fairest possible sharing of these gains.'[24]

ICTU opposed deflationary measures as a response to inflation, stressing the need to maintain high levels of domestic demand by ensuring high wage increases.[25] It was sceptical of the effect of lower wage increases on the rate of inflation.[26] It was sceptical, too,

[24] Ruaidhri Roberts at ICTU SDC on opening new talks in Sept. 1973, ICTU *Annual Report*, 1974: 227.

[25] For example, Ruaidhri Roberts at an *Irish Times* Investment Conference argued that wage restraint contributed to unemployment and thus to deepening the recession (*IT* 4 Dec. 1975); and ICTU rebuffed the Minister for Finance's calls for a 'pay pause' in 1976 (see Chapter 3). Also: 'Congress straight away rejects any deflationary approach to the solution of our problems . . . Its objectives . . . will be related to reducing unemployment, maintaining the real value of social welfare payments and protecting the living standards of wage and salary earners. Its proposals will be based on policies of planned economic growth, equitable income distribution and a more just tax structure.' (Statement submitted at the Tripartite Conference, 4 Nov. 1976, ICTU *Annual Report*, 1977: 260.)

[26] See 'Trade Union Priorities', documentation supplied to SDC 22 Nov. 1974, including Memo No. 3 on 'The Planned Development of Incomes', ICTU *Annual Report*, 1975: 170–85; also documentation supplied to SDC 19 Dec. 1974, which included a discussion of 'conflict inflation' and indexation, ICTU *Annual Report*, 1974: 224–30. Many trade union members had a very unsophisticated understanding of the causes of inflation. Ruaidhri Roberts recounts getting advice from members to secure 'a really *big* increase this time, so big that inflation *can't* catch up' (interview with Ruaidhri Roberts).

of the employers' concentration on the contribution of wages to competitiveness, to the apparent exclusion of factors more immediately within their own sphere of influence. These issues were rarely discussed at any level of sophistication by ICTU or its affiliates, in spite of frequent reiteration of the need for more effective economic and social planning and greater trade union involvement in national planning. The publication *Jobs and Wages* (1983), by a group of socialist economists sponsored by a group of trade unions and individual trade union leaders, was among the few coherent critiques of the government and employer rhetoric which tended to characterize wage restraint as the sole key to competitiveness. This publication argues, *inter alia*, that 'unions should be pushing hard for *productivity improvements* as part of all wage negotiations. Greater efficiency is essential ... *The pursuit of bigger markets abroad ought to be forced on managements.*' This and similar calls for an end to 'defensive trade unionism' (Rabbitte, 1983; Geraghty, 1982—both of the ITGWU), could not, however, by any means be held to be the dominant strand of opinion within the Irish trade union movement.

ICTU's policy statements on unemployment expressed doubt about the beneficial effects on employment of wage restraint, for the sorts of reasons discussed in Chapter 4. The unions' preferred solution involved increasing public expenditure and state enterprise. ICTU's response to the Fianna Fáil government's Green Paper *Development for Full Employment* (June 1978) accepted 'that the primary emphasis of policy must be placed on action to increase employment', but opposed the simultaneous plans for reducing the government's current borrowing requirement.[27] ICTU also opposed the tentative plans for a more vigorous policy of labour market management as largely either illusory or irrelevant. The Minister for Economic Planning and Development's plans for regenerating the capacity of private enterprise were greeted with 'total scepticism' by the trade unions—if private enterprise had failed to provide enough jobs before, why should it start to succeed now, and with an expanding population to cater for?[28] Moreover, the prevailing approach of trade unions to the relationship between wage

[27] ICTU *Annual Report*, 1979: 296–7.
[28] Interview with Ruaidhri Roberts. On state enterprise, see the Coalition's Green Paper *Economic and Social Development 1976–80* (Sept. 1976): 36–7; ICTU's 1979 'Policy Proposals', ICTU *Annual Report*, 1974: 237–48.

increases, competitiveness, and unemployment continued to be shaped to an important degree by the immediate pressures of the membership. As a senior trade union figure commented, 'If there are 16% out of work, there are still 84% in work who are not too put out by the plight of the unemployed and who want their wage increase.'[29]

Direct material benefits were of overriding concern to trade union members, and ICTU negotiators had to take that fact into account. When income tax became a focus of employee grievances, it became possible for ICTU to negotiate the joint pay-tax NWA in 1977. In this agreement, as in others, the 'cash calculus' was what was commonly believed to have swayed the SDC vote. But the belief was also widely shared by employees that reform of the tax structure was required independently of wage agreements. Not every government move to remedy the inequities of the tax system was regarded simply as a legitimate quid pro quo towards a wage agreement.

ICTU BARGAINING STRATEGY

From the foregoing, it will now be evident that ICTU was not committed to a strategy of 'political exchange'. Negotiation at the Employer–Labour Conference was conducted in a manner which has been described as one of advocacy: that is, ICTU negotiators' views on the merits of the employers' case took second place to the most cogent possible presentation of their own.[30] The unions' and the employers' negotiating positions—whatever the perceptions of the individuals concerned—were not within the requisite bargaining distance of one another for a 'bargained consensus' on economic strategy to be possible. The growing interest of government in securing agreements was used by ICTU as an additional bargaining lever. The possibilities of this two-front bargaining strategy were perceived as early as 1973, when the General Secretary of ICTU, Ruaidhri Roberts, suggested that government's evident interest in securing stability through an NWA could be used to press it to make concessions in the form of tax allowances in the next

---

[29] In interview with the author.
[30] The following account draws extensively on interviews with leading figures in the trade union movement and with others who were involved in, and knowledgeable about, the centralized negotiations.

Budget.[31] ICTU would negotiate using as its bargaining counter not the level of wage increases to be agreed, but the ratification of *any* form of agreement. By the late 1970s the trade unions' procedure was to negotiate up to a certain point with the employers and establish a baseline in case talks should break off, then suspend talks on the understanding that a government offer would be forthcoming, with 'the *only* card played . . . being that of continuing talks with the employers', in the words of one of the negotiators on the trade union side.

The ICTU negotiators conducted simultaneous discussions with employers and with government, but the ensuing agreements had to be acceptable to all parties, and this is where the greatest challenge lay. The first task was to present a unified front at the ELC. The second was to secure the government's input in a manner that did not compromise the principles which would be acceptable to an SDC.

The ICTU negotiators at the ELC dealt with the problem of potential 'free-riders' by making sure that they would be accommodated within the agreement negotiated. As one union leader noted: 'We know in the past that it was not the straight increases in pay that won improvements for large sections of workers; it was the ability of workers and unions in given industrial situations to secure fairly substantial increases through productivity and other local bargaining.'[32] This was the reason why so much attention was paid to the 'restrictive clauses' of agreements, both at the ELC and at SDCs, and why the employers and trade unions had such a fundamentally different view of them. It would appear that the negotiators of the 1970 NWA anticipated that the flexibility clauses would decline in significance over the years, as anomalies were ironed out. As we have seen, this proved to be far from the case. Commenting on flexibility clauses, a prominent and impartial figure close to the negotiations remarked that: 'Some of those clauses were made to mean amazing things by negotiators skilled at using them for their own purposes.'

The ICTU negotiators were aware that although a large minority of delegates would vote against any set of proposals, the provisions had to be such as to minimize the chances that these unions would go outside the system altogether. It was generally recognized that,

[31] Ruaidhri Roberts, ICTU *Annual Report*, 1974: 226 ff.
[32] Matt Merrigan (ATGWU), ICTU *Annual Report*, 1975: 505.

as an individual involved in all the negotiations commented, 'Some flexibility clause changes were made to buy the support of particular unions in order to ensure a majority for the package'. Another participant in negotiations, on the trade union side, added that Congress 'could not openly point out the loopholes' in the agreements because they 'would be accused of bad faith by the employers' and the loopholes 'would be closed up in later agreements'. But ICTU officers welcomed the feedback at SDCs on 'where the shoe pinched in the preceding agreements'. Over time, however, the employers 'got cuter at building restrictive clauses'.

The disruptive capacity of this large minority, in the event of a breakdown in the talks and a return to decentralized bargaining, may have contributed to the strength of ICTU's negotiating position at the ELC: one of the leading negotiators has acknowledged that 'if the one-third minority likely to oppose agreements had not existed, they would have had to be invented'.

The regular attenders at ELC negotiations—perhaps three or four from each side—were fewer than the formal strength of the negotiating team, especially on the union side where it has been suggested that some leaders occasionally found it expedient not to be present at difficult or contentious stages of the negotiations. The discussions were led by Ruaidhri Roberts, the General Secretary of ICTU, on the union side and Dan McAuley, the Director General of the FUE, on the employers' side. The negotiators at the ELC thus tended to develop good personal relations on the whole and, it would appear, discuss fairly openly their views on how offers would be received by critical groups on either side. The chairman, Basil Chubb, also engaged in 'a lot of to-ing and fro-ing between the two sides'.

ICTU's discussions with government, conducted in parallel with ELC talks, never committed ICTU to an overt trade-off of any sort. Even in the 1979 NU, in the preamble stating that this 'National Understanding for Economic and Social Development' was negotiated in the context of government's plans for full employment, no explicit connection was stated between pay policy and government commitments. An informal understanding was necessary, but ICTU would go no further than that. 'If government flew a kite on something', ICTU would take account of it, perhaps in altering the pitch it would make for the final settlement. A prominent individual on the trade union side commented that: 'No formal trade-off could possibly be acknowledged and no crude exchange deal could be done, but the Executive Council recognized that if government had moved on something, it should respond in some way'.

This flexibility brought some direct benefits which the trade union movement might not otherwise have obtained. Ruaidhri Roberts, among other prominent leaders in the trade union movement, believed in the late 1970s that the Irish trade union movement was briefly 'the envy of the European trade unions' (that is, those involved in the European Trade Union Confederation) because of its success in obtaining commitments to employment creation through bargaining channels, when 'other trade unionists were taking to the streets for the same objectives'. The leadership of the trade union movement was, of course, well aware of the more stable institutionalization of full employment policies in other European countries, most notably Sweden and Austria. But the job creation guarantees ICTU obtained were definite and unambiguous, whereas in Sweden, at the time when the first National Under-standing was agreed (July 1979), the Social Democrats were in opposition for the first time in over forty years, while in Britain a Conservative government espousing radical neo-liberal policies, under Margaret Thatcher, had just been elected.

Thus through the opportunities presented to it to broaden the agenda of collective bargaining at national level, yet without excessively stringent quid pro quo wage restraint, ICTU found itself having an input on the issues—jobs, welfare, and taxation among others—which might otherwise be considered proper to the agenda of a Labour Party. Even though ICTU retained its historic links with the Labour Party, the party's small size and marginal influence limited its usefulness to the trade union movement. Consequently, the view was taken by many that: 'In the Irish context, the trade union movement has a particular responsibility to articulate the aspirations of workers, given the absence of any real effective political party to do so.'[33]

In effect, then, it may be suggested that ICTU was able to function as a sort of extra-parliamentary Labour Party. Its involvement in increasingly 'concertative' pay agreements tended to take a pluralist, pressure-group form rather than one characteristic of a 'political exchange'. ICTU's role combined pay negotiations

[33] John Kane, ITGWU Branch Secretary, *Liberty*, Feb. 1982.

with the employers with a distinctive kind of lobbying activity in relation to government. What is more, this relationship was apparent over the lifetimes of both administrations between 1973 and 1981. A trade union figure centrally involved in the negotiations commented in restrospect that, for a while, ICTU exercised 'a lot of clout—more than it should have been able to'; and that where this happens in bargaining situations, 'what is implied is ineptitude on the part of the other side'.

However, the foregoing should not give the impression that the trade unions were unequivocal beneficiaries of these political processes. The policy areas in which ICTU was influential were relatively narrow and it made little headway on a number of issues which were of great concern to it. Despite some government concession in the area of PAYE taxation, employees were more heavily taxed by the end of the decade than they had been at the start; the inequity of the tax structure was noted in Chapter 4. Moreover, it took evidence of mass discontent for ICTU to secure these limited improvements in employees' tax position. Another issue on which ICTU was concerned to influence government policy was unemployment. Its support for commitments to direct job creation, as well as to other issues such as welfare policies, was conditional upon government's maintenance of an expansionist, accommodating stance. Yet even then the scope for government action was limited, as Chapter 4 showed, partly by its conflicting commitments to industrial policy and partly by the structural limitations on government control over the economy. The gains made through political channels in the later years of the 1970s were quickly eroded in the early to mid-1980s.

The majority view in the trade union movement supported the existence of centralized wage bargaining. The agreements promoted a degree of orderliness in wage bargaining and avoided the intense competitiveness of free-for-all wage rounds. By disposing of the bulk of wage increases centrally, they were more sparing of unions' limited organizational resources. The mechanisms for channelling and resolving disputes similarly helped to avert industrial action of a sort which might be regarded as wasteful of unions' financial resources. But as we have seen, ICTU's commitment to the centralized agreements was constrained by the rank-and-file pressures within trade unions. Some union delegates were critical of the fact that whatever gains might be made by engaging in pressure on two fronts were conditional on accepting some restraints on workplace bargaining. Unions had to avoid appearing to compromise their members' interests in the manner suggested by one delegate who charged that: 'We are absolute in our belief that Congress is becoming more like a bureaucracy of Government and we realise more clearly than ever that if this continues we might as well hang up the sign in Raglan Road [*ICTU head offices*]: "The Ministry of Co-operation".'[34]

We have seen in the course of this chapter that all unions experienced pressure from the rank and file to service members' interests and grievances at workplace level. This chapter, in conjunction with the evidence of wage trends surveyed in Chapter 4, has shown that this pressure was concentrated on pay and other cost-increasing issues. The clauses governing ATN claims provided the means whereby unions could seek additional gains on behalf of members. The result was an expansion in the scope and volume of local-level bargaining in the course of the 1970s. In view of the centrality of this issue to the themes discussed in this chapter, we now turn to examine some aspects of the intensification of local bargaining activity.

The Intensification of Local Bargaining Activity

'RISING EXPECTATIONS'

Over the course of the 1970s Irish trade union 'pushfulness' (Goldthorpe, 1978) appears not only to have continued but to have intensified. Several commentators have noted that employees' outlook in the 1970s appears to have undergone a 'revolution of rising expectations'. In some of its aspects this has been seen as an innate or unvarying human trait (MacAleese, 1980; Panić, 1978), but more interestingly, it may be argued that during the 1960s and 1970s these expectations gained a normative and not just an empirical grounding (see Goldthorpe, 1978: 208). While normative expectations of this kind gained a firmer hold, the traditional legitimization of existing wage differentials was weakened. The days were gone of bargaining conceived as 'thumping on the

---

[34] Billy Lynch (CPSSA), ICTU *Annual Report*, 1974: 286.

table'.[35] Although comparability remained a core feature of collective bargaining, a more sophisticated approach was taken to the formulation of claims and the identification of bargaining opportunities. In short, a noticeable 'opportunism' came to prevail in patterns of bargaining (Roche, 1981).

Government and employers drew regular attention to the 'aspirations gap' which had allegedly opened between people's expectations and the economic resources of workplace or nation. Participants at the Irish Management Institute Conference in 1976 criticized in particular the ' "special case" mentality in Irish society' which fuelled supplementary wage claims.[36]

But trade unionists also marked the changes. The General Secretary of a large public sector union noted the rapid shift from an older society 'practised in living in frugal comfort' (thus echoing de Valera's well-known 1943 depiction of an idyllic, peasant Ireland), to a society 'almost crazed by the consumer society and the acquisitiveness and aggressions which it generates' (O'Sullivan, 1982). The ex-President of the ITGWU, subsequently Treasurer of ICTU, suggested that:

Perhaps the most enduring consequence for industrial relations of the experiences of the sixties was its generation of what has become the revolution of rising expectations ... I don't think it an exaggeration to attribute much of the current difficulties in handling the economy to the deeply-ingrained belief born of the sixties and early seventies that affluence had arrived and that unless one grabbed one's share it would be appropriated by others. (F. Kennedy, 1981: 7).

Donal Nevin, at this time Assistant General Secretary of ICTU (and General Secretary from 1982), commenting on the fact that the serious disputes in the latter years of the 1970s occurred largely in the public service sector, said that:

Groups convinced themselves, perhaps correctly, that they had fallen behind workers in the private sector. I suspect that most claims today are based not so much on the value of work done, but on what somebody else has ... There is an aspirations gap, heated up by political promises, and how to meet this situation, I don't know. (Cited in Puttnam, 1981: 465.)

---

[35] A reference by Fintan Kennedy, in interview, to the prevailing style of bargaining up to the 1960s and 1970s.

[36] See *IT* 28 June 1976.

THE SCOPE OF COLLECTIVE BARGAINING

The expanded scope of bargaining activity during the 1970s was commented upon thus by the FUE:

Originally, the substantive content of any industrial relations agenda covered wages, hours of work, annual leave and little else. This has expanded in recent years to take in such matters as sick pay, pensions, overtime rates, shift rates, compassionate and maternity leave, recruitment, grievance and dismissal procedure, training and redundancy. (FUE, 1980: 15.)

The increase of 'opportunistic' bargaining was deftly summarized by a public sector manager as 'a variation of one of Parkinson's laws: "The capacity of staff to invent claims is always greater than the ability of negotiators to concede them" ' (J. J. Kelly, 1980: 51).

The importance of relativities as the ground for additional wage claims during the 1970s has already been noted. Pay relativities are often seen as having conservative implications for pay structures. But it was widely understood that, in many cases, unions cast about to identify exploitable analogues and played upon the expansion and contraction of pay scales. Relativities within the public service were a particularly important source of additional claims. Certain grades came to be pivotal to the extent that changes in their rates of pay had repercussions in many directions. These 'knock-on' effects were noted from the early days of the public sector Conciliation and Arbitration (C&A) schemes. But whereas originally they took about ten years to be extended throughout the public service, the pattern of claims in the 1970s increased the velocity with which gains were transmitted, so that they were estimated to take only about two years to work through fully.[37] One union, the CSEU, usually had several 'special' claims pending at once during the 1970s, each at a different stage of the negotiation process.

The structure of pay relativities represented one powerful conductor of wage pressures. Another was provided by the 'leap-frogging' of claims made possible by the existence of several schemes. This led to an effort on the part of the Coalition government, in 1975, to rationalize the arbitration function by appointing a single Arbitrator for all the schemes.

Productivity bargaining and bargaining for change or flexibility, closely related to one another, were also major grounds on which to

[37] Interviews with Séamus ÓConaill, and Brian Whitney, of DPS.

pursue 'special' claims. But the problems and ambiguities associated with this form of bargaining were noted in the last chapter. Bargaining for change or introduction of new technology was not universal, but the FUE was sufficiently concerned about this subject to advise all member companies in 1981 to make acceptance of ongoing change a condition of future wage agreements.

The extension of the range of bargaining and the generalization of gains may be illustrated with brief reference to the issues of 'disturbance' money, maternity leave, and special allowances, to select but three examples.

During the 1970s claims for disturbance money, or compensation for moving to a new work-premises, became common in both public and private sector. Payment was originally conceded in cases where considerable inconvenience or additional travel expenditure was experienced by employees, arising from the relocation of the firm. The principle was pressed to cover a wide range of cases within a relatively short time. Any move, however short, came to involve payment of disturbance compensation of varying amounts to employees. The first Labour Court recommendation (LCR) on this matter concerned a public sector employer, the ESB, in 1969.[38] In the course of the 1970s the Civil Service and the Post Office standardized the rates of disturbance compensation payable, calculated with regard to distance. In 1981 the amounts involved ranged from £100 for the shortest move to £600 for a move of five or six miles.[39] The volume of such claims, while variable, could be significant: of the 195 Reports by the Post Office Departmental Council in 1981, over 100 dealt with claims for disturbance compensation. The great majority of these claims resulted in agreed recommendations.[40] A union official remarked in 1981 that 'from small to big companies, disturbance money has got to be taken into consideration in the overall cost of the move. Those that don't consider it will find the balloon blows up into their faces.'[41]

Maternity leave provides another example of the extension of the scope of collective bargaining in the 1970s, and was an issue concerning which a very rapid change was seen in the course of the decade. At the start of the 1970s maternity leave would have been

[38] See also *IRNR* 33 (4 Sept. 1981).
[39] *Business and Finance*, 7 May 1981.
[40] *The Postal Worker*, May 1982.
[41] Ben Kearney (FWUI), quoted in *Business and Finance*, 19 Mar. 1981: 17.

almost unthinkable as a bargaining issue. Until 1973, for instance, women were expected to leave the civil service upon marriage. Enactment of statutory protection against discriminatory employment practices, the greater participation of women in the workforce, and the move towards the 'harmonization' of EEC welfare provisions contributed to a change in the climate of thinking. The growth of bargaining on this issue appears to have been concentrated in a relatively short period towards the end of the 1970s.

The first LCR for paid maternity leave was in 1975 (LCR No. 3763, a case involving RTE). Between 1978 and 1980 the Court issued approximately twenty-five recommendations on this subject. But the extent of bargaining without recourse to the Court was indicated by the ITGWU Research Department. In 1978 it noted 38 such agreements in the private sector. The total grew to 92 in 1979 and to 110 in 1980, including 27 in the public sector, and even this was not a complete count.[42] In 1981 the Maternity (Protection of Employees) Act was passed, making paid maternity leave a statutory right. Political commitment to this issue was secured partly through the piecemeal extension of the entitlement through collective bargaining in individual employments, and eventually by including it among the 'non-pay' elements secured by ICTU in centralized bargaining leading to the NU of 1980 (of which see para. 15). Protective legislation of this sort, providing a 'floor of rights' for all employees, provides a baseline from which further bargaining advances may be made. Evidence for this trend was seen in the rapid extension of bargaining for severance payments in excess of the statutory minimum as provided by the Redundancy Payment Act, 1967 to 1979.[43]

The 1970s also saw a growth in the variety of grounds on which supplementary allowances were claimed—further evidence of the opportunism and inventiveness of claim formulation. In general, allowances are sought for job-related expenses and for arduous or otherwise unusual working conditions. A number were well-established by the early 1970s, for example protective clothing

---

[42] See *Paid Leave for Maternity, Paternity and Marriage*, ITGWU Research Dept., Feb. 1980; also *IRNR* 30 (31 July 1980); 33 (3 Sept. 1980); 71 (20 Aug. 1980).

[43] See the *IRNR* occasional series on 'Redundancies: Variations in Agreed Settlements': 36 (2Sept. 1980); 47 (10 Dec. 1980); 11, (13 March 1981); 26 (3 July 1981); 30 (31 July 1981); 8 (19 February 1982); 1 (7 January 1983) Also FUE *Bulletin*, November 1983.

where necessary, tool allowances for craftsmen, meal and sub-sistence allowances, and allowances for exposure to dirt, noise, danger, or extremes of temperature. In the five-year period 1966–70 the number of grounds on which extra allowances were sought in cases before the Labour Court totalled 24, of which a maximum of 11 was used in any one year. Under these headings approximately 45 allowances were sought, or an average of nine each year. The contrast with the late 1970s is marked. In 1979 the grounds on which claims for allowances were sought before the Court numbered 37, and 100 claims were advanced, and in 1980 42 headings covered 140 claims. Over the two years 1979 and 1980 the total number of grounds for seeking allowances was approxi-mately 65.[44]

LOCAL BARGAINING IN CONTEXT

This section has shown some of the consequences of the intensifi-cation of local bargaining during the 1970s. Earlier in this chapter we explained the structural and ideological features of the trade union movement which made this possible, and the incentives which unions had to continue to rely upon their labour-market power. But the outcome, termed a 'wrong balance' between central and local bargaining by the FUE, was not exclusively the product of trade union 'pushfulness'. It was also the consequence of employers' role in collective bargaining and their willingness and ability to resist unions' claims. Equally, the terms on which the increasingly 'politicized' agreements were concluded were, in principle, capable of being actively shaped by the employers as much as by unions and government. Therefore the employers' 'capacity for strategy' needs further investigation, and their contribution to the outcomes of the centralized agreements must be evaluated. This, then, is the subject of Chapter 6.

[44] Labour Court *Annual Reports* 1966–70; 1979; 1980. An example of employee inventiveness is the LCR in 1979 in which it was reported that Aer Lingus air hostesses and stewards sought (among other claims) special allowances for suitcases and telephones (LCR No. 5173). The employees' case was that these were cost-increasing job-related items, even though it may be supposed that they had previously accepted these costs without question as their own responsibility.

6

Employers' Associations and Centralized Bargaining

Associability and Collective Purpose in Employers' Associations

Organization has long been recognized as the key 'power resource' of employees, but employers' need of organization to advance their common interests has frequently been accorded less than adequate attention (although recent exceptions include Schmitter and Streeck, 1981; Windmuller and Gladstone, 1984). A lack of interest in employers' capacity for collective action may be linked with an overvaluation of the structural advantage enjoyed by capital in relation to the state. Private business clearly shares substantial interests in common with government: each depends upon the successful performance of private enterprise. Business interests depend upon accumulating adequate levels of profit and investment capital. In addition to the obvious need to sustain a healthy economy, government requires buoyant revenue sources. Some authors would argue that government therefore experiences as a 'technical' constraint the need to protect the interests of capital, so closely identified are their interests (see for instance Lindblom, 1977; Poulantzas, 1973). Another line of analysis recognizes that governments may have to satisfy other demands through social expenditure commitments. But in this view, crisis tendencies are likely to develop from the contradictory logic of state involvement in the economy and society: the state is constrained to protect capital interests, but it must also implement a range of social policies. The attempt to fulfil both objectives may prove excessively costly; alternatively, the justifications for doing both may come to appear incompatible, resulting in a 'legitimation crisis' (see for instance Habermas, 1976; Offe, 1975; Offe and Ronge, 1982; O'Connor, 1973). However, each of these approaches, albeit in different respects, tends to treat the functions of the state as invariant in changing political and economic conditions. In contrast, the approach adopted in the present work, while recognizing the structural constraints on government policy in capitalist society, seeks to be attentive to the variability of the policy 'mixes' which government may adopt, which may at times run counter to some of the manifest preferences of business interests. Business interests are not necessarily accorded preferential treatment by government, even though business efficiency may suffer as a consequence. Employers' associations may well be obliged to have recourse to organization and collective action to advance their interests in the political process.

A second reason why employers' problems of associability may be underestimated may follow from overstatement of the contrast between the logics of collective action proper to employers and employees. Employees must combine in order to wield any economic power. In Chapters 1 and 5 it was argued that employees may share two 'orders' of collective interests. In contrast, the primary level of concern for employers is that of their own firm, the interests of which are directly revealed through the mechanism of the market. Where collective action may be required, the objectives sought are often seen as a relatively straightforward aggregate of the interests of individual firms (Offe and Wiesenthal, 1980). However, this view tends to underestimate the degree to which solidarity and collective purpose among business interests may be hindered or facilitated by a variety of conditions, including the competitive relationship between firms, and similarity or difference in their market situations, size, and capital intensity. The tendency of business or employer interests to form a common purpose may also vary with the perceived need for collective action, which may depend upon the unity and strength of the trade union movement and the partisan character of government, among other factors.

Centralized collective bargaining, at industry or national level, requires employers' adherence to a collective strategy. The terms of centralized agreements must be observed by all members of the employers' association if the policy is to be implemented success-fully. A less than sturdy commitment among employers facilitates 'free-riding' among trade unions and risks undermining the whole arrangement. This suggests that similar organizational features may be important in the case of the employers' associations as proved important in the case of the trade unions. The main requirement is that the leadership of the federation should be able to commit members authoritatively to a common strategy. Chief among the historical experiences through which the extent of employers' centralization and authoritative co-ordination is shaped is the nature and timing of industrialization. The character of relations and conflicts between employers and unions may also be important; these are shaped by the developing organizational characteristics of the trade union movement. Changes in current and prospective economic conditions would also be expected to affect employers' preferences regarding the level of bargaining, just as in the case of the unions.

Two factors might be expected to create difficulties for a strategy of collective action among Irish employers. First, the diversity of the Irish economy, discussed in Chapter 2, meant that employers were in heterogeneous competitive conditions, and even in the area of collective bargaining their interests were by no means uniform. Second, employer organization in Ireland tended to develop in response to the challenges of trade unionism. Employers periodically recognized a need to improve their associations' internal co-ordination, but their experiences of employee wage pressures differed because of variations in trade union activity. Although employers came to hold that they needed an equivalent organization to ICTU, it proved difficult to co-ordinate the relevant aspects of employer activity.

In this chapter the structure of the main employers' associations is surveyed. Their approach to devising a strategy for collective action is examined, and the implications for their views on collective bargaining and industrial relations are discussed.

Membership and Functions of Employers' Associations

MEMBERSHIP OF ASSOCIATIONS

Before the period of the centralized wage agreements of the 1970s employers' associations were not strongly centralized. A variety of employers' associations was in existence in 1941 when all organizations engaging in collective bargaining, whether trade unions or employers' associations, were obliged to register to obtain negotiation licences under the terms of the Trade Union Act 1941. Some were industrial bodies, some regional. The embryonic FUE was the only one with a universal orientation and industrial relations as its exclusive concern. Throughout the 1950s and 1960s over twenty associations were registered as having negotiating licences. There were twenty-three in 1957 and twenty-one by 1972; the number declined to eighteen in 1977 and sixteen in 1982.[1] Membership of the employers' associations still operating in the early 1980s (and listed under their present names) is given in Table 6.1 for selected dates, to show the trend in membership from the end of the protectionist era, through the 1960s, to the period in which centralized agreements were functioning.

In 1981 the member companies of FUE were estimated to employ about 50% of the occupied labour force (excluding the public services, agriculture, and the self-employed). Membership of the

TABLE 6.1. *Membership of Employers' Associations in Selected Years*

	1957	1963	1969	1975	1981
Irish Flour Millers' Union	36	19	15	15	10
Irish Pharmaceutical Union	1,156	804	1,061	1,609	1,402
Limerick Employers' Federation	106	98	89	76	61
Federated Union of Employers	1,220	1,435	1,630	1,957	2,563
Irish Printers' Federation	30	44	61	49	59
Dublin Master Victuallers' Association	202	249	240	234	227
Construction Industry Federation	303	n.r.	750	1,200	2,166
Petroleum Employers' Association	15	18	10	10	21
Society of Dublin Coal Importers	14	12	11	11	11
Society of the Irish Motor Industry[a]	888	901	945	998	1,119
Irish Master Printers' Association[a]	89	79	56	75	69
Licensed Vintners' Association[a]	410	n.r.	560	556	676
Irish Commercial Horti-cultural Association[a]	1,058	360	300	275	275
Irish Hotels Federation[a]	327	n.r.	473	412	403
Cork Master Butchers' Association[b]	18	n.r.	51	55	57
Retail Grocery, Dairy and Allied Trades Assn.[b]	4,689	4,273	3,000	2,442	1,350

[a] The figures for these associations are for the years 1958, 1964, 1970, 1976, 1982.
[b] The figures for these associations are for the years 1956, 1962, 1968, 1974, 1980.
n.r.: No reply.

Source: Department of Labour triennial returns.

[1] Information from the Dept. of Labour.

CIF was estimated to comprise 46% of all construction firms and 75% of employees in private building. SIMI's members were estimated to employ about 70% of employees in the motor industry. (See *Report of the Commission of Inquiry on Industrial Relations*, 1981: 41–3).

ATTEMPTS AT UNIFICATION

Table 6.1 shows the diversity of employers' associations. During the 1960s a greater need was quite widely perceived among employers' associations for an overarching organization, an employers' equivalent to ICTU.[2] They came to this view partly because employers' representation was sought in the new institutions of national planning; but changing conditions of collective bargaining also provided an important stimulus to greater employer co-ordination.

Where employers did not display solidarity trade union pressures in decentralized bargaining could bring about an early collapse of their collective position. Individual firms could be 'picked off' and the concessions won from these would be extended fairly rapidly as other employers sought to avert industrial action in their workplace. Employers felt some need for a central federation with the establishment of new consultative and advisory bodies in the early 1960s, but industrial disputes may have provided a stronger incentive. Two strikes in particular during the 1960s underscored for employers the need to improve their internal co-ordination: first, the building workers' strike in 1964, and second, the maintenance craftsmen's strike of 1969. The strike in the construction industry in 1964 was undertaken by employees seeking a reduction in weekly hours worked. A National Wage Agreement was in operation, but the two sides disagreed over the admissibility of the building workers' claim for the duration of the agreement. However, it was conceded by some employers and quickly spread throughout the construction industry and then, more importantly for the purposes of the present discussion, to other employments in

---

[2] This aspiration dates from the earliest days of the Federated Employers Limited, established in 1937, which preceded the establishment of the FUE in 1941. A resolution stated that 'there is an imperative need for an employers' central authority (similar to the Trades Union Council) which will be kept informed of all demands and give advice to employers on whom demands have been made'. See FUE *Bulletin*, Aug.–Sept. 1983.

the private sector. The intractability and bitterness of the maintenance craftsmen's strike in 1969 has already been referred to. The unions' picketing practices were not systematic: some firms which employed no maintenance craftsmen were picketed while others which did were not. This strike found the private sector employers in disarray. The FUE attempted to co-ordinate a policy, but the pattern of settlements in this dispute bore little relation to the FUE policy, as employers did separate deals with the unions.[3]

During the 1960s there were two moves to co-ordinate private sector employers in an overarching federation. In 1963 a loosely structured Joint Committee of Employer Organisations was set up. This provided the employer representation at the negotiation of the short-lived NWA of 1964. But the Joint Committee had little cohesion and did not survive the building workers' strike. That strike, and later industrial disputes, pointed out the need for greater employer co-ordination. In 1967 a report commissioned by a group of employers proposed the integration of all Irish business organizations into a 'National Irish Business Organisation' (NIBO). It was proposed that this would incorporate employers' associations and the Federation (later Confederation) of Irish industry, the representative organization for Irish industry in matters other than collective bargaining and industrial relations. But there was no agreement among employers that one big national organization was desirable, and the matter never even came to a vote at the FUE's National Council.[4]

The maintenance craftsmen's strike of 1969, however, represented a turning point for the employers as it did for the unions, resulting in an effort to work for greater unity among employers. Towards the end of 1969 the major private sector employers' associations formed a new umbrella organization, the Irish Employers' Confederation (IEC). The original members were seven employers' associations, representing about 4,000 companies which employed over 200,000 workers. Chief among these associations were the FUE, the construction industry employers, and SIMI.[5] These were

---

[3] The firm of the chairman of the FUE negotiating committee was one such firm. Apparently the private settlement was made without his knowledge. See Charles McCarthy, 1973: 167.

[4] Interview with a senior FUE official.

[5] The others were the Irish Printing Federation, the Association of Electrical Contractors, the Dublin Master Victuallers' Association, and the Limerick Employers' Association.

joined in 1970–1 by three more associations, representing vintners, victuallers, and electrical contractors.

The objectives of the IEC were stated thus:

to devise a formula to counter . . . leap-frogging in wage claims . . . [and] the playing off of one industrial group against another.[6]

The main objectives of IEC will be the formulation and application of policies to improve industrial relations; examination and co-ordination of the activities of employer organisations in the field of industrial relations and related matters; the provision of advice, information and guidance to constituent organisations. (Press release.)

Although it may be argued that centralized collective bargaining improved the conditions for employer co-ordination, the IEC never became a united and powerful organization. It had no funds or staffing of its own. It remained a loose federation and never acquired a strong independent identity. The FUE did not lose the monopolistic position it enjoyed in some aspects of the representation of employers' interests; it was, for example, the sole employer body designated for the purpose of nominating employer representatives to the Labour Court. In consequence, the IEC never exhibited any strong unity of purpose. The third largest employer organization, SIMI, left the Confederation in 1972.[7] The FUE and the CIF, moreover, did not always share a common perspective, as will shortly be seen, and the leading role of the FUE was a matter of some irritation to the CIF. In October 1977 the CIF withdrew from the IEC altogether, although it continued to be represented at the Employer–Labour Conference. The character of employer organization in Ireland must therefore be explored further by looking at the changing role of the main individual associations during the period of centralized bargaining.

THE FUNCTIONS OF EMPLOYERS' ASSOCIATIONS

With the advent of centralized bargaining in the 1970s, it was no longer incumbent upon individual employers to conduct negotiations for the main pay increase of each round, and industry-level

---

[6] *IT* 31 Dec. 1969.
[7] In a statement at the time SIMI pointed out that it had never formally joined the IEC even though it had been associated with its foundation and early work (see O'Brien, 1981: 72).

agreements similarly ceded to national agreements negotiated through the ELC. But the 1970s also saw an increase in local collective bargaining pressures, as surveyed at the end of Chapter 5. Consequently, employers tended to have greater recourse to their associations on various matters connected with collective bargaining and industrial relations. The growth in the membership of the main associations may be seen in Table 6.1. Some associations had greater resources than others to respond to the increased demand for services. These tended to experience the most rapid growth in membership. The very rapid growth for instance in the CIF's membership during the 1970s may be seen. The FUE, however, had various advantages when it came to increasing its membership. It represented employers across all sectors of economic activity, and was able to characterize itself as the sole employers' organization to encompass the whole of the economy. It was also the only organization whose exclusive concern was collective bargaining and industrial relations. It had the resources and full-time personnel to provide the kind of service which members sought during the 1970s. It would appear that a number of employers who belonged to other trade or industry associations were also members of the FUE, principally for purposes of advice or assistance. One association, the Master Printers' Association, transferred its functions directly to the FUE, but retained its name and identity within the FUE.

A breakdown of requests for information in the FUE's *Annual Report* for 1981 showed that 'the greatest demand for information related to wages and salary levels, detailed information on conditions of employment, employment legislation, statistical data and industrial practices'. Similarly, the CIF noted in its *Annual Report* for 1980–1 that 'the demand for the [industrial relations] services increased substantially, resulting from more union demands, more labour law and increased membership'. These developments parallel the British experience, where Brown (1981) found that British employers had greater recourse to the information services of the CBI on account of the increased complexity of laws regulating pay and employment practices.

Some differences would appear to exist between the uses made of employers' associations' services by international companies and Irish-owned companies. Foreign-owned companies tend to take up membership of employers' associations and it is general practice for them to recognize and negotiate with representative trade unions. In a 1980 study the FUE found that 96% of international companies surveyed had a signed agreement with a trade union, just over half of which had been signed before production began.[8] Information from an Industrial Development Authority study suggests that foreign-owned companies had somewhat less frequent recourse to employers' associations for assistance in the conduct of negotiations, compared with Irish-owned companies, and tended to use the employers' associations mainly for information. This study was undertaken in 1984 when centralized agreements were no longer in operation. Two-fifths of Irish-owned companies reported that they conducted negotiations as part of a group, but almost all the foreign-owned companies stated that they conducted negotiations as an individual company (IDA, 1984: 53). This helps to explain what seems to be a greater involvement of the Irish companies with their employers' associations.

The FUE and the CIF were the two leading employers' associations during the 1970s. We now turn to look more closely at their composition and functions.

MEMBERSHIP AND FUNCTIONS OF THE FUE

Table 6.2 shows the pattern of growth of FUE during the 1970s. (The figures are based on a slightly different reckoning than those used in Table 6.1.[9]) The membership of the FUE spans a wide variety of sectors, and its representative character is strengthened by the fact that the membership density among large and medium-sized companies is high. The distribution of membership by sector and by size is shown in Table 6.3. Similarly, within the manufacturing sector FUE organizes members both in the predominantly indigenous industrial sector and in the 'new' industrial sector, much of which is foreign-owned, as Chapter 2 showed.

The FUE derives no income from the state. FUE income in 1970 was £110,525; in 1975 it was £337,898; in 1980 it was £1,137,157. Almost all of this came from members' contributions.[10]

---

[8] Information from FUE.

[9] These membership figures include information members. Dept. of Labour statistics, returned in compliance with the Trade Union Act 1941, give lower totals for negotiating purposes.

[10] Information from the Registrar of Friendly Societies, courtesy of FUE.

TABLE 6.2. *Membership of the FUE*

Year	Membership	Year	Membership
1962	1,415	1976	2,149
1970	1,651	1977	2,292
1971	1,983	1978	2,485
1972	1,708	1979	2,796
1973	1,777	1980	3,036
1974	1,909	1981	3,247
1975	2,022	1982	3,364

Source: Registrar of Friendly Societies, courtesy of FUE.

TABLE 6.3. *Member Firms of the FUE by Sector and Size in 1979*

Sector	% of member firms	Employees as % of total employed by member firms
Manufacturing	50	60
Distribution	28	17
Services	19	18
Institutions	3	5
Number of personnel		
<15	24	2
16–100	57	30
101–500	16	44
501–1000	1	12

Source: Report of the Commission of Inquiry on Industrial Relations, Report 1981: 42 (from the FUE).

The topics on which the FUE provides advice and information were mentioned above. In addition to its consultative role, the FUE's services to members include participation on the management side in negotiations with trade unions, and representation at the hearings of third-party conciliation talks and at hearings before the tribunal established in connection with protective legislation. The demand for the FUE's services increased considerably in the course of the 1970s, partly because of the greater complexity of the issues involved and partly because of the growth in the number of firms seeking access to these services. Table 6.4 indicates the nature and extent of the FUE's main activities during the 1970s.

TABLE 6.4. *Representation and Negotiation on Behalf of Member Companies by the FUE, 1975–1981*

	1975	1976	1977	1978	1979	1980	1981
Representation							
Labour Court Investigations	164	152	174	235	233	322	355
Labour Court Conciliation	512	423	515	592	634	691	987
Redundancy/Employment Appeals Tribunal	60	71	71	69	83	116	172
Investigation by Rights Commissioner	155	190	247	238	347	431	506
Equal Pay Officer	–	–	7	12	17	19	26
JLC and JIC	–	–	47	46	54	43	43
Consultation with members	3,765	4,196	4,601	5,299	6,138	6,909	7,187
Participation in trade union negotiations on behalf of members	2,473	2,492	2,422	2,621	3,013	3,019	2,961
Other meetings (e.g. with government departments and agencies, ELC, internal)	987	1,103	903	987	1,629	1,798	2,100
Total number of formal meetings serviced	8,116	8,627	8,987	10,099	12,150	13,348	14,337

Source: FUE *Annual Reports.*

MEMBERSHIP AND FUNCTIONS OF THE CIF

In 1979 the CIF comprised twenty-nine employer trade associations;[11] it is the sole employers' federation in the construction industry. It represents all its associations and their member companies in industrial relations matters, with the exception of a few individual firms which have their own industrial relations functions. Membership grew rapidly in the course of the 1970s, as the data in Table 6.1 shows.

The construction industry employers had a particular incentive to retain their organizational identity, besides the fact that the construction industry was a sizeable and important sector of economic activity. Collective bargaining in the construction industry was conducted through a Joint Industrial Council (JIC), under the provisions of the Industrial Relations Act, 1946 (see e.g. O'Mahony 1964). The agreements reached at the JIC were binding on all firms and their employees in the industry, whether or not they had been directly represented through the CIF. During the period of the National Wage Agreements supplementary claims in the construction industry were channelled through the JIC. The CIF's member firms thus continued to maintain in use the bargaining machinery through which decentralized negotiations would also take place. In this they differed markedly from most other private sector employers. But the CIF also provided industrial relations services akin to those of the FUE. The CIF's *Annual Report* for 1980–1 stated that 'members were represented at more than 1,000 meetings, mainly at individual firm level'.

Implications for Employers' Solidarity

During the 1970s the FUE and the CIF were the leading private sector employers' associations. The private sector and public sector employers, moreover, sought to present a common front at the Employer–Labour Conference, where Dan McAuley, Director General of the FUE and a joint secretary of the ELC, tended to take a leading role in negotiations on behalf of employers.[12] Yet we have seen in Chapter 4 that the employers were unhappy throughout the decade with the extent of above-the-norm bargaining and wage

[11] Information from the Dept. of Labour.
[12] Interviews with Dan McAuley, Ruaidhri Roberts.

drift, and with the volume of industrial action undertaken in support of supplementary claims. It was suggested at the end of Chapter 5 that the level of resistance among employers and the extent to which they were able to promulgate a unified position must be seen as an important influence on these developments.

Two dimensions of employers' co-ordination may be identified: intra-organizational solidarity, inherently more problematic for the industrially heterogeneous FUE than for the CIF, and inter-organizational co-ordination, between organizations such as FUE and CIF, and also between these and the government as employer. It is more difficult to document the decision-making procedures of employers' associations than of the trade union movement, since they do not publish detailed annual reports, nor are internal debates publicly accessible as are those of the unions. Nevertheless, it may be argued with some confidence that the employers' associations were beset by problems of co-ordination within their organization (or more specifically, within the FUE) and between organizations, and also by differences over the role played by government.

FUE'S CO-ORDINATING ROLE

FUE claims a role of authoritative leadership with regard to its members. But it regards as inappropriate the use of any disciplinary means of enforcing this authority. Only on one occasion was expulsion used as a discipline on FUE members: two member companies were requested to leave because of their conduct in the course of the maintenancemen's dispute in 1969. But FUE leaders stress that such a situation would never arise again; what is more, FUE is obviously keen that new foreign companies should become members, but American companies in particular, in the words of one employers' representative, 'would run a mile' at the suggestion that FUE might use compulsion to enforce its policies. FUE, both officers and members, see the main role of the federation as one of providing services to members and representing the interests of employers whenever the need may arise. They see its role as one of co-ordination rather than of rule-enforcement. All members of the federation were expected to comply voluntarily with the terms of the NWAs and NUs, and members are expected 'to undertake upon request to consult with the Federation about trade union claims where the member or the Federation may have cause to believe that the concession of such claims either in whole or in part would be contrary to general Federation policy or would adversely affect the interests of other members'.[13]

But as Chapter 2 showed, the spread of opinion on the issue of pay and competitiveness was likely to be very great. The FUE had the task of formulating a policy on pay which would be acceptable to all, yet the views member companies held on what could be afforded were diverse. Fogarty *et al.* (1981: 29) presented an account of the FUE's role as follows:

... individual employers may find it difficult to ignore headlines set by others or the pressure for comparability which results from them. Irish employers are remarkably heterogeneous, and even more so now than in the past. Some are in unsheltered industries, some in sheltered but competitive and relatively unorganised sectors such as distribution, some in sheltered sectors with industry-wide negotiations which ensure that a headline setting award will not affect any employer's competitive position. This is notably the case in construction which over the years has been an important source of pay headlines. Some have monopolies. Many firms in manufacturing are offshoots of trans-national companies with limited commitment to the Irish economy. The FUE and other employer organisations have certainly a responsibility to do all they can to prevent undesirable headlines being set ... But the FUE is also a voluntary organisation and no more able than Congress to impose a maximum on increases in its members' pay bills, even if a majority of its members voted to do so.

FUE engaged in a regular process of consulting member companies and canvassing opinion on pay and industrial relations policy in general and on NWAs in particular.[14] Its general membership is organized in local or regional branches; there also exist industrial branches for some of the more important industries. Local branches meet regularly and were extended during the 1970s. The President and Vice-President of each branch sit, ex officio, on the National Executive Council of about fifty members. In principle the officers and committees of the FUE are responsible to the National Executive Council. This Council meets monthly and

[13] FUE *Rules and Byelaws*, 16. iii.
[14] This information is drawn from interviews with prominent individuals in the FUE and from details of FUE's organizational structure given in its *Rules and Byelaws, Annual Reports*, and other sources.

formulates policy which is ratified by the General Council, membership of which numbers between two hundred and fifty and three hundred. Representation from each region is not weighted by any indicator of company size (whether numbers employed or annual turnover), but there is a weighting for the number of companies in each region. In theory, therefore, companies of all sizes and in all competitive situations had a say in formulating policy on the national agreements.

When each agreement was due to expire, special meetings of regional branches would be convened to discuss the issue of entering into talks for a new agreement. Branches tended to return unanimous views; meetings were regarded as forums for discussion rather than solely as devices for registering votes. In addition, a sample of members would be canvassed and asked to complete a questionnaire to give FUE officers more information on members' experiences during the agreement then current. No figures on the outcome of this opinion-sampling were ever made public. Unlike their ICTU counterparts, FUE negotiators at the ELC were not obliged to refer proposed terms of agreement to a vote of the membership, and the breakdown of opinion within the National Exective Council is not available. It has been claimed that the usual level of support obtained from member companies for opening negotiations was between 80% and 90%. There was no fixed lower limit of support below which the FUE leadership would not open new talks, but individuals closely involved in the negotiations on the employers' side have suggested that if support was as low as, for example, 75% of members, the leadership could not have proceeded with them.

But there were marked differences in the capacity of member firms to tolerate increased wage costs, and differences also in the degree of resistance companies were prepared to offer to union pressures at local level. These followed from differences in the capital–labour intensity in manufacturing, differences in export orientation, and differences in the cost-structure of domestic firms and local branches of multinationals. The unwillingness of employers to offer strong resistance could stem from a number of sources, as the Fogarty quote cited above suggested, following from the diversity of FUE's membership. In some years, such as 1977–9, when many companies were doing well, some companies were prepared to tolerate more drift than could be accommodated by the agreements (see Fogarty *et al.*, 1981: 19). Wallace (1982: xii. 8) found that 56% of firms in the Limerick area had paid in excess of the national awards during the 1970s:

Of those firms who had paid above the national award, only 17% said they had done so after strong management opposition, thereby indicating a high degree of acquiescence by management in these payments . . . management most frequently cited productivity reasons for giving an award above the national level but in one-third of these cases, no real increase in productivity was actually forthcoming.

On the other hand, some companies could not withstand protracted disputes because they were in a particularly exposed or vulnerable competitive position. In such cases, companies might accommodate additional cost-increasing pressures even if it resulted, whether sooner or later, in rationalization and redundancies. In other instances, the concession of ATN claims could be attributed to managerial inexperience. For example, senior FUE officials believed that a number of firms conceded the 2% 'kitty bargaining' increase permissible under the terms of the 1978 NWA with relatively little bargaining input on their part, while looking to FUE to hold down wage costs through centralized bargaining.

Thus the diversity of the industrial structure made it impossible for FUE to promote a strong, uniform policy in centralized agreements: enough scope had to be left for the wide variations in local conditions. For most employers control of wage costs remained highly desirable. Yet the variety in employers' situations increased the difficulty of securing a common commitment among employers to resist union pressures at local level, even though, as Fogarty *et al.* noted, in Ireland 'there is no such thing as an isolated pay settlement' (1981: 44).

'Local' bargaining generally meant firm- or plant-level bargaining during the 1970s. Industry-level bargaining, whether on issues arising from the centralized agreements or on other issues, tended to decrease, and this left individual employers somewhat more isolated.[15] This is mainly attributable to the nature of the issues

---

[15] Industry-level bargaining took place among certain groups, particularly those for whom there existed JIC negotiating structures, the most important of which was the construction industry. Other sectors in which industry-wide bargaining took place included banking, oil and petroleum companies, printing, engineering contract shops, electrical contractors, furniture, hosiery and knitwear, and agricultural co-operatives (which reverted to local bargaining in 1983). Information from the Dept. of Labour.

which were likely to arise once the basic pay terms had been disposed of by the national agreement. Complex issues of work organization, work practices, productivity bargaining, and changes in wage payment systems all have to be dealt with at firm or plant level (see Mooney, 1982). Employees' intensified bargaining pressures, described in Chapter 5, were primarily focused on the individual firm level.

The recency of industrialization, the low level of industrial concentration, and the diversity of sources of ownership in Ireland precluded the development of a strong sense of collective purpose among employers. There was little of the collective emphasis which characterized the employers' associations in some European countries, and unlike their counterparts in Germany or Sweden, for example, Irish employers rarely if ever had recourse to solidaristic lock-outs. Individual employers quite frequently sought the support of the law to forestall unions' intentions to picket certain premises. The level of *ex parte* and interlocutory injunctions was high during the 1970s, and quite frequently this in itself would undercut the support for industrial action.[16] The option of proceeding with the civil claim for damages was rarely entertained, however, since such a step was generally considered to be inimical to the restoration of 'good industrial relations'.

The FUE saw its main role as one of support for individual employers in promoting good industrial relations, rather than one of advocacy for a collective strategy which would quickly have encountered irresolvable contradictions among such a diverse membership. Thus FUE concentrated on providing services to members, the range and volume of which were indicated in Table 6.3. In addition, it assisted with improvements in companies' industrial relations and the development of procedures for handling grievances, claims concerning improved pay and conditions, and discipline and dismissals. It also counselled on the criteria which ought to prevail in negotiating productivity or other cost-increasing agreements, manning levels, flexibility agreements, and other issues with implications for managerial control (see e.g. FUE, 1980; 1981). But where members chose to depart from FUE guidelines, whether in industrial relations practice or in pay policy, the association held no brief to discipline them or to maintain a unified collective front.

[16] See Casey, 1969; Stewart, 1975; also 'Injunctions and the Worker: A Critical Examination', *IRNR* 9 (4 Mar. 1983).

INTER-ORGANIZATIONAL TENSIONS

The industrial homogeneity of the CIF presented it with far fewer problems of co-ordination than FUE. The construction industry employers, with their well-established industry-level bargaining, and their practice over this period of making collective agreements binding by registering them with the Labour Court under the provisions of the Industrial Relations Act, 1946, might be expected to experience less disruption in a return to decentralized bargaining than would most other private sector employers.[17] The collective interests of the construction industry employers were sometimes at odds, therefore, with the preferred policies of the more diverse FUE. During recessionary periods when construction was depressed, the CIF was strongly opposed to what it regarded as the excessive pay increases awarded through the centralized agreements. Early in 1977, for example, a joint report by the CIF, the Irish Farmers' Associations (IFA), and the Association of Chambers of Commerce called for the abolition of the NWAs and a return to decentralized bargaining. This alliance was formed because its members 'shared the ethic of private enterprise', according to IFA President Paddy Lane. The Managing Director of the CIF stated that this alliance represented 'the beginning of the fight back of private enterprise.'[18] But at other times, when the construction industry was prospering (and when some firms may have been experiencing skilled-labour shortages), many firms regarded the NWA clauses on ATN increases as unduly restrictive. In the autumn of 1977, for example, the CIF wanted to concede a pay claim by craftsmen, in spite of an initial Labour Court recommendation for deferral in order to keep increases in line with the terms of the current NWA. Relations between CIF and FUE became very strained over this issue, which contributed to the withdrawal of the CIF from the Irish Employers' Confederation in October 1977. Although it continued to be represented at the ELC, it did not rejoin the IEC.

As we have seen, SIMI was not a member of the IEC for most of the 1970s. Its reason for remaining outside was that 'it was felt that

[17] In fact, however, collective bargaining in the building industry in the early 1980s, proved to be fraught with difficulty. The JIC was adjourned *sine die* in 1982; the CIF withdrew on account of its 'growing frustration regarding a number of unions repeatedly flouting the disputes procedures while claiming the benefits, sometimes by process of law' (CIF *Annual Report*, 1982/3).

[18] *IT* 21 Jan. 1977.

membership of the IEC would create difficulties for some of its multinational manufacturing companies' (O'Brien, 1981: 166). The international company policy of such firms was to undertake their own pay and industrial relations negotiations rather than become involved in collective negotiations with other employers. This preference led, on occasion, to conflicts within SIMI between manufacturing and retailing companies, as well as to tensions between SIMI and the IEC (O'Brien, 1981: 166 nn. 8, 9).

GOVERNMENT AS EMPLOYER

During the second half of the 1970s both the FUE and the CIF became increasingly critical of what they saw as a lack of co-ordination in public sector pay policy. In the FUE's view, neither government over the period had a consistent approach to the development of public sector pay. It was particularly critical of the concession of 'special' awards to various public sector employments, which owed more, the FUE suggested, to pressures from the unions than to any plan for public sector pay. Thus although government in its role as a major employer shared many interests in common with the private sector employers, and government representatives as well as representatives of public sector companies were included at the ELC, the FUE came to believe that the calculations of government as the supreme political authority overrode the criteria appropriate to government's employer function (see Fogarty *et al.*, 1981: 21–4, 25–31).

The CIF was also critical of government's contribution to pay policy as a major employer. Strong relativity relationships existed between craft workers and other categories of employees in public sector employments and in the private sector construction industry. Higher rates of pay in public bodies by the late 1970s and early 1980s meant that claims for similar 'special' increases were brought against private sector construction employers. The CIF complained in 1983 of the volume of 'special' wage concessions made by public bodies in recent years and it gave its view that, over the years, the Department of the Public Service 'has failed dismally in its main function, that of controlling the cost and numbers of employees in the public service' (*Annual Report* 1982/3). It should be noted, however, that the Department of the Public Service also had cause, on occasion, to be critical of the CIF's pay policy, most notably with regard to the previously mentioned relativity claim conceded to construction workers in mid-1977. This had direct implications for the cost of public sector construction, frequently contracted out to private companies; it also had knock-on effects on the 'special' pay claims of public sector craft and construction employees during 1977 and 1978.

The organizational features of the employers' associations, reflecting as they did the diversity of the economic structure in the 1970s, were not conducive to the development of effective employer solidarity. As the fate of the IEC demonstrates, the private sector employers showed little capacity to present a united front in collective bargaining and industrial relations more generally. The different priorities which tended to prevail in private and public sectors further cut across the possibility of employer unity. As a consequence, the employers came increasingly to hold that the key to a more satisfactory pay policy and more peaceful industrial relations lay with government. FUE, in particular, increasingly expressed the view that the balance of advantage in industrial relations rested to an excessive degree with the unions and that legislative action was needed to correct this imbalance.

Three areas of government policy were the focus of FUE concern: first, the growing gap between total labour costs to the employer and employees' disposable income; second, the volume of protective legislation enacted during the 1970s; third, the law on trade disputes, long the subject of FUE criticism, which was held to provide excessively wide legal immunity for employees engaging in industrial action. In none of these was the FUE's lobbying successful. Indeed, on the third issue, reform of trade disputes law, the only new statute enacted over the period was passed in the face of FUE's opposition. The next section sets out briefly the nature of employers' grievances in relation to government policy.

Employers' Associations and Government Policy

TOTAL LABOUR COSTS

During the 1970s, as Chapter 3 showed, the FUE was anxious that government should become more directly involved in centralized agreements, to offset pay agreements with tax and welfare commitments in a form of a social contract. The talks leading to the 1977 NWA had been convened at its suggestion. By 1981, however, the FUE had grown disillusioned with the outcome of increasingly 'politicized' agreements, holding that government had misjudged the role it played to the disadvantage of employers. By this time, as was seen in Chapter 4, employers' labour costs had increased considerably although union wage pressures had not abated. The FUE was highly critical of the manner in which the second NU was secured in 1980, when the Taoiseach, Charles Haughey, made it clear to private sector employers that the government wanted an agreement to be negotiated. Although the early NWAs had been comparatively successful from the employers' point of view, and they were prepared to accept later NWAs as a better alternative to free-for-alls, much had changed by the early 1980s. When the talks on a new centralized agreement broke down at the Employer–Labour Conference towards the end of 1981 the employers were unwilling to intervene to rescue them, even though it might mean the loss of a centralized framework for wage negotiations. By this time the FUE was also expressing determination to engage in more public, more overtly political lobbying activities. The intention was to represent the employers' case to government in a forcible manner and thus to counterbalance the influence which it believed the unions exerted.[19] The FUE argued, for example, that the increased burden on employers of pay-related social insurance contributions and other employment levies (apart from those voluntarily entered into under the terms of NUs) represented a disincentive to additional employment creation.[20]

PROTECTIVE LEGISLATION

The FUE was also critical of the pace at which a range of employee entitlements such as equal pay and paid maternity leave were introduced in spite of the difficulty these measures could cause to employers. In 1977 three major pieces of employment protection legislation were enacted: the Unfair Dismissals Act, the Protection of Employment Act, and the Employment Equality Act. The FUE's views on these pieces of legislation were clearly stated in an article

[19] Interview with E. P. Galvin, President of FUE, in *Business and Finance*, Easter 1982.
[20] See E. McCarthy, 1983; FUE *Bulletin*, Apr. 1981, Aug.–Sept. 1981, Feb. 1982.

featured in the FUE *Bulletin* of November 1976 entitled 'Tough Provisions on Dismissals Could Discourage Recruitment', which cited a report by the British Manpower Services Commission in support of this contention.[21] Moreover, the FUE was also unhappy at the government's commitment to a statutory maternity leave scheme in the second NU. In 1980 the FUE *Annual Report* argued that:

While particular pieces of legislation may be considered socially desirable, the cumulative effect of the labour and social legislation introduced in the last ten years is probably now having a disincentive effect on the creation of new employment . . . Proposals for further legislation should be shelved. Social progress cannot advance at a rate greater than the growth of the economy.

Much of the protective legislation introduced during the 1970s and early 1980s was made necessary by EEC directives. But in the FUE's view, the nature and timing of these measures, and particularly the introduction of those not strictly required in order to comply with EEC standards, resulted from what it viewed as an undesirable degree of political influence of the trade union movement.

TRADE DISPUTE LAW

The same contention was made with respect to trade dispute law. In the view of the FUE, the inheritance of British labour legislation gave too much latitude to trade union action without obliging the unions to observe a corresponding 'responsibility'.[22] The disputes which concerned employers most, such as unofficial strikes and strikes in breach of procedures, enjoyed the protection of the Trade Disputes Act 1906. The FUE wished the range of immunities to be narrowed and specific disputes procedures to be made mandatory. For many employers the case of *Gouldings Chemicals* v. *Bolger*

---

[21] FUE *Bulletins* between Oct. 1976 and Mar. 1977 contained much discussion and comment about the various pieces of protective legislation then being enacted.

[22] This theme has been put forward by FUE for quite some time, e.g.: 'A major force in society has power without any corresponding responsibility and changes which in a democratic society emerge through representative institutions are made the subject of wars of attrition in the industrial sphere. Until there is a clear understanding of the role which trade unions should play in society, and this can only be shaped by legislative process, the problems of industry in the field of management–labour relations will remain largely unresolved.' (FUE *Bulletin*, June 1966.) See also FUE *Bulletin*, Mar. 1977, Aug.–Sept. 1977, July 1981.

(1977) occasioned particular interest in and concern for the reform of labour law.[23] The case concerned a group of employees of Gouldings Chemicals who refused to accept the redundancy settlement negotiated on their behalf by the trade union of which they were members and who then proceeded to picket the plant. One of the Supreme Court Justices (Mr. Justice Parke) commented that:

Whatever may be the practical result of the defendants' actions, what they have done appears to be a defiance of the normal democratic procedures and to strike at the whole principle of orderly collective bargaining under the authority of properly elected union representation . . . As the law now stands it is a step which the Court is powerless to restrain.

The FUE wrote to the Minister for Labour in April 1977 as follows:[24]

We consider it essential that the Government introduce amending legislation to remove the right to picket in the circumstances of the case before the Supreme Court and also, as requested last week by the President of the FUE, that an expert group be set up to advise on the kind of labour law reforms which are necessary and desirable.

A Commission on Industrial Relations (CIR) was duly established by the Fianna Fáil government in 1978, to report on industrial relations generally and in particular on: '(1) the practices of employers and their organisations and of workers and their trade unions under the system of free collective bargaining, (2) the relevance of statute law to industrial relations, and (3) the operation of institutions, structures and procedures and to make recommendations' (terms of reference of the CIR). But ICTU withdrew from it at an early date in protest over the government's refusal to enact a statutory measure for which it had been lobbying, concerning amendment of the Trade Disputes Act 1906. Case-law in Ireland, over the years, had had the effect of excluding workers not employed 'in trade or industry' from the protection of the Act. This effectively excluded public services employees from legal protection for strike action (McCartney, 1964; id., 1965; Casey, 1972; *Irish Law Times and Solicitors' Journal*, 1953). This had become a matter of concern to ICTU, and this concern increased as

---

[23] See FUE *Bulletin*, Mar. 1977, May 1977.
[24] FUE *Bulletin*, May 1977.

public service employees took industrial action to a greater extent than in the past. The recommendations of the ensuing CIR report, published in July 1982, would inevitably be compromised by appearing to reflect primarily an employers' point of view. However, the employers were unhappy that the government showed no apparent interest in implementing the recommendations of this report. Their dissatisfaction was increased when in June 1982 the government enacted the Trade Disputes (Amendment) Act 1982, providing the amendment which ICTU had sought and FUE had opposed. Moreover, this move seemed to the employers to run directly contrary to the main thrust of the CIR's deliberations. It occasioned an 'unprecedented' refusal by FUE to meet the Minister for Labour to discuss the recommendations of the Commission's report.[25]

A second piece of legislation was passed in 1982 to which the employers also took exception, contending that it strengthened the unions' position in industrial disputes in a manner which could be seen as increasing the incentive to take strike action. This was the Social Welfare (No. 2) Act 1982. It provided for the establishment of a Social Welfare Tribunal which would decide upon the payment in certain circumstances of social welfare benefits to workers who were on strike. The admissible reasons concerned the precipitating actions of the employer leading up to the decision to strike. FUE circulated its members with a memo calling for protests to individual TDs and arguing in strong terms that this Act was 'neither necessary nor desirable'.[26]

EMPLOYERS' SOLIDARITY AND GOVERNMENT ACTION

In conclusion, we have seen in this chapter that the private sector employers were unable to devise a collective strategy on pay developments; furthermore, they held that this was not in any case their proper function. They argued that the deficiencies of trade union organization gave rise to pressures on individual employers which were difficult to withstand. However, it should also be noted that with the recession of the early 1980s employers tended to take a 'harder' line both on pay developments and on work organization

[25] *IT* 29 June 1982.
[26] FUE *DataBank*, 1/2 (July 1982).

and managerial prerogatives.[27] This point is developed further in Chapter 8.

The activities of trade unions and bargaining groups were subject to some degree of legal regulation. But the employers held that the 'rules of the game' of industrial relations failed to provide adequate disincentives to contravention of agreed procedures and collective agreements. They looked primarily to government to remedy this state of affairs. Yet they had been unable to influence government to adopt the measures to which they attached so much importance. They recognized that throughout the 1970s governments attached a high value to maintaining centralized agreements, and they came to hold that this increased the political influence of the trade unions on some issues which were of vital interest to employers. Some employer representatives and leading industrialists considered it a disadvantage that neither of the two main political parties were expressly partisan to employers' interests. At any rate their view was that 'governments have all had a touch of fear about coming into conflict with the unions.'

Earlier chapters have shown that in so far as the unions may be said to have exercised political influence on matters such as trade disputes legislation, their power was largely a power of veto. The unions' impact on public policy was confined in its scope. Chapter 4 referred to the complex but confused role of government in public policy on industrial relations, pay policy, and economic management, and contrasted it with the policies which would be expected from a government trying to give effect to a concertative approach. That chapter suggested that government was responsive to diverse political pressures. We must now examine the underlying reasons why governments were attentive to some pressures and not to others, and why governments seemed to lack a 'strategic' approach.

[27] See 'The New Hardliners', *Business and Finance*, 5 July 1984, examining employers' stance in pay negotiations in recessionary conditions.

7

Economic Interests and Party Politics

The Significance of the Role of Government

In the discussion in Chapter 1 of the role government may play in securing concertative agreements it was argued that no institutional prerequisites may be identified with confidence and that the partisan colouring of the governing party or coalition, while important, is not in itself decisive as a predictor of success. What is crucial is that government should play a mediating role in employer–labour bargaining, so that it should be worthwhile for the unions to rely relatively heavily on political processes for benefits rather than to exert to the full their labour-market power. Government must therefore be alert to all the implications of the antagonistic interests involved in distributive conflict, if it is to be successful in facilitating an agreement. It was earlier argued that a stable employer–labour 'consensus' can only be secured through bargaining between the two sides, each capable of authoritatively representing collectively-defined interests. The government's input must be directed purposefully in a consistent strategy for economic management. Therefore, as noted in the first chapter, it will be better able to mediate employer–labour conflicts if it already has good 'sectoral corporatist' relations with each peak federation, a concept which embraces the political articulation and effective co-ordination of economic and class-related cleavages.

Two political models were set out in Chapter 1 as a means of clarifying possible conditions for concertation. The 'Social Democratic' model assumes the dominant role of a Social Democratic party in the political system, close ties between party and trade union federation, and consequently what might be termed 'Social Democratic hegemony' in political economy. The 'consociational' model is not dependent on the dominance of a working-class based party, but assumes some means of clearing policy priorities across parties. These parties may draw upon cross-class electoral support, as in the case of the Netherlands, or the primary political cleavage may be that of class, as in the case of Austria. However, it would appear to be important for mediating co-operative agreements between unions and employers that economic interests should be directly represented in the political system.[1]

The two preceding chapters have shown that in Ireland neither trade union movement nor employers possessed the degree of authoritative co-ordination which would seem to be vital for a strategy of political exchange. But important though the organizational and political features of the trade union federation in particular may be, they should not be discussed in isolation from party politics. The nature of trade union links with political parties may have important consequences for the way trade unions organize themselves, how they perceive their interests, and the collective identity which predominates. The trade unions' strategy is devised against the backdrop of their expectations concerning the nature and reliability of government commitments and the degree to which government's inputs are in turn conditional upon their own actions.

Two aspects of the political system would therefore be expected to be of particular importance for the government's chances of mediating economic conflicts: first, the manner in which economic interests are represented in parliamentary politics; and second, the nature of the links between parties and the peak federations of unions and employers.

PROBLEMS IN THE IRISH CASE

The economic strategies pursued by the Coalition and the Fianna Fáil governments in the 1970s were fundamentally similar. Each adopted the logic of concertative policies and each went to some lengths to maintain centralized agreements. Chapters 3 and 4 showed that both governments between 1973 and 1981 on the whole pursued expansionary, deficit-financed fiscal policies at the same time as seeking to secure wage regulation agreements. But Chapter 4 argued that the diversity of the governments' own policy

[1] This, it has been suggested, is an important reason for the greater stability of Austrian concertation. The departure of the Dutch Social Democratic party from the governing coalition in 1959 has been identified as a crucial contributory factor to the breakdown of the post-war incomes policy in the Netherlands in the 1960s (Lehmbruch, 1979b; Flanagan et al., 1983).

commitments made it difficult for them to devise a consistent and integrated approach to wage regulation.

Moreover, it was seen in Chapter 5 that the trade unions were able to pursue benefits on two fronts simultaneously. ICTU was able to bargain for policy concessions from government in the context of a centralized framework pay agreement with the employers, while affiliates were pressing additional claims on employers at local level. This raises the question of why governments supported centralized bargaining as they did. Their evident support for the agreements contributed to consolidating the influence of the trade union movement both in employer–labour bargaining and in bargaining with government. This fact contributed in turn to a sort of 'ratchet effect' in the late 1970s whereby the trade unions pressed to obtain greater concessions on various policy commitments. Yet the results, in terms of either wage regulation or strike mitigation, fell far short of those intended. As we have seen in Chapter 5, ICTU was not in a position to exercise significant control over its membership. Yet governments continued to cultivate its co-operation.

ELEMENTS OF AN EXPLANATION

A number of related features of the Irish political system must be looked at in order to explain the contribution of party politics and governments' policy 'mix' to the political economy of Ireland in the 1970s.

First, the nature of representation of economic interests must be considered. The alternative political models which were set out in Chapter 1 each involve a means of directly addressing and mediating important political cleavages in the society, and each model would provide a means of attempting concertative policies. It was noted earlier that the lack of strong class differentiation in Irish society was regarded by many as a boon to government attempts to promote bargained consensus. This chapter will argue that the weak representation of class differences and the weak ideological differentiation of parties in Ireland had quite the reverse implications: they contributed to the difficulty of mediating distributive conflict, while giving organized interests access to the shaping of 'accommodating' policies.

Second, the logic of electoral competition strengthened the

tendencies for policies to be pursued on an *ad hoc* basis, even where this led to an implicit conflict between the priorities being pursued. There was little incentive for the parties to seek to reflect social cleavages more consistently or to try to devise more cohesive strategies. In consequence governments continued on the whole to show diffuseness of political purpose and an eschewal of ideological consistency.

Third, the political difficulties of implementing an alternative approach in relation to the trade unions were great. The trade union movement was not 'strong' in Korpi and Shalev's sense (see Chapter 1), and was not fully committed to the logic of a strategy of neo-corporatist concertation. But the costs for government of adopting an alternative approach would have been perceived by politicians as excessive; and, in view of the strength of voluntarist practices, such a move would have been unlikely anyway to achieve the desired effect of controlling pay pressures and the incidence of industrial action. The strategy of industrial development on which further growth, including employment expansion and protection of existing levels of employment, was founded depended on optimizing the conditions for investment by foreign capital. Governments found it impossible to devise a class coalition which would accord primacy to the prevailing development strategy. Yet they could neither depart from this industrial policy, nor could they formulate an approach which would not depend upon some form of bargained co-operation from the trade union movement. The political economy of the 1970s may be seen as the product of competing political and economic priorities which governments had few resources to mould and co-ordinate in a decisive way.

The Parliamentary Representation of Interests

THE STRUCTURE OF THE PARTY SYSTEM

It has been argued that a relatively small number of social cleavages have structured the political systems of most West European countries (see Lipset and Rokkan, 1967). The Irish political system, however, is 'exceptionally unstructured'; the social indicators normally used to predict voting behaviour provide so unreliable a guide that the Irish case has, with some exaggeration, been termed 'politics without social bases' (Whyte, 1974). This is far from suggesting that Irish society somehow lacks real social divisions. The political parties, however, are not primarily based on these differences, and the economic and social divisions of interest in the society find no direct organizational expression in parliamentary politics.

Of the three main parties, only the Labour Party makes any explicit claim to represent class interests. But of these three main parties, the Labour Party is the smallest. The two larger parties, Fianna Fáil and Fine Gael, drew unequal levels of political support for many years, though during the 1970s Fine Gael made greater efforts to narrow the gap. But Fianna Fáil occupied a dominant position in the political system (see Sartori, 1976), regularly winning a plurality of the popular vote, spread across all social classes. Table 7.1. shows the percentage distribution of support for parties at the general elections between 1965 and 1981.

TABLE 7.1. *Support for Political Parties, 1965–1981*

	1965		1969		1973		1977		1981	
	% vote	Seats	% vote	Seats	% vote	Seats	% vote	Seats	% vote	Seats
FF	47.7	72	45.7	74	46.2	68	50.6	84	45.3	78
FG	34.1	47	34.1	50	35.1	54	30.5	43	36.5	65
Labour	15.4	21	17.0	18	13.7	19	11.6	16	9.9	15
Other	2.8	3	3.2	1	5.0	2	7.3	4	8.3	8
TOTAL	100	143	100	143	100	143	100	147	100	166

Source: Election data; see Gallagher, 1985; id., 1978; Chubb, 1982; O'Leary, 1979.

THE CLASS BASIS OF PARTY SUPPORT

As Chapter 2 indicated, both Fianna Fáil and Fine Gael owed their origins to the Sinn Féin movement of the early years of the twentieth century and to the splits which followed independence in 1922. The political divide which was based on nationalist Civil War issues continued to dominate the political system and provided the basis of differentiation among these two parties on 'the national question' and relations with Northern Ireland (see Garvin, 1982a; Carty, 1983). The original issues cut across class lines; the two main parties continued to draw upon cross-class support.

But some systematic differences may be seen in the sections of the electorate in which each party was strongest and also in the spread of support available to each (see Gallagher, 1985; Laver, 1986a and 1986b; Sinnott, forthcoming). Table 7.2 indicates where this support came from in the course of the 1970s. From the two parts of this table it may be seen that the Labour Party had its strongest support among the urban working class, with some pockets of middle-class support, and also had support in rural areas in which unionization of farm workers had early been established. In a 1969 Gallup Poll survey trade union membership and council house tenancy were found to increase the likelihood that an elector would support the Labour Party (Whyte, 1974: 632–4). However, so great was the preponderance of Fianna Fáil in the electorate as a whole that it even had a plurality among these two categories. Whereas the Labour Party drew most of it support from the working class, it was not the major party of the working class. Fianna Fáil drew more support from the working class than did either of the other two parties, while also obtaining a plurality of the popular vote across most other social groups. Fianna Fáil was the most successful cross-class party and a true 'catch-all' party (see Kirchheimer, 1966; Chubb, 1982; Laver, 1986a). Fine Gael's support was less consistently diverse. It tended to be rather more successful than Fianna Fáil among the professional middle class and among larger farmers (not shown separately in this table, but see Laver, 1986a and 1986b). During the late 1970s and early 1980s it would seem also to have extended its support among the lower tiers of white-collar and service employment.

All three parties also retain residual features of a regional differentiation of support which was more marked at the time of the state's foundation. During the 1920s, it has been argued, the distinction between Republican sympathizers (the proto-Fianna Fáil support, drawn to a large extent from the 'have-nots') and the supporters of the Free State (many of whom supported the antecedent to Fine Gael, commonly seen as 'the party of the haves') corresponded with a west–east political divide which had been evident in earlier nationalist and land-war conflicts (see Rumpf and Hepburn, 1977; Garvin, 1974, 1982a). By the 1970s these associations had been blurred, but some continuity was evident in the regional support for parties. Voting behaviour and party identification tended to be influenced strongly by earlier familial

TABLE 7.2. *The Class Basis of Support for Parties, March 1980*
(%, No. = 1058)

	Reported vote in 1977 General Election				
	Upper & middle	Skilled working	Semi-/Un-skilled	Farmers	All classes
Fianna Fáil	52	52	53	46	51
Fine Gael	27	20	15	40	26
Labour Party	7	14	19	3	11
Sinn Féin–The Workers' Party	1	1	3	0	1
Don't know, Others	14	11	10	12	12
TOTAL	101	98	100	101	101

	Party allegiance				
	Upper & middle	Skilled working	Semi-/Un-skilled	Farmers	All classes
Fianna Fáil	38	39	41	34	38
Fine Gael	25	22	16	42	26
Labour Party	6	13	19	3	11
Sinn Féin–The Workers' Party	1	1	2	0	1
Don't know, Others	28	25	23	21	24
TOTAL	98	100	101	100	100

Notes: 1. Totals sometimes add up to more or less than 100% due to rounding error.

2. There are two reasons for presenting both tables here. First, the 1977 election produced an unusually large majority for Fianna Fáil and an unusually small vote for Fine Gael, so some comparison is desirable; second, any survey of this sort must be treated with some reserve, so both tables should be treated as illustrative rather than as definitive.

Source: Courtesy of Irish Marketing Surveys Ltd.; also in Garvin, 1982b: 173, 174.

political allegiance; Table 7.2. suggests that the votes which may be identified as floating or uncommitted (i.e. those involved in the change in reported party preference between the two sections of the table) were slightly more numerous among the (largely Dublin-based) urban middle class.

Irish politics features no strong ideological cleavages, any more than it features important class-based cleavages. It is not uncommon for all parties to view themselves as being 'a little bit left of centre' (Gallagher, 1981). A survey of perceptions of party location on a left–right spectrum, undertaken in 1976, produced the result shown in Figure 7.1. The typical respondent located himself or herself roughly in the centre, with the Labour Party somewhat further to the left. The two main parties were perceived to have very similar profiles, and respondents' answers place them over a very broad spectrum, undoubtedly indicating the difficulty of locating these parties in left–right terms. The Coalition government, in contrast, was seen by the typical respondent as a centrist government, and the distribution of people's perceptions of its location resembled that of people's self-location.

THE COALITION QUESTION

The two main parties were cross-class catch-all parties, and according to their electoral profiles they resembled one another more closely than either resembled the Labour Party. This makes the possibility of a Fine Gael–Labour coalition prima facie, difficult to explain. Two reasons may be advanced, both pertaining to the ideological diffuseness of Irish politics.

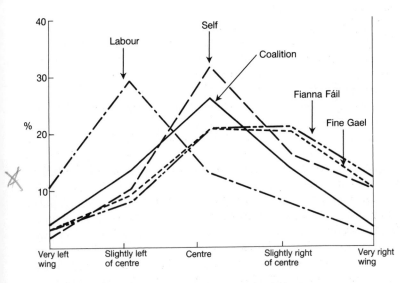

FIG. 7.1. Right, Left, and Centre in Irish Politics

Source: Courtesy of Irish Marketing Surveys Ltd., survey undertaken in 1976 for RTE; also reproduced in Chubb, 1982: 110.

First, the logic of electoral competition poses coalition as an option for Fine Gael and Labour (see Cohan, 1982). Fianna Fáil is the only party which has hitherto been capable of forming a government by itself. Party competition is structured such that the main difference is between Fianna Fáil and the other parties. Despite their apparent incompatibility in view of the differences in the social bases of their respective support, an electoral alliance between Fine Gael and Labour has been seen as the only realistic alternative to uninterrupted Fianna Fáil rule.

Second, the policy preferences of the two parties proved not so difficult to combine during the 1970s. The Labour Party was more self-consciously leftist than either of the two major parties. But the party's orientation on economic matters may be characterized as one of centrist Social Democracy. Neither Fianna Fáil nor Fine Gael professed any strong ideological orientation. But whereas Fianna Fáil was chary of committing itself to any distinctive position, Fine Gael embraced some more clear-cut policy preferences. One section of the party retained an allegiance to economic conservatism and a 'strong' position on law and order, but another section was distinctly more liberal on most issues: this difference corresponded to a large extent with a generational difference within the party. Enough support was forthcoming within Fine Gael to work out a Coalition programme with the Labour Party as a condition of making a realistic bid for power. Thus Labour's moderation, the result of divided opinions within its own ranks, combined with the dispersion of opinion within Fine Gael, made possible a Coalition between the leading sections of each party.

Some indication of parties' ideological positions may be gleaned from analysis of their election manifestos and policy statements. In a content analysis of these materials, Mair (1982a, 1987) established that the Irish parties may be differentiated on several axes of policy issues, including those of state intervention in the economy, public morality, and Irish unity. During the 1970s Fine Gael shared a greater affinity on some issues with the Labour Party than might immediately be apparent. All parties were fundamentally committed to the development strategy which relied primarily on private enterprise, supplemented by public enterprise and active state intervention, though Labour would prefer more extensive state intervention than the others, according to this evidence. But the public positions of both Fine Gael and the Labour Party were closer together than either was to Fianna Fáil on other issues; Fianna Fáil's position was rather conservative on issues of public morality and, on the whole, more strongly in favour of a united Ireland.

However, these suggestions should be treated with considerable caution. Each of the issues mentioned above proved divisive for all the parties and each party comprised a coalition of different opinions on various issues. The tendencies which distinguished the two main parties, in particular, must be seen as differences of degree and not of kind, and changes of personnel on the front benches could result in important shifts in dominance among the different internal coalitions of opinion.

THE STABILITY OF NON-IDEOLOGICAL POLITICS

The main features of the party political system have been remarkably stable over a relatively long period. Most significantly, they survived the economic and social transformation of Irish society in the 1960s and 1970s. Two features of party politics merit further exploration: first, the significance of the early nationalist cleavage for the articulation of class interests; and second, the adaptation of the party system to changed social and economic conditions.

There has been considerable debate over which elections may be considered 'critical' for the formation of the political system of the new state, but all are agreed that it was during the period between 1918 and 1932 that the fundamental patterns were established which continued to prevail, in spite of the occasional intrusion of small parties, right into the 1980s (Farrell, 1970; Pyne, 1969; Sinnott, 1978).

As we have already seen, the parties which had developed in the course of the early nationalist conflicts continued to dominate the political scene thereafter. In the opinion of certain commentators, there was some potential for the Civil War cleavage to produce 'an enduring and recognisable left–right, conservative–radical polarisation of some kind' (Garvin, 1978: 331), not least because certain serious political problems had been disposed of in the period prior to independence, including the religious cleavage, most marked in the North, and the land question (see Lynch, 1966). But the Labour Party was unable to extend its share of electoral support. It was undoubtedly hindered by its weak social structural basis, but the consolidation of the nationalist divide proved perhaps its greatest obstacle: 'More than any other party, Labour has suffered from partition, from emigration, from the division of the trade union movement . . . and from the competing claims of republicanism' (David Thornley, political scientist and Labour Party TD, cited in Chubb, 1970: 83; cf. Hardiman, 1981; Orridge, 1977; Garvin, 1978).

From an early date Fianna Fáil was better able than the Labour Party to claim the 'radical' position, and after its accession to power in 1932 it passed a number of pieces of social legislation. But it simultaneously secured the image of its leader, de Valera, as 'a pious, bourgeois conservative' (Chubb, 1970: 77). More generally, 'in the context of Irish politics . . . the left or radical position was held by those who stood for basic constitutional change—the republicans' (Mitchell, 1974: 235). But this radicalism did not necessarily entail social radicalism. Rather, social issues tended to take a secondary place:

Nationalism in Ireland, as elsewhere, has been more directly concerned with securing the power of the nation to direct its own destiny than with achieving prosperity or social progress as such. The two aims of national aspirations and lower-class striving for increased political voice appeared to coincide, prior to independence: the class enemy was the national enemy . . . [after independence] the left had, in effect, been captured by radical republicanism. (Rumpf and Hepburn, 1977: 219; see also Mitchell, 1974: 291; Garvin, 1974.)

If this was the situation which prevailed in the early post-independence period, it might none the less be expected that the scale of social and economic change in the 1960s and 1970s would have brought about a restructuring of the political system. However, although the substance of party competition altered and economic issues became more central to political debate, no change occurred in the basic form of the party system. Rather, each of the parties adapted successfully to the changing context in which it operated (see Mair, 1979; Gallagher, 1981; Girvin, 1984). But the persistence of the older bases of differentiation might suggest that the party system had thus necessarily become even more removed from the social and economic realities of the rapidly modernizing society.

The Labour Party was disappointed in its efforts to break out from its marginal position during the 1960s. But even if social conditions were more favourable to it during the 1960s, political and ideological conditions had improved but little. The Catholic authority structure was dominant throughout the period of national independence (see Whyte, 1980), but more significantly, its ethos was shared by the Labour Party itself (see Mitchell, 1974; Gallagher, 1982).[2] When it came to assert a less apologetic leftist position during the 1960s, it was still vulnerable to 'red smear' tactics from the other parties (see Busteed and Mason, 1970); and the new policies garnered far from unanimous support from its own rural membership. The prevailing ideological climate was not very sympathetic to socialist ideas, however moderate. The other two parties could encompass similar policies among their catch-all range without attracting the same opprobrium, leading to the complaint from Labour leaders that 'Fianna Fáil and Fine Gael stole Labour's programme'.[3]

In the late 1970s and early 1980s the Workers' Party tried to win new support for class-based party politics. It seemed possible that expansion in the younger section of the electorate, at a time of acute economic difficulties, heralded a longer-term change in established voting patterns and consequently in the shape of the party political system. But although the Workers' Party won three seats in the election of February 1982, reduced to two in November 1982, these were gained in constituencies in which the Labour Party had once been strong. No major change of electoral allegiance seemed imminent.

Fine Gael adapted to the new conditions of the 1960s and 1970s through the efforts of a younger, more politically liberal wing of the party which evinced a stronger concern with issues of social policy and social justice than that which characterized the leadership of the 1950s and 1960s, and a more ambitious conception of the responsibility of the state for effecting change in these matters. This section of the party became more prominent during the 1970s, and with Garret FitzGerald's accession to the leadership in 1977 was

---

[2] Brendan Corish, then leader of the Labour Party, identified his philosophy as one of 'Christian Socialism' (interview, *IT*, 9 June 1964). In response to Labour's ostensible move to the left in the mid-1960s, Seán Lemass said in the Dáil (on 8 July, 1966) that 'far from the Labour Party going "red", they are not going anywhere . . . they are a nice, respectable, docile, harmless body of men—as harmless a body as ever graced any parliament' (cited in 'Backbencher' column, *IT* 10 Oct. 1966).

[3] See *IT* 14 Sept. 1964.

widely seen to have moved into the ascendant. Nevertheless, it had to coexist, at times somewhat uneasily, with the more traditional elements of the party which had different views on issues such as public morality and law and order.

Fianna Fáil had the advantage in adapting to new conditions of having presided over the inception of growth and economic planning. It accomplished the feat of retaining its traditional support and its traditionalist associations while also securing widespread support for its development initiatives. Fianna Fáil presented its change of policy direction as being continuous with the party's concern for and identification with 'the national interest'. The party established close links with the newly prosperous business class and enjoyed the support of a fund-raising organization of businessmen, Taca, until it was disbanded in the late 1960s. It also put itself forward as the party with greatest concern for the least well-off, since the climate of opinion was favourable to issues of social policy.[4] In the opinion of the political scientists Rumpf and Hepburn (1977: 223):

Fianna Fáil was the most successful nationalist *and* radical party in Ireland since 1921 ... [even though it] changed its character almost entirely between the 1930s and the 1960s. Nationalist-radical parties in general possess considerably more political flexibility in areas of the world which have nationality problems than do Labour parties, which tend to appear by contrast as very colourless when confronted with the state's most burning issues.

Fianna Fáil's retention of its nationalist image, combined with its cultivation of extensive constituency-level contacts and good local-level organization, enabled it to retain broad cross-class support throughout the period of social and economic change (see Carty, 1983; Farrell, 1983; Garvin, 1982a). 'Pragmatism' was a frequently used watchword for Fianna Fáil politicians, who prided themselves on precisely the flexibility of party policy. The party's position was summarized by Charles Haughey in 1982, when he was leader of Fianna Fáil in opposition: 'The party is neither hostage to the left

[4] David Thornley, political scientist and later Labour Party TD, wrote in 1965 that 'one can scarcely exaggerate the influence of Pope John upon the Irish political climate. In 1951 the language of Catholic social teaching was still of vocationalism, subsidiarity and the duties of the family. In 1965 it is of socialism, welfare, economic rights.' (*IT* 31 Mar. and 1 Apr. 1965.)

nor slave to the right, but operates a pragmatism of the centre.'[5]

Fine Gael had traditionally relied heavily on local notables for its party organization, but during the 1970s it came to emulate Fianna Fáil's example and to organize much more effectively at local level. Thus, in summary, far from being prey to problems of party discipline (at least until comparatively recently) and consequent electoral volatility, the two largest parties combined a relative lack of interest in policy partisanship with highly developed party organization. Both adjusted to the new issues and new style of party competition in the 1960s and 1970s by adapting their cross-class, non-ideological approaches.

Non-Ideological Politics and the Electoral System

There was obviously no possibility that an Irish government could operate the sort of 'Social Democratic hegemonic' strategy outlined in Chapter 1. But it would not seem in principle to be out of the question that parties could develop a 'consociational' strategy, whereby parties, agreeing on the substance of economic policy and priorities, might press for employer–labour agreement within the limits of what was agreed to be politically and economically tolerable.

But in the consociational countries political parties had the resources with which to make the framework for a bargained agreement acceptable to both sides. Deep denominational or ideological scissions in the society contributed to the acceptability of a consociational style of politics. In Ireland, however, the cross-class basis of governments' support and their flexible ideological orientation did not have this consequence. For one thing, the two main parties lacked 'partisan' organizational or political links with the trade union and employers' federations. But more fundamentally, the way the parties were constituted and the logic of party competition induced them to gloss over economic conflicts instead of attempting to clarify them, and to try to accommodate the separate pressures from each side instead of mediating a compromise on new terms.

[5] Interview on radio programme 'This Week', RTE, 19 Dec. 1982. In his 1978 Budget speech George Colley, Fianna Fáil Minister for Finance, said: 'Our approach is a pragmatic one. It is not dictated by ideological dogma.' (*Dáil Debates* 1 Feb. 1978, vol. 303, col. 394).

In Chapter 1 it was argued that the class basis of distributive conflict must be given organizational expression, and that economic interests must curtail sectional competition and approximate to class-oriented organizations, if a bargained agreement is to be possible. This means that the government must facilitate the articulation of class-oriented interests, within parliament and without. As Przeworski argues (1980*b*: 42, and 1985; see also Chapter 1), there are many potential collective identities which might shape individuals' political and electoral behaviour:

> Class shapes the political behaviour of individuals only as long as people who are workers are organised politically as workers. If political parties do not mobilise people *qua* workers but as 'the masses', 'the people', 'consumers', 'taxpayers', or simply as 'citizens', then workers are less likely to identify themselves as class members and, eventually, less likely to vote as workers.

This argument, applied to the Irish case, helps to clarify the inefficacy of government concertative strategies. Governments did not articulate class-related interests through the parties. Nor were they able to provide the ideological pivot on which the trade union movement might be able to turn towards a concertative strategy. The very factors supposed by many to facilitate consensus themselves contributed to the failures of the consensus-oriented strategy.

The way this came about may be looked at under two headings: first, the conduct of electoral competition, and second, the nature of the relations between each government and the organized economic interests. Therefore the present section looks at the role of the electoral system in shaping and perpetuating a non-ideological approach to politics, and the following section looks at the consequences for patterns of policy-making and for the role of the trade union movement in the policy process.

ELECTORAL COMPETITION

No major issues of principle divided the parties at national level, but party discipline and constituency organization were strong among the two larger parties (the Labour Party was very weak in many parts of the country). Only relatively recently has any systematic work been done in identifying the importance of the electoral system itself in shaping this distinctive style of party competition (see Carty, 1983). Constituencies are multi-seat, each generally returning between three and five candidates. The polling system is one of proportional representation with the single transferable vote (see Chubb, 1982: appendix C, for details). Inter-party competition tended to be concentrated on allocation of the last seats in constituencies reckoned to be marginal, so a great deal depended on the rank-ordering of preferences among candidates and on the extent to which people vote a full party slate; party discipline and party organization aimed to ensure that voters' preferences were structured along party lines (see Gallagher, 1978). Voter volatility was not high and party allegiances in electoral behaviour were fairly stable during the 1960s and 1970s (see Mair, 1982b).[6] Nevertheless, some quite small shifts in support could be decisive for the allocation of marginal seats, and the electoral system tended to result in disproportionate gains in numbers of seats for the largest party contesting all or most seats (O'Leary, 1979: ch. 9). For the Coalition parties electoral success depended to a considerable extent on ensuring an efficient transfer of preferences between the two parties, and this also required them to pay close attention to constituency campaigning.

These features of the electoral system concentrate competition at constituency level. Strong local loyalties constrain party head offices in the choice of candidates they can advance for nomination by the constituency parties (Gallagher, 1980). An extra dimension to this pervasive localism is the intra-party competition for rank-ordering of preferences, which further personalizes candidates' campaigning. In such circumstances politicians have every incentive to concentrate on providing local services, engaging in the 'politics of the parish pump'. Correspondingly, constituents expect their representatives to 'go about persecuting civil servants' (Chubb, 1963). Any politician who neglects the primary importance of brokerage politics may expect to pay a heavy price in loss of electoral support (see Carty, 1983; Komito, 1984). This servicing function often involves no more than provision of information

[6] The election of 1977 was the first in which those aged between 18 and 21 were entitled to vote, and because of the age-structure of the population first-time voters constituted fully 25% of the total electorate in that year (O'Leary, 1979: 90). The sizeable gains made by Fianna Fáil were attributable in part to the influx of new voters, and in part to effects of the changes in constituency boundaries undertaken by the Coalition government—which, in the event, operated to the disadvantage of the outgoing government.

which is otherwise available. But it also typically involves local clientelist relationships; even government Ministers have to engage in the most parochial transactions and negotiations. Politicians without access to state power also cultivate local support bases using precisely the same techniques (Bax, 1976; Sacks, 1976). 'Organisationally and spiritually, parties remain tightly tied to the immediate concerns of local communities; there is no mechanism, no incentive, and little opportunity for them to discover or express the needs and claims of the larger society. Inevitably, a system rooted in community breeds a conservative politics.' (Carty, 1983: 141.)

Consequently, parties have been highly susceptible to the demands articulated by different sections of their support. The electoral system shaped and perpetuated party competition among parties with effective national-level organization and close ties to localist issues. Small shifts of opinion could have major cumulative consequences at national level. The governing party had a strong incentive to try to secure such support by acceding to the demands made, and the opposition party or parties, equally, had an incentive to try to exceed that offer in the promises they built into their election manifesto.

SUSCEPTIBILITY TO DIVERSE PRESSURES

Irish political parties are, on the whole, cross-class and non-ideological in character; they are strongly rooted in localist politics; and they are inclined to try to extend support by 'upping the philanthropic ante'[7] in electoral competition. But general elections are contested only every few years, and all sorts of organized interests press for political attention in between times. Most important among these have been the major economic interests. Governments are highly conscious of the need to retain support from diverse quarters, and a short time span geared to electoral advantage tends to prevail. Therefore, governments are likely to be susceptible to pressures from different quarters even where, as in the case of unions and employers, these claims may not be mutually compatible in the broader context of economic management.

Governments do not depend directly on organized interests for electoral success. They do not rely, for example, on the mass-

[7] Antóin Murphy, 'The Economic Policies: Spot the Difference', *IT* 6 May 1977.

mobilizing electoral capacity of the trade union movement. There is relatively little continuity between the collective identities of workers *qua* trade union members and *qua* electors. Indeed in many respects the activities of trade unions tend to be unpopular among the electorate. Yet trade unions have been drawn increasingly into the political domain because of their economic power and its implications for economic management. There is therefore quite a discrepancy between the vote-mobilizing and the extra-parliamentary significance of the trade union movement. This is, of course, also true of employer and industrial interests, although in a different way, as discussed in Chapter 6.

The reason why parties make electoral calculations relating to the economic interests is because of their considerable indirect significance for parties' electoral success. Governments in Ireland, from the early to mid-1960s on, were primarily evaluated on the basis of their perceived ability to manage the economy. Economic issues regularly topped opinion poll surveys of electoral priorities in the 1970s and early 1980s, even at times when political opinion formers may have wished to stress the urgency of other issues, such as Northern Ireland. This may be seen from Table 7.3.

TABLE 7.3. *Voters' Perceptions of Leading Election Issues (%)*

	1973[a]	1977[b]	1981[c] (June)	1982[c] (Feb.)	1982[c] (Nov.)
Prices/inflation	28	76	27	19	16
Unemployment	11	76	48	46	45
Rates	18	–	–	–	–
PAYE/taxation	–	54	5	3	4
Stable government	–	–	–	7	17
Reducing govt. debt	–	–	–	11	8
Social welfare etc.	17	27	3	1	3
Housing	8	27	–	–	–
Northern Ireland	12	20	6	1	1
Security/crime	3	20	3	1	2

Note: Only the columns marked "c" may be directly compared with one another. This table is intended only to be indicative of electoral priorities. The scores are derived from the following questions:

[a] 'Which of the problems listed on this card would you personally like to see the newly elected Government tackle first?', IMS poll in the *Irish Independent*, 26 February 1973.
[b] 'Which of these issues do you think will be important in the election?', *Irish Times*/National Opinion Poll Survey in *IT*, 2 June 1977.
[c] Key issues identified by electors in IMS polls immediately before the General Elections, in Des Byrne, 'Ireland at the Polls' (IMS Ltd.).

Governments in the 1970s therefore strove to secure working agreements with the main economic interests which would ensure reasonable levels of economic performance. But the nature of electoral competition also affected the priorities that governments observed. Governments became increasingly conscious of the direct electoral importance of public service employees. A number of disputes in the late 1970s and early 1980s in public service employments were regarded as politically sensitive, and the governments were reluctant to engage in confrontation with the relevant unions. Furthermore, strikes, especially those affecting key services and utilities, of which there was a series during the closing years of the 1970s, were unpopular among the broader electorate in measure with their disruption of everyday life. Politicians' connections with their constituency bases of support provided a direct channel for citizens' grievances of this sort, and government frequently experienced a good deal of pressures to 'do something' about particular strikes.[8] This could result in direct ministerial intervention in a dispute—for example, by referring it to the Labour Court for investigation, under the powers accorded the Minister for Labour by Section 24 of the Industrial Relations Act, 1969.[9] The short time-scale which normally prevailed tended to favour action to resolve immediate disputes and to avert imminent disputes. This was not conducive to the formulation of the sort of longer-term approach which would be required by a concertative strategy for economic development.

'ACCOMMODATION' VERSUS 'MEDIATION'

The primacy of electoral considerations and the short time-horizons associated with this led governments during the 1970s to try to satisfy the immediate demands of many diverse interests. This tendency was strengthened by the 'catch-all' character of non-ideological politics.

The main parties' conception of what would be required by the

---

[8] Interviews with Michael O'Leary and Gene Fitzgerald. In a study of the 'Irish value system', Fogarty, Ryan, and Lee (1984) discovered that politicians were held in very low regard by respondents—no surprise to any Irish citizen. They found also that trade unions have an unenviably low public standing.

[9] Between 1946 and 1969 only one dispute was referred to the Labour Court under Sect. 24; between 1969 and 1983 forty-four disputes were so referred by Ministers for Labour (Labour Court *Annual Reports*, 1946–83).

logic of a concertative strategy was limited. Unlike those of other countries in which such a strategy was implemented, Irish political parties had few full-time party workers and little interest in academic policy input. Governments' ideas on a prices and incomes policy, the value of tripartism, and the extension of budgetary policy to complement collective bargaining resulted from the confluence of diverse intellectual streams. The native nationalist tradition was certainly important, so too were the British experiments with a prices and incomes policy in the 1960s and the Social Contract of the 1970s. But there was also an important element of *ad hoc* policy-making. Fianna Fáil was the self-avowed 'party of pragmatism', but the Coalition also showed marked evidence of a pragmatic response to political contingencies.

This 'pragmatism' was closely bound up with the parties' need to maintain their electoral support. The very diversity of that support, in the case of the two major parties, would make it difficult under any circumstances to retain high levels of approval simultaneously from all groups. Yet this was what the electoral logic required of the parties. Thus if, as Chapter 1 suggested, an effective concertative wage regulation agreement required the commitment of state policy to the interests of working people, Irish governments were limited in the extent to which they could do this by their need simultaneously to protect the interests of other groups. Some of the policy consequences of this need to satisfy a broad range of interests were discussed in Chapter 4.

Priorities in Public Policy

In this section we shall examine the consequences of non-ideological politics for the formation of public policy priorities. We shall then examine in more detail the relationships between the different parties and the trade union movement, looking in particular at the shortcomings in the approach of each government to securing wage regulation agreements.

POLITICS AND POLICY-MAKING

The non-ideological character of party politics, combined with the localist pressures associated with electoral competition, introduced a number of important constraints into government processes of policy-making. These constraints would make it difficult for any government consistently to pursue a strategy of mediating distributive conflict. But the problems of developing and implementing a consistent strategy were compounded by other, more general features of the political system which tended to encourage an expansionary approach to management of the public finances and which contributed to the narrowness of the criteria which governed public policy-making.

The institutional seat of decision-making was the cabinet, following the British model of government, and the cabinet in Ireland was synonymous with the government (Chubb, 1974). No other institution, whether civil service, Central Bank, or economic interest, formally played more than an advisory role in decision-making. But this meant that 'the party élites have a virtual monopoly of formulating policy' (Carey, 1980: 264), with all the implications discussed above for the play of short-term electoral pressures as against pursuit of a longer-term set of objectives.

The dominant role of the cabinet is all the more significant because, in the words of one political scientist, 'the Dáil is one of the worst organized, equipped and informed parliaments in the democratic world' (Chubb, 1982). The opposition party or parties had few facilities for scrutinizing or evaluating government policy proposals, particularly those involving expenditure commitments. The most common objection to spending proposals was that they were inadequate, and opposition parties were rarely disposed to call for downward revision of departmental estimates when these were presented before the Dáil.[10] Governments found it very difficult to withstand the pressures from the opposition benches, and indeed from their own back benches, to accommodate diverse demands. As an earlier section argued, these pressures played upon governments' electoral calculations. Of course it may be argued that such pressures are, to some extent, common to all liberal democracies, and 'election-year economics' is a recognized phenomenon in many societies. One author has written of the United States as follows:

A bribe to the voters is, after all, a bribe to the voters. In election years, unemployment drops, social welfare programmes expand, and beneficiary payments to millions of people increase. The months before the election are

[10] Interviews with politicans from all the major parties.

the 'liberal hour', replacing the administration's efforts earlier in the term to build 'business confidence' . . . Perhaps the electoral–economic cycle should be accepted as one of the externalities and inefficiencies resulting from the democratic—and consequently political—control of the economy. (Tufte, 1978: 149.)

However, the pressures under discussion in the Irish context are not confined to election periods but tend to occur, albeit at a lesser intensity, throughout a government's period of office, intensified by the fact that government and opposition are competing for the support of similar constituencies of interest.

The government itself was the final arbiter (notwithstanding Central Bank advice; see Whitaker, 1983c) of all policy decisions, and had a virtual monopoly on relevant information and on establishing the criteria which would guide the eventual decisions (McDowell, 1982). Few guidelines were sufficiently well established to override or curtail the pressures of localism and electoral calculation. There was little tradition of non-party-political public policy-making which might increase the political influence of other institutions such as, for example, the Central Bank. For several decades after the independence of the state, fiscal policy adhered to conservative guidelines of fiscal orthodoxy. But this had been a largely conventional restraint on decisions concerning management of the public finances. During the 1970s, when the convention was abandoned of not permitting a deficit on the current account, public policy in this area was left without definite guidelines emanating either from public institutions or from party ideology and strategy. The resultant tendencies were summarized by George Colley, then the Fianna Fáil spokesman on Finance, replying to the Coalition's 1977 Budget: 'Every Minister for Finance is tempted to allow expenditure to grow more than he knows it should grow and more than the economy can bear at a particular time. He is tempted because there are some very worthwhile things he can do, and he is tempted for purely political advancement.'[11]

[11] *Dáil Debates* 26 Jan. 1978, vol. 296, cols. 309–10 (citing himself on 10 May 1976). A widely-held view of politics in the 1970s and 1980s was expressed in interview by a prominent industrialist: 'The institutions of Irish society are in severe disequilibrium as a result of the tendencies on all parts to go after short-term and expedient answers, irrespective of the consequent or related problems.' A similar comment was passed by an individual long prominent in public life: 'No one twenty years ago would have believed the amazing strength which trade unions, employers, and farmers now possess compared with the political parties.' (Interview with T. K. Whitaker.)

Party élites therefore tended to have considerable discretion in formulating fiscal policy, and the most significant constraints tended to be those emanating from within parties. The differences across governments must be explained not only in terms of differences in the economic conditions facing them but also with reference to the previous traditions and accustomed priorities of the political parties. Both the Coalition government and the Fianna Fáil government adopted expansionary policies, but each then experienced political difficulties in reducing the current account deficit and the public sector borrowing requirement. The differences in the economic circumstances of the two administrations has already been discussed. But the Coalition's adoption of policies of retrenchment in 1976 must also be seen as a course of action shaped to an important degree by Fine Gael's traditional attachment to fiscal orthodoxy. The same may be said of the proposals contained in the Coalition government's White Paper *A Better Way to Plan the Nation's Finances* (July 1981), although the specific recommendations it contained were never given effect.[12]

In mid-1982 the Fianna Fáil government adopted a more stringent approach to the public finances than it had previously been pursuing. In this instance too the pressure of external economic conditions alone does not account for the shift in government priorities, and changes of opinion within the party (and lobbying pressures to which politicians are subject) should also be taken into account to provide a full explanation; however, a detailed examination of this sort is beyond the scope of the present work. The reorientation of policy towards the public finances in the early 1980s, though widely accepted to be inevitable, was not easy to accomplish; it contributed to the rapid alternation of governments in 1981–2. Even in November 1982, after a Coalition government had taken office, Fianna Fáil won considerable support by characterizing the Coalition's policies as 'monetarist' and 'uncaring'.

TRADE UNIONS AND ELECTORAL PRESSURE

In Chapter 5 it was shown that the trade union movement came to have a distinctive sort of pressure-group relationship to government

[12] In one attempt to increase electoral sympathy for the measures needed to reduce the public sector borrowing requirement, Fine Gael minister John Bruton used an uncharacteristic metaphor in calling for 'a war of national economic independence' (interview in *IT* 2 Sept. 1981).

in the course of the 1970s. The present chapter has set out the main features of the political system which account for the importance attached to achieving co-operation with the trade union movement, and for the accommodating fiscal policies on which that co-operation was largely based. The private sector employers considered that the political influence of ICTU was considerable in those areas with which they were most concerned, in particular the reform of industrial relations legislation. Yet as Chapter 4 showed, on the issues with which ICTU was most concerned during the 1970s, principally the incidence of PAYE taxation and the level of unemployment, its political influence was limited. To some degree the unemployment problem was the result of the structural limitations of state control of an economy experiencing rapid changes in composition. However, as Chapter 4 showed, it was also the product of a particular combination of policies pursued by successive governments, over which the trade union movement did not by any means have a dominant influence. Although ICTU may have been able to exercise a power of veto over proposals for industrial relations reform, its ability to bring about substantive changes in policy was limited. This is particularly noteworthy in the case of taxation. ICTU lobbied throughout the 1970s for greater equity in the tax system, which would have required drawing the agricultural sector into the tax net. But farmers' organizations, especially the two largest, the Irish Farmers' Association and Irish Creamery Milk Suppliers' Association, were well-organized and united in their resistance to any extension of the tax system to include farmers. Moreover, both Fianna Fáil and Fine Gael draw considerable electoral support from the farm sector. Both shied away from electorally damaging confrontation with the farmers.

RELATIONS BETWEEN ICTU AND POLITICAL PARTIES

Although ICTU developed close relations with both the Coalition and the Fianna Fáil government, in neither case did this amount to a 'sectoral corporatist' relationship in Lehmbruch's sense (see Chapter 1). The trade unions affiliated to the Labour Party if they affiliated at all, but because of its small size and lack of internal unity there was little scope for a strong alliance between ICTU and the Labour Party. Fianna Fáil was the dominant and governing party for a long period. ICTU preferred to keep open the possibility of negotiating with either government. But while each government sought to establish a working relationship with ICTU, both lacked a coherent approach to the mediation of distributive conflict. Yet the nature of relations between ICTU and government differed, depending on the party composition of government.

The Labour Party and the Coalition government

During the 1970s only nineteen of the ninety or so trade unions were affiliated to the Labour Party: some of these had affiliated, or reaffiliated after a lapse of some years, in the course of the 1960s. This group included some of the largest unions, such as the WUI (later renamed FWUI) (1964), the ITGWU (1967), and the ATGWU (1970). Affiliated unions were represented at party conferences, including those convened to decide whether or not to enter into a coalition agreement with Fine Gael. Each delegate cast one vote, and the union delegation usually amounted to about one-tenth of the total of about 1,500 delegates. Their financial contributions covered only about 8% to 10% of the party's spending in the 1970s. Some unions, such as the ITGWU, had political funds which considerably exceeded the political levy paid to Labour. However, these funds were mainly used to give direct support to trade union Labour Party candidates in elections.

ICTU and unions affiliated to the party frequently used the Labour Party over the years as a channel through which to articulate political grievances. At the Annual Delegate Conference of the Federal Workers' Union of Ireland in 1983, in a debate on a recurring theme for many unions, a proposal to withdraw the political levy paid to the Labour Party until it withdrew from Coalition, it was reported that:

The most practical and beneficial advantage of this union's affiliation to the Labour Party is reflected in the representations and assistance afforded to the General Officers, Industrial Officers, members in industrial disputes and the pursuit of trade union objectives in particular situations by Labour Party TDs and the Party... Hardly a Branch of this union has not benefited by this co-operation ... Unfortunately, much of this work is of a confidential nature and tends not to be publicised.[13]

The top leaders of the largest unions have tended to be Labour Party members and these connections were used, whether the

[13] Reported in *IRNR* 21 (1 June 1983).

Labour Party was in or out of office, to channel trade union opinion in the Dáil. But Fianna Fáil leaders expressed 'disappointment' when the largest union, the ITGWU, reaffiliated to the Labour Party in the late 1960s, because Fianna Fáil wished to depict itself as 'the workers' political party'.[14] Similar themes were repeated over the years by Fianna Fáil, perhaps most insistently during periods in which Labour Party participation in government coincided with recession.[15]

Relations between the trade union movement and the Coalition government of 1973–7 were far from easy. The five Labour Party ministers did not form a cohesive bloc in cabinet, and it has been said that divisions of opinion in cabinet during the Coalition's period in government never occurred on party lines (Gallagher, 1982: 219).

The same government's conception of how to secure the 'national partnership' which it sought lacked unity of support from its own side and coherence of purpose. The Minister for Labour, Michael O'Leary, introduced several important pieces of protective legislation between 1973 and 1977. He expressed the view that the state should show itself to be committed to workers' interests, since only if its commitments were seen to be 'to the left' in matters of social policy would the trade union movement have any incentive to co-operate with other government objectives.[16] But when ICTU began to lobby for a change in the Trade Disputes Act, 1906, to remove the restriction on industrial action which applied in principle to public service workers (see Chapter 6), the Minister resisted on the grounds that 'the unions have enough of that sort of power already'.[17] He also took the view that if employment levels were to be protected, an incomes policy was essential. However, it must be concluded that these aspirations were not translated into an effective strategy during the Coalition's period of office. The trade union movement tended to take for granted the enactment of the protective legislation, much of which was passed to comply with EEC directives anyway. The emphasis placed on an incomes policy was indistinguishable, from the point of view of many trade

[14] Paddy Hillery (Fianna Fáil Minister for Labour 1963–6), quoted in *IT* 11 Dec. 1967, 27 Nov. 1967; see also *Hibernia*, Jan. 1968.
[15] See e.g. 'Fianna Fáil Sets its Eyes on Labour-Linked Unions', *New Hibernia*, Oct. 1984: 13.
[16] Interview with Michael O'Leary.
[17] Interview with Michael O'Leary.

unions, from the traditional Fine Gael emphasis on fiscal controls even at the expense of cuts in real wage levels. Personal relations between some union leaders and the Minister for Labour (a Labour Party minister and erstwhile ITGWU official) were also, at times, difficult.

The coalition between the Labour Party and Fine Gael proved highly contentious for the trade union movement as much as for many Labour supporters. The alternative to sharing power in coalition was 'principled socialist opposition', the preferred course of the party's left wing. The party would be excluded from political power by adopting such a strategy. But participation in coalition tended to blur the party's electoral identity, and it fared worse in 1977 than in 1973. By the early 1980s many within the Labour Party feared that Labour was being outflanked on the left by the Workers' Party. A major row erupted at the Labour Party conference as early in the Coalition's period of office as 1974, in which the ITGWU delegates accused the Labour Party of having 'sold out to Fine Gael'.[18] In 1973 the unions did not have a united position on the issue of coalition, but opinion had shifted against it by 1977. In 1981 and 1982 the policies of the two main unions, the ITGWU and the FWUI, were opposed to coalition.[19] The trade union view notwithstanding, the Labour Party formed another coalition with Fine Gael. The party's commitment to coalition, and its recognition of the extent of the problem in the public finances, resulted in somewhat uneasy relations between ICTU and the party when in government.

Fianna Fáil

Labour Party voters were more likely to be trade union members than not. But as Chapter 5 showed, the nationalist cleavage in the party system had its counterpart in the trade union movement. More trade unionists evidently voted regularly for Fianna Fáil than for Labour, and quite a number voted regularly for Fine Gael (though the latter party had virtually no presence in intra-union politics[20]). In the opinion of a senior ITGWU official, about 80% of the union's membership were Fianna Fáil voters.[21] In spite of the

[18] See *IT* 12 Nov. 1974.
[19] Joseph O'Malley, 'Why the Trade Unions Fear Another Coalition', *Sunday Independent*, 25 June 1981.
[20] Interview with Richie Ryan.
[21] In interview with the author.

union's institutional links with the Labour Party, Fianna Fáil had reason to seek good relations with it. In this case, Fianna Fáil's quest for union support was undoubtedly facilitated by personal ties between some individuals, but party political expediency also pointed to the desirability of securing good relations with the trade union movement in general and of convincing it, in the words of Jack Lynch on becoming Taoiseach in 1977, that the basic objectives of Fianna Fáil and ICTU were 'close and perhaps identical'.[22]

It has already been seen that the concertative strategy implicit in the Fianna Fáil government's initiatives was no more thoroughly worked out than were the Coalition's plans for a 'national partnership'; but Fianna Fáil's accommodating stance resulted in largely good relations with the trade union movement. The government's approach required close co-operation with ICTU on pay policy, but government policies were not well integrated to this end. Relations between government departments, particularly the Department of Finance and its offshot the Department of Economic Planning and Development (DEPD), were not always smooth. Moreover, the Minister for EPD subsequently acknowledged that the early fiscal concessions had had little to do with winning the unions' confidence for a pay policy and more to do with securing votes and returning to power.[23] Opinion was widely believed to have been divided in cabinet on the developing trends in the public finances and the proper role of government in economic management.[24] An opposition deputy, commenting on the division then believed to exist in relation to the government Green Paper *Development for Full Employment* (June 1978), said that 'the more hard-nosed and realistic members of the Cabinet—Deputy Haughey and Deputy Brian Lenihan—freely admit that the basic assumptions behind the document are quite impractical at best'.[25]

The leadership succession in December 1979 caused a rift within the party, and, as Chapter 3 noted, it was widely held that the development of pay policy in 1980–1 owed not a little to the intensified electoral pressures experienced by the new leadership, in

[22] This was the phrase used when Jack Lynch met ICTU representatives shortly after the 1977 general election; see *IT* 24 Sept. 1977.
[23] Interview with Martin O'Donoghue.
[24] See e.g. the report on a Cabinet debate on the economy, *IT* 3 June 1978.
[25] Barry Desmond (Labour Party), *Dáil Debates* 29 June 1978, vol. 307, cols. 2353–4.

its wish to secure a decisive electoral victory for the party.[26] For reasons already discussed, the logic of electoral benefit militated against making cuts in expenditure once spending commitments had been made.

In 1981, surveying Fianna Fáil's period in office, one journalist went so far as to say that over the preceding four years, 'with a seat in the Cabinet, the trade unions could hardly have done better or secured more from Fianna Fáil'.[27] Whatever the truth of this, several commentators have suggested that the trade union movement 'regards the Labour Party as the natural party of protest and Fianna Fáil as the natural party of government'.[28] Matt Merrigan, General Secretary of the ATGWU and a founder-member of the short-lived Socialist Labour Party, made the same point in 1978 when he said: 'Labour has offered no alternatives, but Fianna Fáil has delivered the goods'.[29]

Thus it may be concluded that neither the Coalition nor Fianna Fáil possessed an intellectual tradition or ideological orientation conducive to developing the implications of a concertative approach to collective bargaining. Government priorities tended to be formed by a variety of short-term considerations which counselled the minimization of conflict between the government and important organized interests. For these reasons the 1970s have been seen as a period dominated by 'manifesto politics' (Fintan Kennedy, 1981).

Earlier in this chapter it was suggested that two aspects of the Irish party-political system would have to be explored in order to account fully for the approach taken by successive governments to pay policy and economic management more generally. The first concerned the conditions which made possible the 'accommodation' of conflict, and this has been the subject of the chapter thus far. The second concerned the pressure on government to adopt a quasi-concertative approach to pay policy and collective bargaining because of the constraints it encountered in adopting an alternative

[26] With reference to the concession of a number of trend-setting 'special' increases in 1981 and 1982, one public sector union leader was heard to comment that a militant approach to pay claims paid off and was like pushing an open door on the other side of which sat a welcoming Taoiseach presiding over a large cash-box (personnel communication).

[27] Joseph O'Malley, 'Why the Trade Unions Fear Another Coalition', *Sunday Independent*, 25 June 1981.

[28] Ibid.; also Gallagher, 1982, 1985.

[29] See M. Foley, 'The Unions: The Revolutionary Purpose', *IT* 12 Oct. 1978.

approach. The constraints should not be regarded as absolute, nor should it be concluded that governments had no option but to act as they did. But the constraints felt by governments shaped their approaches to pay policy and relations with the trade union movement. The next section therefore surveys some to the limits governments encountered to adoption of an alternative approach.

The Dominance of the Concertative Approach

GOVERNMENTS' CONSTRAINED CHOICE OF STRATEGY

The logic of what each government attempted during the 1970s was implicitly that of concertation as discussed in Chapter 1. But the cross-class, non-ideological approach of each government made it difficult for it to devise a consistent and effective approach to wage regulation agreements. Neither government analysed distributive conflict in terms which recognized its origins in class-related differences. Therefore the mediating role of government was not conceived as one of 'trans-sectoral' concertation. The importance of overcoming trade union sectionalism was recognized by successive governments. But the implication—that a strengthening of class identity and shared interest was needed—was not clearly perceived. Governments have frequently sought to strengthen the authoritative centralization of ICTU, recognizing that this would greatly facilitate the objective of making collective bargaining compatible with improved performance. Indeed, one trade union official wryly noted, in interview, that governments were usually keener to have a strong trade union leadership than were trade unions themselves. But political parties could provide no convincing ideological model in terms of which trade unions might spontaneously perceive their interest in a centralized collective strategy. Thus government efforts to enhance ICTU authority, in the view of many in the trade union movement, amounted to no less than an effort to extent coercive controls over rightful trade union autonomy (Kelly and Roche, 1983).

Neither government in the 1970s had a well worked out conception of how to implement a mediating role in collective bargaining. This was evident in the weakness of the conditions attaching to negotiation with the trade union movement. It was evident, too, in the *ad hoc* decisions taken by government on what issues to draw into the bargaining arena. Therefore governments were more inclined to accommodate pay pressures than to cultivate bargaining towards a class-compromise, positive-sum outcome. The results, as Chapter 4 showed, were hardly encouraging to a belief in the success of the general strategy.

But the strategic options governments were faced with were very limited. The dominance of such a very imperfect concertative approach during the 1970s emerged in a field of constrained choice. A key shortcoming in the centralized wage agreements of the 1970s was the strength of decentralizing tendencies. But governments had few means by which to contain these in any other way than through negotiation with ICTU, and promotion of the conditions under which the trade unions would engage in voluntary reform of their structures and strategies. Quite apart from the immense political difficulties involved in any government attempt to restructure the trade union movement, there were substantial constitutional limitations to government's freedom of action in this area.[30] The voluntarist features of the industrial relations system were also jealously preserved by the trade unions, who tended to be highly suspicious of the extension of legal regulation. A voluntarist system is not of itself inimical to the operation of wage regulation agreements—indeed, the legal reinforcement of such agreements is not very common in those countries where they have been successful. But a system which is both voluntarist and decentralized presents problems for the success of concertation.

Governments were regularly drawn towards strengthening the statutory measures governing trade union activities and the auxiliary institutions (in Kahn-Freund's sense, 1977) charged with responsibility for assisting in dispute resolution. But they commonly had recourse to such plans at times when processes of voluntary negotiation, whether in the field of pay policy or of trade union or industrial relations reform, had broken down. Proposals for the most radical statutory and institutional reforms of this sort were generally abandoned as soon as the climate for negotiation improved. As we saw in Chapter 2, the proposals for change in the Trade Union Bill 1966, and the Industrial Relations Bill 1966, were not put into effect. Similarly, successive governments in the 1980s

[30] See e.g. Shillman, 1960; McCartney, 1964, 1965; J. Kelly, 1980; Redmond, 1982. The only major attempt to effect a restructuring of the trade union movement by statute was Sect. 3 of the Trade Union Act 1941. However, in *NUR* v. *Sullivan and others* (IR 77 (1947); 81 *Irish Law Times Review* 55), this sect. of the statute was found to be repugnant to the Constitution (see Charles McCarthy, 1977b).

proved equally reluctant to implement the proposals of the CIR for a greater role for the law in industrial relations (see Chapter 6).

Because of the inadequacies of the concertative approach and the difficulties of making it effective, governments were inclined to take an alternative, more 'coercive' approach. But the latter could not become the dominant approach. The trade union movement possessed considerable labour-market power and disruptive capacity, and governments generally acted on the assumption that if ICTU perceived that the vital interests of trade unions were under threat, it would have the capacity to make such a strategy very difficult to implement. It is unlikely that either government during the 1970s would have risked a straight confrontation of this sort with the trade union movement, on prudential grounds. Besides, all parties lacked the sort of ideological support that, for example, a neo-*laissez-faire* philosophy might give, and the electoral constraints discussed earlier would quickly come into play if a government seemed to adopt such a course. The common Irish political attachment to concepts of 'community' and 'national interest' did not facilitate a concertative strategy, but neither would these sentiments be conducive to a systematic attempt to weaken or control trade unions' market power and traditional freedoms.

Therefore governments tended to oscillate between supporting negotiation with the trade unions and sustaining voluntary employer–labour agreements on the one hand, and threatening statutory controls on the other. The threat to legislate on a statutory pay norm was sometimes used as a means of hastening a voluntary agreement, and to that extent had to be in some measure credible (instances include the proposals to enact a statutory prices and incomes policy in 1970, a wage freeze in the summer of 1975 and at various points during 1976, and a binding pay guideline in 1979). But it is none the less striking that governments always withdrew from confrontation when it seemed that a voluntary agreement could be secured, even on terms which departed significantly from the content of the original legislative proposals.

We have seen in this chapter that during the 1970s governments were unable successfully to implement concertative agreements. We have argued that much of the explanation for this can be traced to the weak political representation of class interests and to the electoral incentives to perpetuate a non-ideological approach to policy-making and electoral competition. But if governments were unable to play a concertative role, they were also unable to deal with trade unions' market power and their consequent political significance in any other way. There was therefore a compelling case for both the Coalition and Fianna Fáil governments to attempt to reach an understanding with the unions, even where, as this chapter has argued, their strategies were inadequately worked out. An *ad hoc* approach to industrial relations and pay policy tended to predominate.

The experiences of centralized bargaining and of a concertative government approach during the 1970s produced very mixed benefits for all concerned. By the early 1980s it was not clear that any party to them could be said to have benefited unequivocally: there were no 'winners'. The new problems of economic management owed something to the failures of the concertative orientation of the 1970s. However, the political difficulties in devising a strategy adequate to the changed economic context also showed strong continuities with the experience of the 1970s. The period of decentralized collective bargaining in the altered economic context of the 1980s is the subject of the next and final chapter.

8

Postscript: Collective Bargaining
in the 1980s

THE economic climate of the 1980s proved to be very different from that of the preceding decade. As Chapter 3 noted, the second oil crisis and the international economic downturn affected Ireland badly, yet these were the years in which difficult adjustments would have to be made in the public finances. In this context, it is hardly surprising that major changes may be identified in the conduct of collective bargaining.

It has already been noted that following the termination of the second National Understanding of 1980, subsequent 'rounds' of collective bargaining reverted to industry or firm level. This pattern prevailed until 1987. Towards the end of that year, a new centralized agreement, the first for seven years, was negotiated, involving the FUE, the CIF, ICTU, farming organizations, and public sector employers in an agreement which once again linked a pay settlement to government policy commitments: this was to be a 'Programme for National Economic Recovery'.

It would be misleading to suggest that a return to centralized negotiation linking pay with other policy objectives was in any sense inevitable. It followed from the policy initiatives of the Fianna Fáil government which was formed following the general election of February 1987. The new agreement, moreover, was negotiated on very different terms from the previous NUs, and in what was obviously a dramatically altered economic environment. Quite clearly, the unions no longer enjoyed the bargaining advantages they had previously possessed. The private sector employers and the governments which had held power during the 1980s had both striven to alter the terms of debate on the relationship between pay increases and economic performance. But the possibility of negotiating a new centralized pay agreement had emerged from discussions publicly conducted in the mid-1980s over how best to plan for medium-term economic recovery. This chapter traces the changes in collective bargaining practices in the 1980s in the context of markedly worsened economic performance and, in the light of this discussion, seeks to set in context the emergence of a new centralized agreement.

Employers' Experiences of Collective Bargaining in Recession

The impetus for change in the organization of wage determination during the 1980s came from the private sector employers, and more specifically from the FUE, who were acting on the policy recommendations contained in the report they had commissioned, *Pay Policy For the 1980s* (Fogarty *et al.*, 1981; see Chapter 6).

The private sector experienced some improvement in performance in the course of the 1980s. Industrial output began to recover after 1981 and 1982, the years in which recession hit hardest. Manufacturing production growth showed a strong recovery in 1983 and 1984, mainly as a result of strong export growth. Growth in 1985, at 2.75%, was considerably slower than in the two preceding years: although firms oriented to the domestic market improved their performance, export performance was less buoyant. Nevertheless, an index of industrial production of 100 in 1980 had reached 133.8 in 1986.[1] The main impetus came from the newer high-technology sectors of industry such as electronics and chemicals, though other manufactured exports also performed well. A survey carried out by the Industrial Development Authority in 1984 reported that 78% of all firms surveyed experienced an upward trend in productivity over the preceding three years, with not much difference between Irish and foreign firms (IDA, 1984: 7–8). However, these recorded increases in productivity were mostly attributable to new capital investment and to labour shedding. The closure of enterprises and the decline in employment varied greatly by sector, hitting the labour-intensive, traditional industries, mainly Irish-owned, hardest of all (NESC No. 67, 1983), but also affecting companies in the new, largely foreign-owned sector. Furthermore, the subsequent viability of firms also varied by sector: according to the IDA study mentioned above, 60% of the foreign-owned plants declared a substantial degree of profitability over the preceding three-year period, compared to just 40% of Irish establishments (IDA, 1984: 7–9).

[1] *Economic Review and Outlook*, 1984, 1985, 1986; Central Statistics Office information.

Following the demise of centralized bargaining, the challenge of adapting to the altered economic climate focused anew private sector employers' concerns about the rate of increase of earnings. The FUE sought to shift collective bargaining away from the notion that a specific norm should prevail in each wage round—and, if possible, from the idea that wage rounds ought to follow one another automatically. Rather, pay increases ought to be much more closely tied to what the individual firm could bear. In its periodical statements on pay policy and its regular communications with member firms it stressed that the primary considerations were to be the profitability and competitiveness of the enterprise, especially in relation to cost developments in competitor countries, and the ability of the enterprise to sustain pay increases while preserving incentives for investment. Neither wage relativities nor the cost of living in general ought to prevail over these considerations as a basis for settling pay claims. Furthermore, the FUE recommended that consent to changes in work practices and the introduction of new technology ought to be an integral part of pay agreements, not bargained for separately.[2]

The transition to decentralized bargaining occurred quite smoothly, from the employers' point of view. By 1984 and 1985 it was evident that they had been relatively successful in their efforts to limit pay increases to the basic amount negotiated in each round of collective bargaining. There was a clear reduction over these rounds in the number and range of supplementary cost-increasing pay claims, and changes in conditions of employment apart from pay, such as hours worked, were infrequent. A trend appeared to be emerging towards what employers saw as greater 'realism' of trade unions at enterprise level.[3] The FUE *Annual Review* for 1986, summarizing recent wage round data, concluded that 'there seems to be a growing willingness to accept the need for changes in working practices and methods'.

One consequence of successive rounds of decentralized wage bargaining was a greater dispersal of termination dates for different sectors. The pay settlements of various bargaining groups in the first decentralized round of 1982–3 terminated within a three-

[2] See e.g. policy statements in FUE *Bulletin*, Mar. 1983, June 1985; 'Six Priorities for 1986: Policy Statement by the National Executive Council', Jan. 1986; 'The Technological Imperative', Aug/Sept. 1987.

[3] FUE *Bulletin*, Nov. 1986; see also 'The New Hardliners', *Business and Finance*, 5 July 1984.

month span. But over time some difference in the phasing of wage rounds developed between public and private sector bargaining groups. By 1986 the first claims were being advanced for a new round of increases in private sector employments, while for significant numbers of workers, largely in the public sector, the 1985–6 round of agreements still had some considerable time to run. This prompted a comment from the FUE that:

The wage round has ceased to exist as a concept which produced separately identifiable and non-concurrent cohorts of wage agreements . . . This scattering out of entry dates, which is likely to be further accentuated in 1986–7, is one of the most spectacular changes in this field in recent times.[4]

However, despite this dispersal of termination dates of settlements, and notwithstanding some variation in the level of settlements, there was little evidence of any fundamental change in the pattern of wage bargaining. Employers, though relatively successful in containing additional cost-increasing wage claims, remained concerned over the rate of increase of basic nominal wages and the transmission of increases throughout broad sectors of the workforce with each successive round.

Gross hourly earnings rose by more than three-quarters in Ireland between 1980 and 1985. During this period gross hourly earnings rose by less than half in competitor countries, expressed in domestic currency rates. This difference was offset by sharp improvements in productivity in Ireland and by the depreciation of the Irish pound in relation both to sterling and to EMS currencies over this period; thus, expressed in common currency terms, Irish wage costs per unit of output rose by only 7% between 1980 and 1985, compared with a 37% increase in competitor countries overall and about 29% in Britain.[5] Private sector employers nevertheless stressed the continued importance of curbing the rate of nominal wage increase: exchange rate adjustments, in their view, could not be relied on in the longer term to ensure competitiveness and to compensate for what they saw as excessive cost increases.[6]

Furthermore, at a time of falling inflation, the FUE became more

[4] FUE *Industrial Relations Databank*, Oct. 1986. See also Dept. of Labour *Annual Reports*, 1984, 1986.
[5] *Economic Review and Outlook*, 1986; tables 7a and 7b; Paul Tansey, 'We Have to Learn to Sell Ourselves', *Sunday Tribune*, 3 Aug. 1986.
[6] See e.g. 'Competitiveness: Recent Trends in Wage Costs', FUE *Bulletin*, Oct. 1987.

concerned that wage increases should reflect the stabilization of the rate of price increase. 'Cost of living', in the FUE's view, should no longer feature as a significant basis for wage claims.[7] In 1981 and 1982 average price increases outstripped earnings, but in each subsequent year, though the rate of increase of both prices and wages slowed, gross pay increases again exceeded prices.[8]

In summary, the employers were relatively pleased with their successes in resetting the agenda of collective bargaining in the 1980s. However, the rate of increase in nominal earnings remained, in their view, less flexible and less closely linked to local conditions than the FUE would wish.

The Trade Unions' Responses to Recession

The trade union movement overall was much weakened by unemployment and recessionary conditions. Trade union membership and density both peaked at the end of the 1970s. In 1980 membership reached its highest level ever at 524,000, while density peaked at approximately 56%. But numbers declined steadily over the following years, and an initial estimate of trade union membership in 1984 was 501,000, with density estimated at approximately 50% (Roche and Larragy, 1987).

Clearly, and in sharp contrast with earlier years, unions' capacity to engage in industrial militancy had been reduced, and each wage round showed a decreasing tendency for disputes to be brought as far as the Labour Court for third-party mediation. The total number of strikes declined, and the number of days lost was considerably lower over the period 1980–5 than in the preceding five-year period. Moreover, in the years after 1979 there was a continuing decline in the proportion of strikes which were unofficial. In every year after 1982 the number of official strikes exceeded the number of unofficial, the ratio being about two-thirds official to little more than one-third unofficial by the mid-1980s, a very significant reversal of the typical distribution of the 1960s and 1970s. An even more marked decline is evident in the number of days lost in unofficial disputes. In 1980, for example, 46% of days lost were due to unofficial disputes, but a downward trend in each

---

[7] See e.g. the FUE National Executive Committee Policy Statements in FUE *Bulletin*, Jan. 1986, also Oct. 1986.
[8] See e.g. Labour Court *Annual Report*, 1984, 1985.

subsequent year brought the figure to a mere 12% in 1985 and 6% in 1986. These trends are summarized in Table 8.1.

Unemployment, always an issue of grave concern to ICTU, worsened markedly during the 1980s. Overall unemployment rose rapidly during the 1980s; it increased from 8.9% in 1981 to 10.7% in 1982, as recession first made its impact (Conniffe and Kennedy, 1984: 22). It then rose steadily to 16.6% in 1984, 17.5% in 1985, and 18.1% in 1986.[9] This placed Ireland close to the top of comparative OECD performance on unemployment. While the rate of increase slowed during 1986 and 1987, there seemed to be little prospect of a substantial fall in the immediate future.

TABLE 8.1. *Number of Strikes and Days Lost, 1980–86*

Year	Strikes				
	Total	Official	%	Unofficial	%
1980	132	51	39	81	61
1981	117	56	48	61	52
1982	131	76	58	55	42
1983	151	93	62	58	38
1984	191	116	61	75	39
1985	116	70	60	46	40
1986	101	63	62	38	38
	Days lost				
	Total	Official	%	Unofficial	%
1980	404,000	219,000	54	184,500	46
1981	436,000	305,000	70	131,000	30
1982	437,000	363,000	83	74,000	17
1983	311,000	253,000	81	58,000	19
1984	364,000	313,000	86	51,500	14
1985	412,000	364,000	88	48,000	12
1986	315,500	295,000	94	20,500	6

Source: Department of Labour *Annual Reports*.

The data cited earlier on the rate of increase in nominal wages would suggest that aggregate trends in wage increases were relatively little affected by high levels of unemployment. But this would be a mistaken conclusion. The decline in industrial conflict noted above is indicative of this; but more tellingly, the Labour

[9] ESRI QEC, Nov. 1986: 22.

Court, in its *Annual Report* for 1984, commented that 'in terms of the effect on wage bargaining the numbers becoming unemployed and redundant probably has a greater effect than the absolute level of unemployment' (p. 4). Redundancies accounted for an alarming proportion of the growing numbers of unemployed people. The recorded number of notified redundancies—covering only those with two or more years of service—shows a steady upward trend. In the late 1970s the figure was below 10,000 per annum and in 1980 it was 14,664. This rose sharply to over 26,000 in 1982 and over 30,000 per annum for the next two years. By 1985 and 1986 it had dropped somewhat, to a little more than 22,000 each year.[10] The total number at work declined each year after 1980—from 875,000 in 1983 to 837,000 in 1985 and 816,000 in 1986. The manufacturing workforce dropped from 243,000 in 1980 to 204,000 in 1985.[11]

The high dependency ratio in the population, and the large numbers of new labour force entrants each year, further increased the numbers of the unemployed. On the basis of projections made in 1984, and assuming no change in the migration patterns of the early 1980s, the growth in the population aged 15–24 would virtually have ceased during the mid-1980s, but the number aged 25–44 would be expected to increase by more than 20% between 1976 and 1981, by the same amount between 1981 and 1986, and by 16% in the following five-year period.[12] However, it became clear by the mid-1980s that the rate of increase of unemployment was being offset to some degree by the growth in the rate of emigration, once the scourge of Irish society, now re-emerging after the years of net in-migration during the 1970s. Labour force and census data available in mid-1986 made it clear that emigration was running at about three times the rate previously assumed.[13] It was estimated that total net emigration was once again approaching the very high levels of the mid-1950s. Between 1981 and 1986 75,000 people were estimated to have left the country, 31,000 of these in the twelve months to April 1986 alone, and the upward trend appeared to be continuing (NESC No. 83, 1986).

ICTU was no longer expected to provide a co-ordinating role for

---

[10] Dept. of Labour statistics.
[11] *Economic Review and Outlook*, 1986: table 10.
[12] Kennedy and Conniffe, 1984; 38; National Planning Board, 1984: 24.
[13] ESRI *QEC*, Nov. 1986: 27.

trade union pay policy, although it issued guidelines to affiliates on the priorities they should observe in formulating wage claims. Meanwhile it sought to influence public policy priorities, especially on the issues of tackling unemployment, but also on issues such as PAYE tax relief and protection of the value of benefits to those dependent on social welfare.

ICTU's guidelines on pay policy repeatedly recommended that claims should be 'based on the need to protect the living standards of workers'. They also came to include a recommendation that claims for a reduction in working time should also be made 'in line with the demands being made throughout the European Community'. Furthermore, they mentioned that: 'it is desirable that unions in particular industries and employments should co-operate with each other . . . and, as far as possible, co-ordinate claims and negotiations.'[14] In its July 1986 recommendations ICTU made specific reference to its hope that claims would also cover special provisions for low-paid workers and part-time workers,[15] for many of whom decentralized wage bargaining presented particular difficulties.

However, ICTU was in no position to ensure that any of these was put into effect. Living standards declined in the course of the 1980s, as PAYE income tax eroded the real wage increases gained in the years after 1981. The OECD estimated that the average real cost of employing an industrial worker increased by between 5% and 10% between 1979 and 1985, while real after-tax earnings declined by about 15% over the same period.[16] The terminal dates of the various agreements became ever more dispersed; reduction in hours worked had only a marginal place in pay settlements. There was no collective mechanism of any sort to ensure equity in pay developments or protection of the interests of the low-paid, still less of the unemployed.

ICTU's stance on unemployment also remained unchanged in substance. In February 1984, for example, the Executive Committee of Congress issued a statement

rejecting the crude propaganda campaign by Government spokesmen and employers that sought to imply that the closures and job losses and the high level of unemployment could be attributed to the pay levels of Irish

---

[14] Pay guidelines, ICTU *Annual Report*, 1984: 134.
[15] 'Guidelines for Pay Policy', July 1986 (press release).
[16] OECD *Economic Survey*, 1984–5: 38.

workers ... There are a number of reasons for closures and layoffs, particularly market changes, management deficiencies, poor marketing. As regards competitiveness, factor price is but one element and labour costs part only of that element . . .[17]

Congress continued to stress an alternative perspective: 'the reduction in purchasing power which would be the result of a pay freeze would have serious implications for employment.'[18]

ICTU recognized that in certain central areas of concern to the trade union movement political intervention would be required to secure significant change. The most obvious issue was perhaps the heavy burden of personal income tax on employees and the distribution of taxation more generally. But ICTU also took the view (in *Confronting the Jobs Crisis*; see Chapter 5) that unemployment is 'a *political* issue', and that direct government action would be required to ensure that an improvement in employment levels would form part of any plan for economic and social recovery.

However, ICTU no longer had the direct access to government it had enjoyed during the 1970s. The state of the public finances allowed governments little scope for action on the issues of greatest trade union concern. By 1982 all the major parties in the Dáil agreed on the overriding need to stabilize the ratio of the national debt to GNP. It was generally agreed that the scope for increasing tax revenues was limited, and that the employee tax burden could not be reduced significantly in the foreseeable future. Thus sharp cuts in public spending would be needed. Parties differed in their assessment of the space for manœuvre on each of these issues, but the general thrust of public policy was not fundamentally disputed. A government-established body, the Commission on Taxation, conducted a series of investigations into the tax system between 1982 and 1985, but although it recommended several far-reaching reforms, these were held to involve too much uncertainty at a time of tight fiscal constraint. Equally, it was held that no scope existed for public spending on job creation; indeed, recruitment to the public service was sharply curtailed over these years. It was evident during the period of Coalition government (1982–7) that influential Fine Gael members of the cabinet were not willing to accord ICTU

---

[17] ICTU *Annual Report*, 1984: 129.
[18] ICTU *Annual Report*, 1984: 135 (text of ICTU's response to the government's statement on pay policy).

special status in consultations over economic policy; they viewed its role as that of one among a number of lobbying interests.[19] During these years, moreover, ICTU's relations with the Labour Party members of government grew considerably more strained. Although the Labour Party disputed the level and range of public spending cuts introduced by the government in which it participated, the party's shared responsibility for these policies soured its relations with ICTU.

No overt attack was made on the organizational capacity of the trade union movement. Nevertheless, its exclusion from political influence contributed to a new reflectiveness within ICTU on the subject of its representative capacity and the objectives for which, in these altered economic and political conditions, it ought to be striving. A shared feeling began to become apparent that unless it could effect internal changes the trade union movement would lose any sense of collective purpose and would increasingly find itself unable to exert effective influence over public policy debates.

The fragmentation of trade union interests due to decentralized bargaining came increasingly to be criticized. At ICTU's Annual Delegate Conference in 1985 one general secretary noted that: 'The trade union movement can hardly now be called a movement; it is more a loose federation of organisations each dismally engaged in pursuing sectional interests.'[20] The Conference adopted the report of a sub-committee chaired by former ICTU President Paddy Cardiff, which argued that trade unions would have to become fewer in number (there were still 75 trade unions in 1985) and consequently stronger and better organized. These points were underlined by the outgoing President of ICTU, Matt Merrigan, in his opening address, in which he noted that the 'massive decline in membership' had left most unions with staff and officers in excess of their current requirements, representing a dissipation of trade union resources.[21]

Trade unions' declining effectiveness both in collective bargaining and in political influence was increasingly a matter for concern. Billy Attley, General Secretary of the second largest union, the Federated Workers' Union of Ireland, commented that the terms on

---

[19] 'How the Deal was Done', *Sunday Tribune*, 11 Oct. 1987.
[20] Philip Flynn (LGPSU), reported in ICTU *Annual Report*, 1986, and in FUE *Bulletin*, July 1985.
[21] See *Business and Finance*, 4 July 1985.

which collective bargaining was conducted had shifted decisively
towards the frame of reference imposed by the employers, both
private and public sector:

The government could say with justification that it had defeated unions in
the public sector. The battle in the media has also been lost and
propaganda on the relationship between pay and competitiveness has been
accepted . . . The employers have been successful in dismantling the basis
on which we have traditionally argued in pay negotiations—comparability
and inflation.[22]

Yet ICTU seemed unable to adapt its approach or to make an
effective impact on public policy. The General Secretary of ICTU
warned of the dangers to the trade union movement if it let itself
lose sight of priorities it ought to be espousing: 'Unless we rid
ourselves of complacency, shibboleths and wishful thinking we will
be doomed to go the way of all dinosaur organisations which fail to
adapt.'[23]

Under these circumstances, as Chapter 7 noted, Fianna Fáil in
opposition sought to improve its links with the unions.[24] Recognizing that a general election would soon be held in which the
government parties were likely to lose support, a number of trade
union leaders grew more interested, in the latter half of 1986, in
gauging the disposition of Fianna Fáil towards the unions.[25] A new
Fianna Fáil administration would obviously be tightly constrained
by macro-economic difficulties, but it would be more willing to
involve the unions in policy discussions than the Coalition
government. In the absence of political links of this sort the trade
union movement would be likely to continue to find itself
effectively marginalized from policy debates.

Government's Experiences: Fiscal Policy and Pay Policy

From mid-1982 onwards all the major parties were committed to
curbing the volume of public spending as an essential precondition
for any plan of national economic recovery. But the Coalition
government of November 1982–February 1987 experienced con-

[22] Source as in n. 20.
[23] Donal Nevin; source as in n. 20.
[24] See e.g. 'Fianna Fáil Sets its Eyes on Labour-Linked Unions', *New Hibernia*,
Oct. 1984: 13.
[25] See Stephen Collins, 'Pay Pact Time Bomb Ticks Away', *Sunday Press*, 20
Sept. 1987; Gerald Barry, 'How the Deal was Done', *Sunday Tribune*, 11 Oct. 1987.

siderable difficulty in devising an effective strategy. The onset of international recession, the disadvantageous turn taken by international money markets (with higher interest rates and fluctuations in exchange rates), and the slow-down in rates of inflation all contributed to making the national debt both unsustainably high and increasingly difficult to reduce.

At the end of 1986 the total national debt stood at over IR£24bn., three times larger than it had been in 1980 and representing 148% of annual GNP. Repayments on the interests on the public debt alone rose from 7% of GNP in 1980 to IR£2bn., or 12%, in 1986.[26] The position was eased somewhat by reducing the proportion of the debt borrowed on foreign money markets to about 40% by 1986; this reduced the degree to which interest payments could vary with changing interest and exchange rates.

Fiscal and monetary policy in the 1980s thus entered what one commentator called 'a crushing spiral of constriction':[27] taxes, both direct and indirect, remained high while high interest rates depressed investment and thus reduced the productive capacity of the economy. The total public sector borrowing requirement was 17% of GNP in 1980 and 20% in 1982. This was reduced to 15% by 1986. However, capital spending and the capital budget deficit proved easier to control than current spending. The task was all the more difficult at a time of high unemployment and rapid population growth; government spending on social services increased from 28.9% of GNP in 1980 to 35.6% in 1985. The current budget deficit stood at 6% of GNP in 1980 and 8% in 1982, and despite some improvement in the following two years it stood at 8.5% of GNP in 1986, the highest level on record.[28]

Stabilizing the ratio of debt to GNP required sharp cuts in borrowing and consequently in current spending. Public sector pay, because it accounted for a considerable proportion of current expenditure (see Chapter 4; also Conniffe and Kennedy, 1984: 73), inevitably became the focus of government concern, and much political capital was made of the fact that each additional 1% Civil Service pay increase cost the Exchequer approximately IR£20m.

The tougher government stance on public pay was signalled by

[26] Statistics drawn from *Economic Review and Outlook*, Central Bank *Quarterly Bulletins*, and NESC No. 83, 1986.
[27] Hugh Carnegy, 'A Hard Road or Haughey's Gamble', *Financial Times*, 6 Feb. 1987.
[28] See NESC No. 83, 1986; OECD *Economic Survey*, 1984–5: 29–33.

the Fianna Fáil administration in July 1982 when it initiated a renegotiation with the public service unions of the phasing of the 1981–2 public sector pay agreement. Each of the following pay agreements included a pay pause, of varying duration. The first Budgets introduced by the Coalition government made no initial provision at all for new Exchequer-financed pay increases in that year, a bargaining stance which, although later modified to allow public sector pay increases roughly in line with those prevailing elsewhere in the economy, nevertheless signalled the government's firm intention of restraining pay in the public sector. A similar tactic was adopted by the incoming Fianna Fáil administration in 1987. The Coalition government's medium-term national plan *Building on Reality* (1985) also stressed the need to keep a tight rein on public sector pay: 'The development of public service pay must take express account of the capacity of the public finances . . . The overriding need to restore balance to public finances must be a primary consideration in public sector pay developments.' (1. 15). To this end strict limitations on recruitment for public service positions were also introduced, and an embargo was placed on filling more than one in three of all public sector vacancies.

Public service pay agreements were negotiated with relatively little overt conflict between 1981 and 1985, but quite considerable behind-the-scenes tensions accumulated both over the level and phasing of pay increases and over the conduct of public sector arbitration. A one-day strike in October 1985 brought the grievances of about 170,000 public service workers into the open. The orchestration of this demonstration by ICTU's Public Services Committee masked a diversity of interests and priorities amongst public service employees,[29] but the discontent was manifest. Then in the spring of 1986 the government overturned customary practice by calling a Dáil vote to propose a delay in implementing the recommendation of the public service Arbitrator that teachers should receive a 'special' or supplementary pay increase. This was the first occasion since 1953 that a government had invoked its powers to challenge independent pay recommendations in the public service, and it provoked widespread strike action by teachers' unions.

Each of these major conflicts over public sector pay was

[29] See 'After the Great Strike—A Leadership in Disarray', *Business and Finance*, 24 Oct. 1985.

eventually settled by an agreement on the phasing of the pay increases. But the government's recovery strategy not only encountered resistance from the unions, it also increasingly gave rise to tensions between the partners in government, Fine Gael and the Labour Party. Internal cabinet conflicts reduced the overall sense of direction of the government. Proposals for public spending cuts, an integral part of the recovery strategy, were resisted by Labour Party cabinet members anxious to protect their own constituency of support and to prevent government unpopularity from eroding their electoral base. The government was thus internally divided on how the cuts were to be implemented, and this slowed decisive action of any sort.

Meanwhile, from 1984 on, Fine Gael encountered additional pressure from another flank within the Dáil to adopt a tougher approach on the management of the public finances. This came from the Progressive Democrats (PDs), a new party which originated as a breakaway from Fianna Fáil and had its roots in divisions within the party centring on the leadership of Charles Haughey. The split was occasioned by differences on policy towards Northern Ireland. But on economic issues the PDs' policy profile was close to the 'ideological' branch of Fine Gael, favouring fiscal conservatism and some move towards the privatization of publicly-owned companies (see Laver, 1987).[30] This threatened Fine Gael's potential electoral base and exacerbated the conflicts within the Coalition between Fine Gael and Labour. For although all parties in principle accepted the need to stabilize the public finances, they differed in their views on how this might be achieved. Fianna Fáil, in opposition, was freer than the Labour Party to criticize the incidence of expenditure cuts and thus better able to capitalize on popular—especially working class—discontent with government policy. Fine Gael and the PDs were both believed to offer more unequivocal support for swingeing cuts, and sympathizers with this approach were more likely to be found among the urban middle class.[31]

[30] See e.g. the text of the address given by Des O'Malley, the party leader, to the second PD National Conference, IT, 12 Oct. 1987.

[31] See also Laver, 1986a, 1986b; Sinnott, forthcoming; Stephen Collins, 'PDs in Search of a Role', Sunday Press, 11 Oct. 1987. This characterization of the PDs' support base is borne out by voting patterns in the general election of Feb. 1987; see Trench et al., 1987 (especially the evidence of transfer patterns between Fine Gael and PDs, pp. 12–13).

Thus by the mid-1980s the Coalition government appeared to have made relatively little progress on the main issues on which its credibility rested, particularly control of the public debt, unemployment, and prospects for future recovery. In these circumstances, and notwithstanding its earlier stance, the government became increasingly interested in the prospect of building broad-based support behind a strategy for economic and social recovery among the main economic and social interests in society, and in establishing a tripartite, consensus-building institution to devise and implement plans for national recovery and economic development. The consultative National Economic and Social Council (NESC) produced a report in the autumn of 1986, entitled *A Strategy for Development, 1986–1990*, stressing the need for urgent action on a national plan to tackle the problem of public expenditure. This report had the support of the main interest groups in the economy—trade unions, employers, and agriculture, all of which were represented on NESC. The report was intended to secure agreement on a common analysis of the country's economic and social problems. It concluded that what it termed 'the twin problems of mass unemployment and chronic fiscal imbalance' would have to be tackled simultaneously. This could only be done by adopting an integrated medium-term strategy which, if it was to be successful, would have to command widespread acceptance throughout society. The NESC report was not intended to make recommendations on pay; pay determination, the employers stressed, must be kept at industry or firm level. The report was conceived as a means of giving new life to the recovery plans of a Coalition government which, under the leadership of Garret Fitzgerald as Taoiseach, was increasingly seen as lacking decisiveness and direction. It proved to have established the context for a national recovery plan on quite a different model.

The Approach to a New Centralized Agreement

The results of the February 1987 general election are shown in Table 8.2. The Fianna Fáil government which took office was widely expected to experience considerable difficulty in accepting and implementing the strategy for economic recovery developed under the previous government. It had gained electoral support, particularly from Labour Party supporters and among the urban working class more generally, by its criticism of the preceding government's performance and of the incidence of spending cuts. It was, moreover, a minority government and likely to want to avoid the electoral risk of implementing cuts. However, the government very soon made it clear that it proposed little modification of the outgoing government's budgetary plans. Furthermore, it was supported by Fine Gael's undertaking, given by the new party leader Alan Dukes, not to precipitate the fall of this government over the policies of fiscal retrenchment to which it had itself been committed. Unhindered by the internal divisions which had made the Coalition appear indecisive and lacking in direction, and freed for the time being of immediate electoral considerations, the Fianna Fáil government embarked upon a programme of public sector cutbacks more far-reaching than anything the Coalition had attempted.

TABLE 8.2. *Results of the February
1987 General Election*

Party	% votes	seats
Fianna Fáil	44.1	81
Fine Gael	27.1	51
PD	11.8	14
Labour	6.4	12
Workers' Party	3.8	4
Others	6.7	3

For a number of years during the 1970s governments had been constrained to attend to short-term calculations of electoral advantage. During the 1980s the Coalition government had sought to shift these priorities, but had held back from imposing the stringent policies implied by its own analysis. It now became apparent that the Fianna Fáil government was prepared, despite the unpopularity of many of the measures it undertook and continuing controversy over the incidence of spending cuts, to devise and to implement a medium-term economic strategy broadly guided by the priorities established by NESC's report *A Strategy for Development, 1986–1990*.[32]

For its first few months in office it seemed unlikely that Fianna

[32] See e.g. 'Ireland's Budget Aims to Bolster Public Finances', *Financial Times*, 1 Apr. 1987; 'Health Cuts—Crude Axe or Skilful Scalpel?', *Business and Finance*, 11 June 1987.

Fáil would wish to revive centralized collective bargaining. Its initial stance on public expenditure was highly restrictive, seeming to preclude any concessions to the unions in exchange for wage restraint. Indeed, the Budget targeted 10,000 voluntary redundancies in the public service, to be spread over a three-year period, and a wages standstill in public service pay for the second half of 1987, after the current (1986–7) agreement had expired. Public spending cuts and high tax levels signalled its serious intention of achieving its targeted reduction of national indebtedness.

Within a few months, however, it became clear that the government was interested in securing a three-year pay agreement throughout the economy. To facilitate the negotiation of a pay agreement, the government was willing to modify its restrictive stance on public service pay and discuss tax concessions, job creation targets, and welfare provisions.[33] This became apparent in the course of the series of consultative discussions between ICTU and government representatives which began shortly after the general election, at which ICTU submitted detailed documents on each of the policy issues with which it was concerned. During September and October the possibility of linking negotiations on these issues with a pay agreement was discussed.[34] The government in its capacity as employer was, of course, empowered to negotiate a pay agreement only with public service employees. But it was evident that any such agreement would be regarded as a norm for the private sector and the rest of the public sector as well. Thus once the initiative towards a centralized agreement had been taken by the government and ICTU, private sector interests, i.e. the FUE and the CIF, became drawn into the negotiations.

The trade union movement entered into these negotiations in a much weaker position than during the 1970s, and the agreement eventually concluded was on very different terms from the 'two-track' bargaining strategy discussed in Chapter 5. The talks developed from the links which had been established between ICTU and Fianna Fáil in opposition. They built upon the NESC report, whose analysis of the gravity of the economic situation had secured the support of the trade union movement as well as that of the employers.

[33] See e.g. 'Cabinet Offers Pay Deal for Union Support', *IT* 5 Aug. 1987.
[34] See e.g. Maev-Ann Wren, 'The Phoney War on Economic Recovery Ends', *IT* 26 Sept. 1987.

Several influential trade union leaders had responded warmly to this report, and publicly developed the theme that a pay agreement could help to further its objectives. For example, in a widely publicized speech at the end of 1986 Billy Attley, General Secretary of the FWUI, recommended proposals for a consensual plan for national recovery along the lines of the NESC report, specifically praising the records of Austria, Sweden, and Norway in maintaining high levels of employment through their centralized and consensual approach to economic management. He went on to say that if government and employers in Ireland were willing to negotiate a national plan covering jobs, tax reform, social welfare, and the public finances, trade unions would be willing to agree policies on income determination, and to commit themselves to moderation in the rate of wage increases over a number of years.[35] Similar views were also articulated by John Carroll, General Secretary of the largest union, the ITGWU, and President of ICTU during 1986–7, and by a number of speakers at ICTU's Annual Delegate Conferences in 1986 and 1987. Concern was also widely expressed for low-paid workers, who were suffering most in recessionary conditions because of their weak bargaining position. A centralized agreement would have obvious benefits for these workers.

The government's actions on first assuming office appeared unpromising from ICTU's point of view, and the severity of public spending cuts caused obvious difficulties for trade union leaders, especially those with members working in the health services, in which some of the heaviest cuts were falling.[36] Nevertheless, once it became evident that the government was interested, the opportunity to engage in discussions on a wide range of issues placed a great deal of pressure on ICTU not to abandon the talks.

Thus at ICTU's ADC in July 1987 Billy Attley, one of the principal participants in the developing consultations, warned delegates that the trade union movement was in serious danger of being marginalized 'as British trade unions had been under Thatcherism'.[37] However difficult trade union leaders found it to participate in talks, and however great their inclination to withdraw from the negotiations in the course of the summer

[35] Reported in FUE *Bulletin*, Nov. 1986, among other places.
[36] See e.g. 'Haughey Shadow Hangs over ICTU'. *Business and Finance*, 2 July 1987.
[37] See e.g. Brian Donaghy, 'What the Plan Gives the Unions', *IT* 10 Oct. 1987.

months in protest at the size and incidence of the spending cuts being implemented, most trade union leaders took the view that there were real gains to be made on jobs, tax, and 'social progress' in general by continuing with the talks, and that withdrawal would not be to their advantage. Moreover, as one commentator noted, if the unions failed to do a deal with the government, 'they would have nowhere else to go'. The unions had not openly been consulted by the Coalition government, though they had been able to bring some pressure to bear in private on Labour ministers, and they had also had in Fianna Fáil an opposition which could provide leverage in the Dáil on their behalf. But Fine Gael was now supporting government policy; the unions 'could either do a deal with the government or resign themselves to the politics of protest'.[38]

The terms of the agreement eventually concluded in October 1987 resembled the National Understandings in scope, but not in content. The main points included a modest tapered pay increase over three years; provision for negotiating a minimum cash increase to benefit low-paid employees; a commitment for some income tax reductions and other tax reforms over the three years; and agreement that the ratio of debt to GNP should be stabilized and the Exchequer borrowing requirement reduced to between 5% and 7% of GNP by the end of the three-year period. Extra employment would be expected to come about in both the public and the private sector, but no extra expenditure would be committed to this. The unions were keen to promote a reduction in working time, arguing that this could increase employment levels, but the agreement involved nothing more specific than plans for discussions between government, FUE and CIF, and the trade union movement on reducing working time by one hour for those working forty or more hours per week, to be implemented over the three-year period. Other clauses of the agreement covered general guidelines for the development of policy on health, social welfare, housing, industrial development, and productivity in state-sponsored bodies.[39]

The Executive Council of ICTU recommended acceptance of the agreement to its affiliates, and it was ratified at a Special Delegate

[38] Stephen Collins, 'Pay Pact Time Bomb Ticks Away', *Sunday Press*, 20 Sept. 1987.
[39] See details in e.g. *IT* 10 Oct. 1987; *Irish Independent*, 10 Oct. 1987; *Financial Times*, 9 Oct. 1987.

Conference on 19 November with about 60% of votes cast in its favour.[40] One commentator noted that:

> The union leaders themselves do not make any exaggerated claims for the content of the agreement: for them, the main achievement is almost a philosophical one, being back on the national stage and having at least the appearance of an influential role in decision-making, rather than being marginalized as their fellow trade unionists have become in Thatcher's Britain.[41]

ICTU's explicit hope to avoid the fate of the British trade union movement is borne out by a statement on the significance of the agreement by the Assistant General Secretary of ICTU, Peter Cassells, who claimed that the Executive Council had taken very seriously its responsibility for representing the interests not only of trade union members but also of the unemployed, and all their families as well; Congress could thus be seen to represent 'the interests of the majority of the population'. In their negotiations with government, according to Cassells,

> we took the view that the most acceptable models on which to base a Programme for National Recovery should be successful European countries such as Austria, Denmark, Finland, Norway and Sweden. These countries have rejected the confrontationist approach of the New Right and have lower levels of unemployment than the US or the UK.[42]

The private sector employers were initially far from favourable towards the negotiations which culminated in a new integrated pay agreement. The FUE had responded to the NESC document with cautious welcome. Employers were not willing to lose the benefits of decentralized bargaining through a return to national-level pay determination. In December 1986, and again in June 1987, the General Council of FUE restated the policy position it had held since the early 1980s: it asserted that negotiations with the trade unions on pay and related matters should continue to take place at local level.[43] Nevertheless, the FUE now indicated its willingness to engage in 'consultation aimed at securing a measure of consensus at

---

[40] The outcome was: 181 votes cast in favour, 114 against; see *IT* 19 Nov. 1987.

[41] 'Labour–Union Rift is Total after the Plan', *Business and Finance*, 15 Oct. 1987.

[42] Cassells, 'Unions View Accord as Success over New Right', *IT* 17 Oct. 1987.

[43] FUE *Bulletin*, June 1987.

national levels on matters of major importance to the different interested parties'.[44] In mid-1987 it stated that:

FUE considers that national level discussions involving the government, the employers, the trade unions and the agricultural sector would be valuable if they led to greater understanding of the general direction of economic and social policies, established overall objectives and arrived at criteria which would guide the different interests in their various activities.[45]

Thus the FUE decided to participate in the developing discussions between government representatives, the trade union movement, and farming organizations, in the interests of securing commitment to a national plan for economic and social recovery. Over the months since the Fianna Fáil government had assumed office the private sector employers had been 'gradually wooed into support of the government's wider economic policies in general . . . the swingeing cuts in public spending were the kind the private sector employers have been urging for years.'[46]

Once it became clear that public sector pay negotiations would be conducted in this context, the incentive to private sector employers to participate was greatly increased. If they did not, the public sector agreement would undoubtedly serve as a 'floor' rather than as a 'ceiling' for claims in the private sector. The employers were also under a certain amount of political pressure to participate in a wage agreement, since for them to refuse in these circumstances could be construed as indicating less than full support for the principles guiding social and economic recovery to which their assent had already been given. But ultimately FUE and CIF support for the pay agreement was secured by their recognition that the terms of the settlement were quite advantageous to their members. The basic pay provision of the private sector agreement was for an annual increase of 3% on the first £120 of basic weekly pay and 2% on any amount of basic weekly pay over that amount. At a time when the annual rate of inflation appeared to have stabilized in the region of 3%, these were attractive terms from the employers' point of view. The private sector pay agreement also stipulated that no further cost-increasing claims could be made for the duration of the agreement, thus excluding claims based exclusively on cost of living

---

[44] FUE *Bulletin*, Nov. 1986; see also *Annual Review* 1986.
[45] FUE *Bulletin*, May 1987, June 1987.
[46] 'Why the Bosses Changed their Minds', *Business and Finance*, 8 Oct. 1987.

or comparability, mainstays of above-the-norm claims in the 1970s. The FUE and the CIF, recognizing the advantages of this agreement over the decentralized wage rounds, were therefore willing to give it their support.[47]

The leadership of Fianna Fáil was also pleased with the negotiation of the new agreement. The Taoiseach, Charles Haughey, hailed it as:

a major achievement . . . the basis for a long period of industrial peace . . . We now have the chance to create or improve our competitive edge, without sacrificing living standards. The development and employment policies already being carried out by the government in accordance with its own programme have been supplemented and given greater precision and new possibilities have been identified, both in the private and semi-state sector.[48]

This agreement, so markedly different from earlier centralized agreements, was nevertheless criticized by a number of commentators for being excessively generous in the concessions made on public sector pay and tax relief and for risking loss of momentum and credibility in its commitment to reduce the ratio of debt to GNP and to effect sustained cuts in public spending.[49] However, no concession had been made in increasing tax allowances and tax bands in line with inflation (although some commitment had been given to draw more farmers and self-employed people into the tax net, alleviating somewhat employees' sense of the inequity of the taxation system). The public sector pay agreement defused a number of potentially disruptive conflicts in state-sponsored companies.[50] More strikingly, perhaps, the government's departmental estimates for the 1988 Budget, published within a week of the agreement's negotiation, announced cuts of IR£485m. in annual spending, an unprecedented sum.[51] This undoubtedly

[47] See 'FUE's Hard Sell on Pay Deal', *Business and Finance*, 22 Oct. 1987.

[48] Press release; see *IT* 10 Oct. 1987.

[49] See e.g. Paul Tansey, 'Fianna Fáil's New Plan a Mistake', and 'Recovery Plan is Self-Destructive' (editorial comment), *Sunday Tribune*, 11 Oct. 1987; Sean Barrett, 'Country "Cannot Afford" Public Sector Pay Rise', *IT* 10 Oct. 1987. A Fine Gael front-bench spokesman, Michael Noonan, criticized the agreement in the Dáil as 'a dicky'd-up pay agreement with a fungus of promises attached to it'; see Gerald Barry, 'Maintaining the Dáil Truce at All Costs', *Sunday Tribune*, 25 Oct. 1987.

[50] See e.g. Brendan Keenan, 'Haughey . . . Giving Away a Lot Less than it Seems', *Irish Independent*, 10 Oct. 1987; also the Industrial Relations columns in *Business and Finance*, 11 June 1987, 3 Sept. 1987.

[51] See e.g. *Financial Times*, 14 Oct. 1987.

increased union leaders' difficulties in persuading their activists, before a ballot on the terms of the agreement at a Special Delegate Conference of ICTU in November, that the Programme for National Recovery ought to be accepted; but it unequivocally signalled continuing government commitment to its medium-term fiscal strategy.

The leadership of Fianna Fáil had thus supported the process of negotiation with the 'social partners' and the conclusion of a new centralized pay agreement because of the advantages to be gained in terms of industrial peace and trade union commitment to a painful but, in the government's view, inevitable series of spending cuts. But there were other, political reasons for the government's support for the process of consultation and negotiation. The Coalition government, after all, had initially set its face against any revival of this form of influence by the trade union movement.[52] Fianna Fáil revealed its preference for defusing rather than opposing industrial conflict, and for seeking to obtain trade union support rather than excluding it from political deliberations. These preferences can only fully be understood in the context of the discussion in Chapter 7 of Fianna Fáil's support base and its political culture. But the terms on which 'consensus' was sought were now very different. The severity of the economic situation obliged the government to adopt a much tougher stance than previously. The altered perceptions and strategic reorientation of the trade union leadership made it possible for the government to maintain this stance. The course and outcomes of pay bargaining under the terms of the Programme for National Recovery were still to be worked out, with plenty of scope for further conflict over its implementation. Nevertheless, it was evident that this new era of centralized negotiations stood in marked contrast to its predecessor in the 1970s.

[52] The Labour Party leader, Dick Spring, expressed the view that the Programme for National Recovery was 'a con-trick which failed to tackle the jobs crisis and inequality' (*IT* 17 Oct. 1987). It is difficult not to see this opinion as also reflecting a degree of bitterness on the part of Labour's leadership that the trade union movement's relations with Fianna Fáil proved more cordial than their relations with the Labour Party. See also 'Labour–Union Rift is Total after the Plan', *Business and Finance* 15 Oct. 1987.

Conclusion

THIS study has examined the development of a concertative approach to collective bargaining and pay policy in the Republic of Ireland during the 1970s; it has also surveyed the collapse of centralized bargaining in the early 1980s, and the re-emergence, on very different terms, of a new agreement in 1987. It has involved an explanation of the origins and main features of centralized collective bargaining, and analysis of the interconnecting reasons why, in spite of the initial successes of the pay agreements in the 1970s, it is generally agreed that Ireland's experience with concertative agreements did not succeed in stabilizing a 'virtuous circle' of economic performance.

The investigation turned upon the role of centralized agreements and the process of wage formation in small open economies. At first glance there would appear to be every expectation that Ireland, like many of the other small open economies of Western Europe, would have developed a form of wage determination whereby the outcomes of collective bargaining could be made to complement other aspects of economic management. Rather than allowing decentralized collective bargaining to follow the promptings of fluctuating market conditions, a centralized approach could take cognizance in an integrated fashion of how the economy was performing overall, and some of the costs of adjusting collective bargaining could be offset by government. This is the basic model for a neo-corporatist adjustment of wage formation processes; thus state policy may, under certain conditions, intervene to modify the primary role of the market in shaping the calculations of the peak federations of employers and trade unions.

Much of the logic of adapting collective bargaining in support of macro-economic performance was applicable to Ireland in the period after 1960. However, neither the trade union movement, the employers' associations, nor governments went more than part of the way in accepting it. The distinctive form taken by centralized bargaining in Ireland is attributable to the fact that Ireland only possessed to a limited degree the facilitating organizational and institutional conditions for neo-corporatist agreements. The trade union movement saw the centralized agreements as a means whereby a variety of union interests could be advanced more effectively than through decentralized bargaining. But ICTU had neither the ability nor the mandate to devise a strategy of neo-corporatist bargaining. However, I have tried to show throughout this study that the trade unions' approach was grounded in a rational apprehension of the risks of neo-corporatist agreements in the Irish context and of how best to protect the interests of their members as they understood them. The private sector employers and the government were also constrained in their freedom to adapt their strategic approach to collective bargaining.

Our examination of the details of the Irish experience suggests that the literature on small open economies discussed in Chapter 1 and 2 may be misleading in certain respects. There is no guarantee that an identifiable 'need' for modified wage formation processes at the macro-economic level will in fact be met, or that a feasible strategy *can* be found which will allow all parties' interests to be brought into a workable accord.

Three features of the Irish situation may be highlighted to further explain the special difficulties Ireland experienced in devising wage formation policies. The first concerns the impact of structural economic change, and the significance of the timing and nature of industrialization for the way economic interests came to be perceived. The second concerns Ireland's location in the international political economy, and the constraints imposed on domestic adaptation by Ireland's dependence on economically stronger nations. A third and final aspect of the Irish situation, the distinctive party system, must also feature in explaining the relative strength of 'politics' and 'market' in shaping pay policy during the 1970s.

Structural Change in the Small Open Economy

Chapter 2 argued that Ireland, like other small open economies of Western Europe, became subject to pressures to adapt to the competitive conditions of international trade following its commitment to trade liberalization, closer integration into the European market, and reduction of the scale of dependence on the British economy. In several other small countries domestic political structures adapted in the direction of the 'concertation' of economic interests. The case for a similar adaptation in Irish conditions became an issue of central political importance during the 1960s and 1970s. The logic of this position was that concertative agreements would provide a less damaging means of adjusting to inflationary conditions than free-for-all bargaining, and that this contribution to improving competitiveness would protect existing levels of employment and provide favourable conditions for increasing employment. It would also alleviate problems of public revenue and expenditure linked with public sector pay.

But this study has shown that the logic of this argument is considerably less compelling when the economy in question is experiencing rapid change in structural composition. The scale of the changes in the Irish economy during the 1960s and 1970s was surveyed in Chapter 2 and it was noted that this resulted in great variability in the competitive conditions of different sections of industry and in the importance of labour costs in overall competitiveness. As Chapters 4 and 6 showed, the diversity of employers' situations made it difficult for them to maintain a unified front in response to unions' claims. Ireland was in the process of becoming a developed industrial economy. But it did not necessarily follow that the organizational centralization necessary to be able to engage in effectively centralized collective bargaining would consequently come about.

The timing of industrialization has been stressed by a number of authors as an important factor in shaping the development of economic interests and thus the organizational and institutional basis for the emergence of neo-corporatist practices (Gourevitch, 1978; Ingham, 1974). Ireland's two-stage industrialization, sheltered at first by protectionist tariffs, then increasingly open to international investment and international trading conditions, shaped employer interests decisively. But trade union structures should also be understood against this backdrop. Chapter 5 set out a brief account of the complex interplay of political and economic change in shaping the Irish trade union movement. The formative patterns of organization were established before the period of 'modernizing' industrial development. By the 1960s and 1970s, although it was well recognized that trade union structures needed to be changed, they proved very resistant to proposed reforms.

Katzenstein, among others (1983, 1985; see also Maier, 1984), has suggested that awareness of the economy's vulnerability in international trade will induce a willingness on the part of the peak associations of both unions and employers to negotiate a common 'consensual' strategy which will be in everyone's eventual interest. This observation is certainly relevant to Ireland's experiences. But the organizational structures on both the employers' and the unions' sides, which are important mediating variables, cannot easily be modified. Industrial development in small open economies does not necessarily result in the sort of organizational conditions which facilitate neo-corporatism.

Dependent Development in the Small Open Economy

Neither the trade union movement nor employers' interests in Ireland were highly centralized. But in the opinion of many trade union leaders the value of developing a centralized strategy was itself open to grave doubt. Katzenstein (1983, 1984, 1985) has been impressed by the success of some small countries in developing specialized functions in the international division of labour which enable them to secure high levels of growth and a high standard of living. This interpretation of international economic relations plays down the importance of unequal economic and political resources between nations and the limits on policy choices in a less powerful and more dependent country. This 'positive-sum' conception of international economic relations may well be appropriate for the small nations which were already highly industrialized by the 1960s and 1970s. However, it is less obviously appropriate in the Irish case. As we have already seen, Ireland's industrial development strategy in this period permitted very little active state direction of investment decisions. Governments viewed industrial policy, and therefore many aspects of employment creation, as quite separate from wage formation policy. The logic of 'concertation' was thus weakened to some degree by the state's dependence on foreign sources of investment and the unpredictability of international capital flows.

Furthermore, control of inflation was only open to government influence to a limited degree, because Ireland remained committed until 1979 to a fixed exchange rate between the Irish pound and sterling. Britain continued to be a major trading partner, though no longer virtually the only trading partner as previously; therefore Ireland was open to direct transmission of inflationary trends current in Britain. This further weakened the appeal of a strategy of 'concertation' to the trade union movement.

So the decentralized nature of the trade union movement was not the only obstacle to the development of a centralized strategy such as has been developed in other small open economies. The diversity of the competitive conditions in different employments in Ireland, as has been shown, would have presented a major 'free-rider' problem for any centralized pact. But the guarantees available to the Irish trade union movement that a longer-term strategy would be in their interests were also weak. The unions would not countenance an anti-inflationary strategy which might leave them exposed to unpredictable fluctuations in 'imported' inflation, and consequently they continued to have recourse to their market strength in order to try to protect real disposable income levels.

The issue of employment creation crystallized the problem involved in commitment to effective wage regulation agreements. A curb on employee wage pressures was intended to improve competitiveness, thus increasing output and creating new investment funds which would ultimately result in expanded levels of employment. But there was no guarantee that this sequence would occur. Government contended that unless wage adjustments came about in a planned and co-ordinated manner there would be little chance that employment opportunities would increase. But the trade unions were sceptical of this view. Increased profits, they argued, were all too often simply repatriated by multinational companies or dispersed in dividends, and if reinvested were likely to take the form of capital-intensive investment, with a limited improvement in employment levels. Governments in the 1970s and 1980s would be most reluctant to challenge companies' autonomy by involving themselves in directing investment: this would undercut the rationale of industrial development strategy. Foreign companies, on which heavy reliance was placed for new investment, would be deterred from investing in Ireland; Irish industrial policy could not risk this at a time of increasing international competition for direct foreign investment. Neither could governments conceive of jeopardizing existing investment in this way.

The scope of government control over economic performance and of policy intervention was therefore limited: Ireland was not a 'strong state' in this sense (Gourevitch, 1978; Lange, 1984). Government could not offer the unions any assurance that planned wage regulation would have the desired long-term consequences. The experience of dependent development was to some degree at odds with the rationale for trade union co-operation in a concertative strategy. The risks faced by trade union members in forgoing immediate benefits for the promise of longer-term gains, under the economic conditions which prevailed during the 1970s, would be great. The union movement had little tradition of strategic analysis and collective action in any case; the uncertainties inherent in a strategy of this sort meant that it had little appeal for trade unions.

Centralized Agreements and Class Politics

Many commentators, including the OECD (see Chapter 1), have held that the lack of ideological differentiation in Irish politics and the weakness of any tradition of class-orientated organization should be highly conducive to the development of a negotiated consensus between the 'social partners' on pay policy and economic strategy. This 'non-ideological' approach was the characteristic stance of both governments which attempted to achieve a closer integration of pay developments and other aspects of economic policy during the 1970s. However, this study has argued that these features of the political system are not necessarily helpful to a neo-corporatist approach to wage formation.

Chapter 1 argued that a concertative or neo-corporatist strategy could not be identified with the establishment of any specific set of institutional arrangements. But two conditions have to be fulfilled, both having a bearing on the class-based representation of interests. First, the peak federations, especially that of the trade unions, must possess sufficient authority and an appropriate ideological orientation to ensure that its membership complies with the terms of centralized agreements. Centralized bargaining must address the fundamental issue of distributive conflict as a collective issue, which requires explicit recognition of the basis of employer–labour conflict in class-related differences of interest. This is most likely to be achieved if the trade union movement is organized along lines of industrial unionism. But the ideological coherence of union strategy is likely to be strengthened if the trade union movement can articulate a definition in class terms of collective interests in whatever political exchange agreements it may negotiate with government.

The second condition identified as central to successful concerta-tion is the complement on the part of government to the unions' centralized strategy. Whatever the party composition or partisan orientation of the government, it must be able to command the confidence of the trade union movement that it will promote the collective interests of employees, both in short-term 'side-payments' and in the longer-term policy priorities adopted. The precise identification of these interests may vary in different societies, but employees' general living standards, welfare protection and employ-ment levels would be expected to be important. Two kinds of party system have been identified as helpful for the development of centralized processes of wage formation: one in which a leftist or Social Democratic party is strong, or one in which a 'consociational' style of conflict accommodation is well developed. In either case the governing party would be expected to be particularly partisan towards the interests of working people.

In the Republic of Ireland, however, as Chapters 5 and 7 showed, the organization of political interests did not primarily follow lines of socio-economic cleavage. Chapter 5 argued that the trade union movement lacked the organizational resources and the ideological orientation to support a coherent collective strategy spanning the whole range of employees' interests, defined in terms of class, and that more diverse and sectional interests tended to take priority in trade unions' strategies. Alongside these developments, political party divisions took root which bore little relation to the class structure of Irish society and yet adapted to the structural changes of the society.

As Chapter 7 showed, both the Coalition government and the Fianna Fáil governments during the 1970s drew extensive cross-class support, which meant that each had a very diverse constituency to satisfy. The structure of the electoral system and the established patterns of policy-making militated against ideological distinc-tiveness in government policies. Instead governments had a strong incentive to absorb diverse pressures, including those from economic interests. This resulted in increased government involvement in centralized agreements, without necessarily entailing 'trans-sectoral' *mediation* of conflict on terms which would benefit national economic peformance as well. Governments' attempts to cater to the immediate satisfaction of different interests gave rise to the inconsistencies between elements of public policy analysed in

Chapter 4. Governments were not committed to leftist partisanship: they were unwilling to risk conflict with other powerful interests, for example on issues of taxation and income distribution, trade union pressures notwithstanding. The weakness of the unions' capacity for co-ordinated collective action and the non-ideological character of much of party politics were mutually reinforcing traits in the political system. Only the conditions of economic crisis of the 1980s brought about, by necessity, a revision of government priorities and a corresponding reorientation of trade union interests.

Public Policy and Trade Union Strategy

If there was little attraction in a more fully developed concertative approach for the trade unions during the 1970s, there was also little incentive for them to alter their primary reliance on their market power. Chapter 5 showed that through the centralized agreements the trade unions were able to combine continuation of wage pressures on employers with negotiation on a broader range of issues with government. These agreements provided scope for a continuation of the upward trend of pay pressures and for continued relatively high levels of industrial action. The range of issues involved, though broader than ever before, remained confined to the issues of most immediate concern to trade unions, and even at that, their success in obtaining what they wanted, particularly on the issues of taxation and unemployment, was limited by the other political pressures and constraints to which government was subject. Nevertheless, the centralized agreements gave the trade unions direct access to government and, some would say, an unprecedented input to public policy.

Chapter 7 argued that the accommodating stance of government which made this possible was the result of deep-seated features of the political system, exacerbated by the weak ideological differentiation of the party system. This is not an inevitable tendency in the political system, as is evident from the recasting of economic priorities among all three major parties during the 1980s. The policy 'mix' of the 1970s was a product of contingent economic and political circumstances. But certain persistent features of the political system which contributed to these outcomes may nevertheless be identified, such as the localism and personalism which are bound up with the electoral system, and the weakness of the legislature. Public policy-making had little tradition of coherent intellectual analysis. Consequently, the implications of adopting a 'concertative' approach were never fully explored by governing parties. Policy-making tended to respond to short-term political needs. Relative stability in collective bargaining arrangements had strong attractions for government, in contrast with the uncertainty of 'free-for-alls', even if actual outcomes diverged from those intended. Moreover, governments were faced with constrained options on alternatives to an accommodating approach, chiefly due to the electoral pressures to which they were subject. The range and diversity of electoral support on which each government depended provided an incentive to governments to try to avoid unpopular or difficult measures for as long as flexibility in fiscal policy made this possible. For these reasons the trade union movement found that participation in centralized agreements provided scope to advance union interests on two fronts simultaneously, with employers and with government. But far from signifying trade union acceptance of the logic of political exchange, this should be seen essentially as the continuation of the unions' older pluralist, pressure-group strategy, however changed in form from the 1960s. Central features of the Irish political system, in a specific set of economic conditions, reduced the incentive to the trade union movement to develop an , alternative strategy.

The economic crisis of the 1980s introduced a new set of problems onto the political agenda. The old solutions were no longer sustainable. The political legacy of the 1970s, however, was mixed; although the National Understandings had been abandoned early in the 1980s, the model of centralized consultation and consensual policy analysis was once again revived later in the 1980s, indicating certain strong continuities, albeit on quite different terms, in the political mediation of economic difficulties.

Bibliography

Primary Sources

1. GENERAL

Dáil Debates
National Wage Agreements and National Understandings
Employer–Labour Conference Reports
Labour Court *Annual Reports*
Labour Court Recommendations
Public Service Conciliation and Arbitration Schemes
OECD *Economic Surveys* of Ireland
Economic and Social Research Institute *Quarterly Economic Commentary*
Central Bank *Quarterly Bulletin*
Department of Labour (1983), *Discussion Document on Industrial Relations Reform: Laws, Institutions, Parties, Problems*
Department of the Public Service (1978), *Industrial Relations in the Public Service*
Industrial Development Authority (1984), Survey of Employee/Industrial Relations in Irish Private Sector Manufacturing Industry
Industrial Relations News Report
Business and Finance
Irish Times
Irish Marketing Surveys Ltd. opinion polls.

2. OFFICIAL SOURCES

(All published by the Government Publications Office, Dublin)

Budgets
National Income and Expenditure reports
Economic Review and Outlook (Department of Finance)
Irish Statistical Bulletin (Central Statistics Office)

Government White Papers and Green Papers:
  1957. *Economic Development.* Pr. 7239.
  1958. *Programme for Economic Expansion.* Pr. 4796.
  1963. *Closing the Gap.* Pr. 6957.

1963. *Second Programme for Economic Expansion.* Part I, Prl. 7239. Part II, Prl. 7670.

1968. *Second Programme: Review 1964–7.* Pr. 9949.

1969. *Third Programme for Economic and Social Development 1969–72.* Pr. 431.

1974. *A National Partnership.* Prl. 4141.

1976. *Economic and Social Development 1976–80* (Green Paper). Prl. 5758.

1978. *National Development 1977–80.* Pl. 6836.

1978. *Development for Full Employment* (Green Paper). Prl. 7193.

1979. *Programme for National Development 1978–81.* Prl. 7618.

1980. *Investment and National Development 1979–83.* Prl. 8547.

1981. *Investment Plan 1981.* Prl. 9471.

1981. *A Better Way to Plan the Nation's Finances.* Pl. 299.

1982. *First Report of the Commission on Taxation: Direct Taxation.* Pl. 617.

1985. *Building on Reality.* Pl. 2648.

Other Official Reports:

1968. *Final Report of the Committee on Industrial Relations in the ESB* (Michael Fogarty). Prl. 553.

1969. *Dispute Between FUE and Maintenance Craft Unions: Report of Inquiry* (Con Murphy). Prl. 798.

1971. *Report of Banks Inquiry* (Michael Fogarty). Prl. 1850.

1972. *Review Body on Higher Remuneration in the Public Sector.* Prl. 2674.

1981. *Report of the Commission of Inquiry on Industrial Relations.* Pl. 114.

1981. *Report of the Committee on Costs and Competitiveness.* Pl. 154.

3. TRADE UNION SOURCES

ICTU *Annual Reports*

Trade Union Information (journal published by ICTU)

ITGWU *Annual Reports*

Liberty (journal published by ITGWU)

CSEU *Annual Reports*

Confronting the Jobs Crisis: Framework for a National Plan. Dublin: ICTU, 1984.

4. EMPLOYER SOURCES

Annual Reports of FUE

FUE *Bulletin*

FUE Industrial Relations *DataBank* (from 1982)

FUE publications for member companies:

1971. *A Brief Guide to Industrial Relations in Ireland.*
1980, 1981. *Guide to Industrial Relations.*
1981. *Industrial Relations Practice: Guidelines for Employers.*

Annual Reports of CIF

CII *Newsletter*

Economic Trends (quarterly publication of CII)

5. INTERVIEWS

Interviews were conducted in August–September 1984. Unless otherwise
specified individuals' designations refer to the positions they held at that
time.

Mr DÓNAL CARROLL, Chairman and Managing Director of P. J. Carroll
and Co. Ltd.; Chairman of Carroll Industries Ltd.; Governor of the Bank
of Ireland 1964–70, 1983–5.

Prof. BASIL CHUBB, Professor of Political Science at Trinity College
Dublin; Chairman of the Employer–Labour Conference since its
establishment in 1970.

Mr GENE FITZGERALD, (Fianna Fáil) Minister for Labour 1977–80;
Minister for Finance 1980–1; Minister for Labour and the Public Service
1982.

Mr JOHN HORGAN, Deputy Chairman of the Labour Court.

Mr FINTAN KENNEDY, ITGWU: General Secretary 1959–68, President
1969–81; ICTU: President 1965–6, Treasurer 1966–82.

Mr DAN MCAULEY, Director General of the FUE.

Prof. CHARLES MCCARTHY Professor of Business Studies at Trinity
College, Dublin; ex-President of ICTU; member of the NIEC.

Dr EUGENE MCCARTHY, Divisional Director of the FUE.

Mr TOM MCCARTHY, Director of ITGWU Development Services Division.

Mr MATT MERRIGAN, General Secretary of the ATGWU.

Mr DONAL NEVIN, ICTU: Assistant General Secretary 1959–82, General
Secretary since 1982.

Mr JIM O'BRIEN, Divisional Director of FUE and Head of FUE's Research
and Information Section.

Mr TADHG Ó CEARBHAILL, Secretary of the Department of Labour from
its establishment in 1966 until 1982.

Mr SÉAMUS Ó CONAILL, Assistant Secretary in the Department of Finance,
with responsibility for public sector pay, until 1973; Secretary of the

Department of the Public Service from its establishment in 1973 until 1978; Chairman of the Commission on Industrial Relations 1978–81.

Prof. MARTIN O'DONOGHUE, (Fianna Fáil) Minister for Economic Planning and Development 1977–9; economic adviser to Fianna Fáil since 1970.

Mr MICHAEL O'LEARY, (Labour Party) Minister for Labour 1973–7; Leader of the Labour Party 1981–Oct. 1982; subsequently joined Fine Gael.

Dr RUAIDHRI ROBERTS, General Secretary of ICTU 1959–82.

Prof. LOUDEN RYAN, Professor of Political Economy at Trinity College, Dublin; Chairman of the General Purposes Committee of the NIEC; Chairman of NESC and of the National Prices Commission during the 1970s; Chairman of the National Planning Board since its establishment in 1982; Governor of the Bank of Ireland since 1985.

Mr RICHIE RYAN, (Fine Gael) Minister for Finance 1973–7.

Dr T. K. WHITAKER, Secretary of the Department of Finance 1956–69; Chairman of the NIEC; Governor of the Central Bank 1969–76.

Secondary Sources

ÅBERG, R. (1984), 'Market-Independent Income Distribution: Efficiency and Legitimacy', in Goldthorpe, 1984.

AKKERMANS, T., and GROOTINGS, P. (1978), 'From Corporatism to Polarisation: Elements of the Development of Dutch Industrial Relations', in Crouch and Pizzorno, 1978: vol. i.

ALLSOPP, C. (1982), 'Inflation', in Boltho, 1982.

ANDERSON, B. (1981), 'Centralised Bargaining or National Wage Agreements?', in Pollock, 1981.

ARMINGEON, K. (1981), 'Determining the Level of Wages: The Role of Parties and Trade Unions', in Castles, 1981.

BACON, P., DURKAN, J., and O'LEARY (1982), *The Irish Economy: Policy and Performance 1972–1981*, Dublin: Economic and Social Research Institute.

BAIN, G. S. (1983), ed., *Industrial Relations in Britain*. Oxford: Blackwell.

—— and PRICE, R. (1980), *Profiles in Union Growth: A Comparative Statistical Portrait of Eight Countries*. Oxford: Blackwell.

BARRY, B., and HARDIN, R. (1982), eds., *Rational Man and Irrational Society? An Introduction and Source Book*. Beverly Hills and London: Sage.

BARLOW, A. C. (1981), *The Financing of Third-Level Education*: Dublin: Economic and Social Research Institute, Paper No. 106.

BATSTONE, E. V. (1982), *Reform of Industrial Relations in a Changing Society*, Seventh Countess Markievicz Memorial Lecture. Dublin: Irish Association for Industrial Relations.

—— (1984), *Working Order: Workplace Industrial Relations over Two Decades*. Oxford: Blackwell.

—— (1985), 'International Variations in Strike Activity', *European Sociological Review*, 1/1, 46–64.

BAX, M. (1976), *Harpstrings and Confessions*. Assen: Van Gorcum.

BERGER, S. (1981*a*), 'Introduction', in Berger, 1981*b*.

—— (1981*b*), ed., *Organizing Interests in Western Europe*. Cambridge: Cambridge University Press.

BEW, P., and PATTERSON, H. (1982), *Seán Lemass and the Making of Modern Ireland 1945–66*. Dublin: Gill and Macmillan.

BEYME, K. VON (1983), 'Interest Intermediation: Towards New Corporatism(s)', *International Political Science Review*, 4/2.

BISPHAM, J., and BOLTHO, A. (1982), 'Demand Management', in Boltho, 1982.

BLACK, B. (1984), 'Trade Union Democracy and Northern Ireland: A Note', *Industrial Law Journal* (Dec.).

BOLTHO, A. (1982), ed., *The European Economy: Growth and Crisis*. Oxford: Oxford University Press.

BOWLES, S., and EATWELL, J. (1983), 'Between Two Worlds: Interest Groups, Class Structure and Capitalist Growth', in Mueller, 1983.

BRANNICK, T., and KELLY, A. (1983), 'The Reliability and Validity of Irish Strike Data and Statistics', *Economic and Social Review*, 14/4, 249–58.

BRISTOW, J. (1979), 'Aspects of Economic Planning', *Administration*, 27/2, 192–200.

—— (1982), 'Wages and Competitiveness', paper at the Institute of Personnel Management Conference, Galway.

BRITTAN, S. (1975). 'The Economic Contradictions of Democracy', *British Journal of Political Science*, 5.

BROWN, W. (1981), *The Changing Contours of British Industrial Relations: A Survey of Manufacturing Industry*. Oxford: Blackwell.

BUSTEED, M. A., and MASON, H. (1970), 'Irish Labour in the 1969 Election', *Political Studies*, 18, 373–9.

CAGAN, P. (1979), *Persistent Inflation: Historical and Policy Essays*. New York: Columbia University Press.

CAMERON, D. (1978), 'The Expansion of the Public Economy: A Comparative Analysis', *American Political Science Review*, 72.

—— (1982), 'On the Limits of the Public Economy', *Annals (AAPSS)*, 459.

—— (1984), 'Social Democracy, Corporatism, Labour Quiescence and the Representation of Economic Interests in Advanced Capitalist Society', in Goldthorpe, 1984.

CARDIFF, P. (1982), 'Reform: What Needs to be Done', in Pollock, 1982.

CAREY, M. J. (1980), 'Ireland', in P. H. Merkl (ed.), *Western European Party Systems: Trends and Prospects*. New York: Free Press.

CARTY, R. K. (1983), *Electoral Politics in Ireland: Party and Parish Pump*. Dingle: Brandon Book Publishers.

CASEY, J. P. (1969), 'The Injunction in Labour Disputes in Eire', *International and Comparative Law Quarterly*, 18 (Apr.).

—— (1972), 'Reform of Collective Bargaining: Some Constitutional Implications', *Irish Jurist*, 7.

CASTLES, F. G. (1978), *The Social Democratic Image of Society*. London: Routledge and Keegan Paul.

—— (1981a), 'Politics and Public Policy', in Castles, 1981b.

—— (1981b), ed., *The Impact of Parties*. London: Sage.

CHUBB, B. (1963), 'Going About Persecuting Civil Servants: The Role of the Irish Parliamentary Representative', *Political Studies*, 1, 272–86.

—— (1970), *The Government and Politics of Ireland* (1st edn.). London: Longman.

—— (1974), *Cabinet Government in Ireland*. Dublin: Institute of Public Administration.

—— (1982), *The Government and Politics of Ireland* (2nd edn.). London: Longman.

—— and LYNCH, P. (1969), eds., *Economic Development and Planning*. Dublin: Institute of Public Administration.

CLARKE, R. O. (1980), *Conflict and Consensus in Industrial Relations in Some OECD Countries*, Fifth Countess Markievicz Memorial Lecture. Dublin: Irish Association for Industrial Relations.

CLEGG, H. A. (1979), *The Changing System of Industrial Relations in Great Britain*, Oxford: Blackwell.

COHAN, A. S. (1982), 'Ireland: Coalitions Making a Virtue of Necessity', in E. C. Browne and J. Dreymanis (eds.), *Government Coalitions in Western Democracies*. New York: Longman.

Commission of the European Communities (1980), *Problems and Prospects of Collective Bargaining in the EEC Member States*. Brussels: Office for Official Publications of the European Community, Collection Studies, Social Policy Series No. 40.

CONNIFFE, D., and KENNEDY, K. A. (1984), *Employment and Unemployment Policy for Ireland*. Dublin: Economic and Social Research Institute.

COUGHLAN, A. (1984), 'Ireland's Welfare State in Time of Crisis', *Administration*, 32/1, 37–54.

COX, A., and HAYWARD, J. (1983), 'The Inapplicability of the Corporatist Model in Britain and France: The Case of Labour', *International Political Science Review*, 4/2, 217–40.

COX, B. (1983), 'The Impact of Recession on Industrial Relations', *Industrial Relations News Report*, 12 (25 Mar.).

—— and HUGHES, J. (1987), 'Industrial Relations in the Public Sector', in T. Murphy et al. (eds.), *Industrial Relations in Ireland: Contemporary Issues and Developments*. Dublin: University College, Dublin.

CROUCH, C. (1977), *Class Conflict and the Industrial Relations Crisis.* London: Macmillan.

—— (1978*a*), 'The Intensification of Industrial Conflict in the United Kingdom', in Crouch and Pizzorno, 1978.

—— (1978*b*), 'The Changing Role of the State in Industrial Relations in Western Europe', in Crouch and Pizorno, 1978.

—— (1979*a*), *The Politics of Industrial Relations.* Glasgow: Fontana.

—— (1979*b*), 'The State, Capital and Liberal Democracy', in Crouch, 1979*c*.

—— (1979*c*), ed., *State and Economy in Contemporary Capitalism.* London: Croom Helm.

—— (1980), 'Varieties of Trade Union Weakness: Organised Labour and Capital Formation in Britain, Federal Germany and Sweden', *West European Politics*, 3.

—— (1982*a*), *Trade Unions: The Logic of Collective Action.* Glasgow: Fontana.

—— (1982*b*), 'The Peculiar Relationship: The Party and the Unions', in D. Kavanagh (ed.), *The Politics of the Labour Party.* London: Allen and Unwin.

—— (1983), 'Pluralism and the New Corporatism: A Rejoinder', *Political Studies*, 31/3.

—— and PIZZORNO, A. (1978), eds., *The Resurgence of Class Conflict in Western Europe Since 1968*; vol. i: *National Studies*; vol. ii: *Comparative Analyses.* London: Macmillan.

CROUGHAN, D. (1984), 'Irish Industry Today', in Ryan, 1984.

CURRIE, J. (1979), *Industrial Politics.* Oxford: Oxford University Press.

DANIEL, W. W., and STILGOE, E. (1978), *The Impact of Employment Protection Laws.* London: Policy Studies Institute, 44/577.

DOERINGER, P. B. (1981), ed., *Industrial Relations in International Perspective.* London: Macmillan.

DONALDSON, L. (1966), *Development Planning in Ireland.* New York: Praeger.

DONOVAN (1968), *Report of the Royal Commission on Trade Unions and Employers' Associations* (Cmnd. 3623). London: HMSO.

DOWLING, B. (1978), 'Budget Deficits and Fiscal Policy', in Dowling and Durkan, 1978.

—— (1981), 'The Increasing Tax Burden', *Irish Times* (29 June), 12.

—— and DURKAN, J. (1978), eds., *Irish Economic Policy: A Review of Major Issues.* Dublin: Economic and Social Research Institute.

DURCAN, J. W., McCARTHY, W. E.J., and REDMAN, G. P., (1983), *Strikes in Postwar Britain: A Study of Stoppages of Work Due to Industrial Disputes, 1946–73.* London: Allen and Unwin.

DURKAN, J. (1978), 'The Irish Economy: The Recent Experience and Prospective Future Performance', in Dowling and Durkan, 1978.

DURKAN, J. and McCARTHY, COLM, (1981), 'Some Aspects of Irish Economic Growth', unpublished paper, Dublin Economics Workshop.

DWAN, J. (1981), 'The Shop Steward in Industrial Relations', in Pollock, 1981.

DYSON, K. (1977), *Party, State and Bureaucracy in Western Germany.* Beverly Hills and London: Sage.

—— (1982), 'West Germany: The Search for a Rationalist Consensus', in Richardson, 1982.

ECKSTEIN, H. (1960), *Pressure Group Politics: The Case of the British Medical Association.* London: Stanford University Press.

EDGREN, G., FAXÉN, K.-O., and ODHNER, E. (1973), *Wage Formation and the Economy.* London: Allen and Unwin.

EDWARDS, P. K. (1983), 'The Pattern of Collective Action', in Bain, 1983.

ELSTER, J. (1985), *Making Sense of Marx.* Cambridge: Cambridge University Press.

ESPING-ANDERSON, G. (1978), 'Social Class, Social Democracy and State Policy', *Comparative Politics,* 11.

—— AND FRIEDLAND, R. (1982), 'Class Coalitions in the Making of West European Economies', in M. Zeitlin (ed.), *Political Power and Social Theory,* vol. iii. JAI Press Inc.

—— (1985), *Politics Against Markets.* Princeton, NJ: Princeton University Press.

FANNING, R. (1978), *The Irish Department of Finance, 1922–58.* Dublin: Institute of Public Administration.

FARRELL, B. (1970), 'Labour and the Irish Political Party System: A Suggested Approach to Analysis'. *Economic and Social Review,* 1/4, 477–502.

—— (1983), *Sean Lemass.* Dublin: Gill and Macmillan.

FAXÉN, K.-O. (1982), 'Incomes Policy and Centralised Wage Formation', in Boltho, 1982.

FITZGERALD, G. (1968), *Planning in Ireland.* Dublin: Institute of Public Administration.

FLANAGAN, R. J., SOSKICE, D. W., and ULMAN, L. (1983), *Unionism, Economic Stabilization and Incomes Policies: European Experience.* Washington, DC: Brookings Institution.

FOGARTY, M. P. (1976). *Industrial Relations and Creativity: The Irish Case,* First Countess Markievicz Memorial Lecture. Dublin: Irish Association for Industrial Relations.

—— EGAN, D., and RYAN, W. J. L. (1981), *Pay Policy for the 1980s.* Dublin: Federated Union of Employers.

—— RYAN, L., and LEE, J. (1984), *Irish Values and Attitudes: The Irish Report of the European Value-System Study.* Dublin: Dominican Publications.

GALLAGHER, M. (1976), *Electoral Support for Irish Political Parties 1927–*

1973. London: Sage Professional Papers, Contemporary Political Sociology Series, No. 06–017.

—— (1978), 'Party Solidarity, Exclusivity and Inter-Party Relationships in Ireland, 1922–77: The Evidence of the Transfers', *Economic and Social Review*, 10/1, 1–22.

—— (1980), 'Candidate Selection in Ireland: The Impact of Localism and the Electoral System', *British Journal of Political Science*, 10/4, 489–503.

—— (1981), 'Societal Change and Party Adaptation in the Republic of Ireland 1960–1981', *European Journal of Political Research*, 9/3, 269–95.

—— (1982), *The Irish Labour Party in Transition 1957–1982*. Manchester: Manchester University Press.

—— (1985), *Political Parties in the Republic of Ireland*. Manchester: Manchester University Press.

GALVIN, E. P. (1982), 'Jobs, Wages and Industrial Relations: The Hard Decisions', Institute of Personnel Management Conference.

GARVIN, T. (1974), 'Political Cleavages, Party Politics and Urbanisation in Ireland: The Case of the Periphery-Dominated Centre', *European Journal of Political Research*, 2, 307–27.

—— (1976–7), 'Nationalist Élites, Irish Voters and Irish Political Development: A Comparative Perspective', *Economic and Social Review*, 8/3, 161–86.

—— (1977), 'Belief Systems, Ideological Perspectives and Political Activism: Some Dublin Evidence', *Social Studies*, 6/1, 39–56.

—— (1978), 'The Destiny of the Soldiers: Tradition and Modernity in the Politics of de Valera's Ireland', *Political Studies*, 26/3, 328–47.

—— (1982*a*), *The Evolution of Irish Nationalist Politics*. Dublin: Gill and Macmillan.

—— (1982*b*), 'Theory, Culture and Fianna Fáil: A Review', in Kelly, O'Dowd, and Wickham, 1982.

GEARY, P. T. (1976), 'World Prices and the Inflationary Process in a Small Open Economy: The Case of Ireland', *Economic and Social Review*, 7/4, 391–400.

GERAGHTY, D. (1982), 'Efficient Enterprise: A Mutual Concern', Annual Conference of the Irish Management Institute.

GIRVIN, B. (1984), 'The Dominance of Fianna Fáil and the Nature of Political Adaptability in Ireland', *Political Studies*, 32, 461–70.

GOLDTHORPE, J. H. (1974), 'Industrial Relations in Great Britain: A Critique of Reformism', *Politics and Society*, 4, 419–52.

—— (1978), 'The Current Inflation: Towards a Sociological Account', in Hirsch and Goldthorpe, 1978.

—— (1984), 'The End of Convergence: Corporatist and Dualist Tendencies in Modern Western Societies', in Goldthorpe, 1984 (ed.).

GOLDTHORPE, J. H. (1984) (ed.), *Order and Conflict in Contemporary Capitalism: Studies in the Political Economy of Western European Nations*. Oxford: Clarendon Press.

—— (1987), 'Problems of Political Economy after the End of the Post-War Period', in C. S. Maier (ed.), *Changing Boundaries of the Political*. Cambridge: Cambridge University Press.

GORMAN, L., HYNES, G., McCONNELL, J., AND MOYNIHAN, T. (1975), *Irish Industry: How It's Managed*. Dublin: Irish Management Institute.

GOULD, F. (1981), 'The Growth of Irish Public Expenditure, 1947–77', *Administration*, 29/2, 115–36.

GOUREVITCH, P. (1978), 'The Second Image Reversed: The International Sources of Domestic Politics', *International Organization*, 32/4: 881–912.

—— LANGE, P., and MARTIN, A. (1981), 'Industrial Relations and Politics: Some Reflections', in Doeringer, 1981.

GRANT, W., and MARSH, D. (1977), *The CBI*. London: Hodder and Stoughton.

HABERMAS, J. (1976), *Legitimation Crisis*. London: Heinemann.

HARDIMAN, N. (1981), 'Nationalism and Class Politics in the Republic of Ireland', Political Sociology seminar, Balliol College, Oxford.

—— (1982), 'Pay and Collective Bargaining: Some Determinants of Changing Patterns in the 1970s', Current Research seminar, Economic and Social Research Institute, Dublin.

—— (1983a), 'Curbing Trade Union Power? A Study of Legislative Initiatives in Ireland', Sociological Association of Ireland Annual Conference.

—— (1983b), 'Trade Union Density in the Republic of Ireland 1960–79', *Journal of Irish Business and Administrative Research (IBAR)*, 5/2, 41–6.

—— (1984a), 'Corporatism in Ireland: An Exchange of Views', *Administration*, 32/1, 76–87.

—— (1984b), 'Public Goods, Collective Action and the Myth of National Consensus', Political Economy of Western Europe seminar, West European Studies Centre, St. Antony's College, Oxford.

—— (1987a), ' "Consensual Politics"?: Public Goods and Collective Action in Ireland', in I. Scholten (ed.), *Political Stability and Neo-Corporatism*. London: Sage.

—— (1987b), 'The Paradox of Conservative Adaptiveness: Economic Transformation and Economistic Trade Unionism in the Republic of Ireland', Workshop on Union Politics, Labor Militancy and Capital Accumulation, Cornell University (Apr.).

HARRIS, N. (1973), *Challenge and Irish Trade Unionism: National Wage Agreements*, Dublin: ASTMS.

HART, H., and OTTER, C. VON (1976), 'The Determination of Wage

Structures in Manufacturing Industry', in R. Scase (ed.), *Readings in the Swedish Class Structure*. Oxford: Pergamon.

HEADEY, B. (1970). 'Trade Unions and National Wage Policies', *Journal of Politics*, 32/2.

HEATH, A. (1976), *Rational Choice and Social Exchange: A Critique of Exchange Theory*. Cambridge: Cambridge University Press.

HENIG, S., and PINDAR, J. (1969), eds., *European Political Parties*. London: Allen and Unwin.

HIBBS, D. J., JR. (1976), 'Industrial Conflict in Advanced Industrial Societies', *American Political Science Review*, 70.

—— (1977), 'Political Parties and Macroeconomic Policy', *American Political Science Review*, 71.

—— (1978), 'On the Political Economy of Long-Run Trends in Strike Activity', *British Journal of Political Science*, 7.

HILLERY, B. (1973), 'The Irish Congress of Trade Unions', *Administration*, 21/4.

—— (1985), 'Ireland's Strike Record: The Manifestation of Change in Industrial Relations', Institute of Personnel Management Conference.

—— and KELLY, A. (1974), 'Trade Union Membership 1945–70', *Management* (Apr.).

—— and MARSH, A. (1975), *Trade Union Organisation in Ireland*. Dublin: Irish Productivity Centre.

HIRSCH, F., and GOLDTHORPE, J. H. (1978), eds., *The Political Economy of Inflation*. London: Martin Robertson.

HODGSON, G. (1982), 'On the Political Economy of Socialist Transformation', *New Left Review*, 133.

HONOHAN, P. (1982), 'Is Ireland a Small Open Economy?' *Administration*, 29/4, 356–75.

HUDSON, M. (1980), 'Concerted Action: Wages Policy in West Germany, 1967–1977', *Industrial Relations Journal*, 11/4, 5–16.

HYMAN, R. (1977), *Strikes* (2nd edn.). London: Fontana.

—— (1983), 'Trade Unions: Structure, Policies and Politics', in Bain, 1982.

INGHAM, G. K. (1974), *Strikes and Industrial Conflict*. London: Macmillan.

Irish Law Times and Solicitors' Journal (1953), 'Some Irish Cases Under the Trade Disputes Act 1906' (28 Mar., 4 Apr., 11 Apr.)

JESSOP, B. (1978), 'Capitalism and Democracy: The Best Possible Political Shell?', in G. Littlejohn, B. Smart, J. Wakeford, and N. Yural-Davies, (eds.), *Power and the State*. London: Croom Helm.

—— (1979), 'Corporatism, Parliamentarism and Social Democracy', in Schmitter and Lehmbruch, 1979.

—— (1982), *The Capitalist State: Marxist Theories and Methods*. Oxford: Martin Robertson.

Jobs and Wages (1983), produced by a group of socialist economists and individual trade unionists. Dublin.

JOHANNESSON, J., and SCHMID, G. (1980), 'The Development of Labour Market Policy in Sweden and in Germany: Competing or Converging Models to Combat Unemployment?' *European Journal of Political Research*, 8/4, 387–406.

KAHN, (1976), 'Thoughts on the Behaviour of Wages and Monetarism', *Lloyds Bank Review*, 119 (Jan.).

KAHN-FREUND, O. (1965), ed., *Labour Relations and the Law: A Comparative Study*. London: Stevens.

—— (1977), *Labour and the Law* (2nd edn.). London: Stevens.

KATZENSTEIN, P. J. (1975) 'International Interdependence: Some Long-Term Trends and Recent Changes', *International Organization*, 29/4.

—— (1976), 'International Relations and Domestic Structure: Foreign Economic Policies of Advanced Industrial States', *International Organization*, 30/1, 1–46.

—— (1977), 'Introduction: Domestic and International Forms and Strategies of Foreign Economic Policy', *International Organization*, 31/4, 587–607.

—— (1978), 'Conclusion: Domestic Structures and Strategies of Foreign Economic Policy', in P. J. Katzenstein (ed.), *Between Power and Plenty*. Madison: University of Wisconsin Press.

—— (1980a), 'Capitalism in One Country? Switzerland in the International Economy', *International Organization*, 34/4, 507–40.

—— (1980b), 'Problem or Model? West Germany in the 1980s', *World Politics*, 32/4.

—— (1983), 'The Small European States in the International Economy: Economic Dependence and Corporatist Politics', in J. G. Ruggie (ed.), *The Antinomies of Interdependence: National Welfare and the International Division of Labour*. New York: Columbia University Press.

—— (1984), *Corporatism and Change: Austria, Switzerland and the Politics of Industry*. Ithaca, NY: Cornell University Press.

—— (1985), *Small States in World Markets*. Ithaca. NY: Cornell University Press.

KEENAN, J. G. (1978), 'Unemployment, Migration and the Labour Force', in Dowling and Durkan, 1978.

KELLY, A., and BRANNICK, T. (1983), 'The Pattern of Strike Activity in Ireland 1960–1979: Some Preliminary Observations', *Journal of Irish Business and Administrative Research*, 5/1, 65–77.

—— (1985), 'Strikes in the Public Sector', unpublished paper, University College, Dublin.

—— and ROCHE, W. K. (1983), 'Institutional Reform in Irish Industrial Relations', *Studies* (Autumn), 221–30.

KELLY, J. (1980), *The Constitution of Ireland*. Naas: Leinster Leader.

KELLY, J. J. (1980), 'Industrial Conflict: Causes, Consequences and Choices', *Management* (May/June).

KELLY, M., O'DOWD, L., and WICKHAM, J. (1982), eds., *Power, Conflict and Inequality*. Dublin: Turoe Press.

KENNEDY, F. (1981), 'Forty Years of Collective Bargaining: National Understandings', address to Royal Institution of Chartered Surveyors.

KENNEDY, K. A. (1981), 'The State of the Public Finances', *Administration*, 29/2, 137–52.

—— and DOWLING, B. R. (1975), *Economic Growth in Ireland: The Experience since 1947*. Dublin: Gill and Macmillan.

—— and FOLEY, A. (1978), 'Industrial Development', in Dowling and Durkan, 1978.

KEOHANE, R. O. (1978), 'Economics, Inflation and the Role of the State: Political Implications of the McCracken Report', *World Politics*, 31.

—— (1982), 'Inflation and the Decline of American Power', in R. Lombra and W. Witte (eds.), *The Political Economy of Domestic and International Monetary Relations*. Des Moines: Iowa State University Press.

—— (1984), 'The World Political Economy and the Crisis of Embedded Liberalism', in Goldthorpe, 1984.

KIRCHHEIMER, O. (1966), 'The Transformation of West European Party Systems', in J. LaPalombara and M. Weiner (eds.), *Political Parties and Political Development*. Princeton, NJ: Princeton University Press.

KOMITO, L. (1984), 'Irish Clientelism: A Reappraisal', *Economic and Social Review*, 15/3, 173–94.

KORPI, W. (1978), *The Working Class in Welfare Capitalism*. London: Routledge and Kegan Paul.

—— (1980), 'Social Policy and Distributional Conflict in the Capitalist Democracies: A Preliminary Comparative Framework', *West European Politics*, 3.

—— (1981a), 'Unofficial Strikes in Sweden', *British Journal of Industrial Relations*, 19, 6–86.

—— (1981b), 'Sweden: Conflict, Power and Politics in Industrial Relations', in Doeringer, 1981.

—— (1983), *The Democratic Class Struggle*. London: Routledge and Kegan Paul.

—— and SHALEV, M. (1970), 'Strikes, Industrial Relations and Class Conflict in Capitalist Societies', *British Journal of Sociology*, 30.

—— (1980), 'Strikes, Power and Politics in the Western Nations, 1900–1976', in M. Zeitlin (ed.), *Political Power and Social Theory*, vol. i.

LALOR, S. (1983), 'Corporatism in Ireland', *Administration*, 30/4.

LANGE, P. (1984), 'Unions, Workers and Wage Regulation: The Rational Bases of Consent', in Goldthorpe, 1984.

—— ROSS, G., and VANNICELLI, M. (1982), *Unions, Change and Crisis:*

French and Italian Union Strategy and the Political Economy, 1945–1980. London: Allen and Unwin.

LAVER, M. (1986a), 'Ireland: Politics with Some Social Bases: An Interpretation Based on Aggregate Data', *Economic and Social Review*, 17/2.

—— (1986b), 'Ireland: Politics with Some Social Bases: An Interpretation Based on Survey Data', *Economic and Social Review*, 17/3.

—— (1987), 'The Social Bases of Support for Irish Politics: The Case of the Progressive Democrats', unpublished paper, Centre for the Study of Irish Elections, University College, Galway.

LEHMBRUCH, G. (1979a), 'Consociational Democracy, Class Conflict and the New Corporatism', in Schmitter and Lehmbruch, 1979.

—— (1979b), 'Liberal Corporatism and Party Government', in Schmitter and Lehmbruch, 1979.

—— (1982), 'Introduction: Neo-Corporatism in Comparative Perspective', in Lehmbruch and Schmitter, 1982.

—— (1984), 'Concertation and the Structure of Corporatist Networks', in Goldthorpe, 1984 (ed.).

—— and SCHMITTER, P. C. (1982), eds., *Patterns of Corporatist Policy-Making*. Beverly Hills and London: Sage.

LIJPHART, A. (1968), *The Politics of Accommodation: Pluralism and Democracy in the Netherlands*. Berkeley: University of California Press.

LINDBECK, A. (1979), 'Imported and Structural Inflation and Aggregate Demand: The Scandinavian Model Reconstructed', in A. Lindbeck (ed.), *Inflation and Employment in Open Economies*. Amsterdam: North Holland.

LINDBERG, L. N., ALFORD, R., CROUCH, C., and OFFE, C. (1975), eds., *Stress and Contradiction in Modern Capitalism*. Lexington, Mass.: Heath.

LINDBLOM, C. E. (1977), *Politics and Markets*. New York: Basic Books.

LIPSET, S. M., and ROKKAN, S. (1967), 'Cleavage Structures, Party Systems and Voter Alignments', in id., *Party Systems and Voter Alignments*. Glencoe, NY: Free Press.

LITTON, F. (1982), ed., *Unequal Achievment*. Dublin: Institute of Public Administration.

LYNCH, P. (1966). 'The Social Revolution That Never Was', in T. D. Williams (ed.), *The Irish Struggle 1916–1926*. London: Routledge and Kegan Paul.

MACALEESE, D. (1977), *A Profile of Grant-Aided Industry in Ireland*. Dublin: Industrial Development Authority.

—— (1980), 'Economic Boundaries: A Need for Realism', *Management* (May/June).

McCARTHY, CHARLES (1973), *The Decade of Upheaval: Irish Trade Unions in the 1960s*. Dublin: Institute of Public Administration.

—— (1974a), 'The Future of National Pay Agreements', *Administration*, 22/1.

—— (1974b), 'Irish Trade Unions in the 1930s', *Economic and Social Review*, 5/3.

—— (1977a), 'A Review of the Objectives of National Pay Agreements', *Administration* (Spring).

—— (1977b), *Trade Unions in Ireland, 1894–1960*. Dublin: Institute of Public Administration.

—— (1978), *Problems in the Field of Dispute Resolution*, Third Countess Markievicz Memorial Lecture. Dublin: Irish Association for Industrial Relations.

—— (1979), 'Industrial Relations: Strategies for Change', *Administration*, 27/3.

—— (1980a), 'The Development of Irish Trade Unions', in Nevin, 1980.

—— (1980b), 'The Management of Industrial Relations in the 1980s', *Management* (May/June).

—— (1982), 'Productivity Agreements: The Problem of the Spurious', *Irish Journal of Business and Administrative Research (IBAR)*, 4/1.

—— (1984), 'Moots and Morals in Establishing a Pay Policy', Discussion Paper in Industrial Relations, 2, School of Business and Administrative Studies, Trinity College, Dublin.

—— and PRONDZYNSKI, F. VON. (1981), 'The Reform of Industrial Relations: An Evaluation of the Report of the Commission on Industrial Relations', unpublished paper, School of Business and Administrative Studies, Trinity College, Dublin.

McCARTHY, COLM (1979), 'Economic Recovery: An Alternative Path', *Business and Finance* (30 Oct.), 10.

McCARTHY, E. (1983), 'Employers: Collective Bargaining and Economic Policies: Dialogue and Consensus'. OECD Conference.

McCARTHY, W. E. J., O'BRIEN, J. F., and O'DOWD, V. G., (1975), *Wage Inflation and Wage Leadership: A Study of Key Wage Bargains in the Irish System of Collective Bargaining*. Dublin: Economic and Social Research Institute, Paper No. 79.

McCARTNEY, J. B. (1964), 'Strike Law and the Constitution', *Irish Jurist*, 30/4.

—— (1965), 'Strike Law and the Constitution of Éire: A Note on the Case-Law', in Kahn-Freund, 1965.

McCASHIN, T. (1982), 'Social Policy: 1957–82', in Litton, 1982.

McDOWELL, M. (1975), 'Ireland: The Control of Inflation in a Small Open Economy', *Studies* (Spring), 3–15.

—— (1982), 'A Generation of Public Expenditure Growth: Leviathan Unchained', in Litton, 1982.

McGILVRAY, J. (1968), 'Economic Planning', in J. Bristow and A. Tait (eds.), *Economic Planning in Ireland*. Dublin: Institute of Public Administration.

McGINLEY, M. (1976), 'Pay Negotiation in the Public Service', *Administration* (Spring), 76–95.

MAGUIRE, M. (1984), 'Components of Growth of Income Maintenance Expenditure in Ireland, 1951–79'. *Economic and Social Review*, 15/2, 75–85.

MAIER, C. (1984), 'Preconditions for Corporatism', in Goldthorpe, 1984.

MAIR, P. (1977), 'Labour and the Irish Party System Revisited: Party Competition in the 1920s', *Economic and Social Review*, 9/1, 59–70.

—— (1979), 'The Autonomy of the Political: The Development of the Irish Party System', *Comparative Politics*, 11/4, 445–65.

—— (1982a), *Issue-Dimensions and Party Strategies in the Irish Republic, 1948–1981: The Evidence of Manifestos*. Florence: European University Institute, Working Paper No. 41.

—— (1982b), 'Muffling the Swing: STV and the Irish General Election of 1981', *West European Politics*, 5/1, 75–90.

—— (1987), *The Changing Irish Party System*. London: Frances Pinter.

MANN, M. (1973), *Consciousness and Action Among the Western Working Class*. London: Macmillan.

MANNING, M. (1972), *Irish Political Parties: An Introduction*. Dublin: Gill and Macmillan.

MARIN, B. (1983), 'Organising Interests by Interest Organisation: Associational Prerequisites of Corporatism in Austria', *International Political Science Review*, 4/2.

MARKOVITS, A. (1982), ed., *The Political Economy of West Germany: Modell Deutschland*. New York: Praeger.

MARTIN, A. (1979), 'The Dynamics of Change in Keynesian Political Economy: The Swedish Case and its Implications', in Crouch, 1979.

MARTIN, R. (1980), *The TUC as a Pressure Group, 1868–1976*. Oxford: Clarendon Press.

—— (1983a), 'Pluralism and the New Corporatism', *Political Studies*, 31/1.

—— (1983b), 'Pluralism and the New Corporatism: A Reply', *Political Studies*, 31/3.

MEENAN, J. (1970), *The Irish Economy since 1922*. Liverpool: Liverpool University Press.

MERRIGAN, M. (1976), 'Leadership and Recovery', *Management* (May).

MITCHELL, A. (1974), *Labour in Irish Politics, 1890–1930*. Dublin: Irish University Press.

MOONEY, P. J. (1978), 'Incomes Policy', in Dowling and Durkan, 1978.

—— (1982), *Wage Payment Systems: Ireland*. Dublin: European Foundation for the Improvement of Living and Working Conditions.

MOORE, RHODES, B. J., and TARLING, R. (1978), 'Industrial Policy and

Economic Development: The Experience of Northern Ireland and the Republic of Ireland', *Cambridge Journal of Economics*, 2, 99–114.

MOYNIHAN, M. (1975), *Currency and Central Banking in Ireland, 1922–60*. Dublin: Central Bank of Ireland.

MUELLER, D. (1983), ed., *The Political Economy of Growth*. New Haven, Conn.: Yale University Press.

MÜLLER-JENTSCH, W., and SPERLING, H. J. (1978), 'Economic Development, Labour Conflicts and the Industrial Relations System in West Germany', in Crouch and Pizzorno, 1978.

MURPHY, T. (1982a), 'Results of a Preliminary Investigation of Industrial Disputes in Ireland: Appropriate Plant-Level Procedures Essential', *Industrial Relations News Report*, 20 (21 May).

—— (1982b), 'Strikes in 1982: First Half-Year Results', *Industrial Relations News Report*, 30 (30 July).

—— (1985), 'The Impact of the Unfair Dismissals Act in Industrial Relations Practice: Some Measure of Success', *Industrial Relations News Report*, 5 (30 Jan.).

National Economic and Social Council (NESC) (1975), No. 9: *Report On Inflation*. Dublin: Government Publications Office, Prl. 4576.

—— (1977), No. 33: *Comments on Economic and Social Development 1976–1980*. Dublin: Government Publications Office, Prl. 6221.

—— (1978a), No. 37: *Integrated Approaches to Personal Income Taxes and Transfers*. Dublin: Government Publications Office, Prl. 6684.

—— (1978b), No. 44: *Comments on Development for Full Employment*. Dublin: Government Publications Office, Prl. 7462.

—— (1981), No. 56: *Industrial Policy and Development: A Survey of Literature from the early 1960s to the Present*. Dublin: Government Publications Office, Prl. 9010.

—— (1982), No. 64: *A Review of Industrial Policy*. Dublin: Government Publications Office, Prl. 409.

—— (1983), No. 67: *An Analysis of Job Losses in Irish Manufacturing Industry*. Dublin: Government Publications Office, Pl. 958.

—— (1986), No. 83: *A Strategy for Development, 1986–1990*. Dublin: Government Publications Office, Pr. 4450.

National Industrial and Economic Council (NIEC) (1965a), No. 7. *Comments on Department of Finance 'Review of Economic Programme in 1964 and Prospects for 1965'*. Dublin: Government Publications Office, Pr. 8251.

—— (1965b), No. 8: *Report on Economic Planning*. Dublin: Government Publications Office, Pr. 8367.

—— (1965c), No. 11: *Report on the Economic Situation, 1965*. Dublin: Government Publications Office, Pr. 8552.

—— (1966), No. 15: *Arrangements for Planning at Industry Level*. Dublin: Government Publications Office, Pr. 8879.

National Industrial and Economic Council (NIEC) (1967a), No. 18: *Report on Full Employment*. Dublin: Government Publications Office, Pr. 9188.

—— (1967b), No. 20: *Comments on Department of Finance's Report 'Review of 1966 and Outlook for 1967'*. Dublin: Government Publications Office, Pr. 9362.

—— (1968a), No. 22: *The Economy in 1967 and Prospects for 1968*. Dublin: Government Publications Office, Prl. 29.

—— (1968b), No. 24: *Comments on Second Programme: Review of Progress 1964–67*. Dublin: Government Publications Office, Pr. 311.

—— (1969), No. 25: *The Economy in 1968 and Prospects for 1969*. Dublin: Government Publications Office, Prl. 560.

—— (1970a), No. 27: *Report on Incomes and Prices Policy*. Dublin: Government Publications Office, Prl. 1102.

—— (1970b), No. 28: *The Economy in 1969 and Prospects for 1970*. Dublin: Government Publications Office, Prl. 1119.

National Planning Board (1984), *Proposals For Plan 1984–87*. Dublin: National Planning Board/Government Publications Office, Prl. 2309.

NEVIN, D. (1980a), 'The Trade Union Role', *Management* (May/June).

—— (1980b), ed., *Trade Unions and Change in Irish Society*. Dublin: Mercier and RTE.

O'BRIEN, J. F. (1981), *A Study of National Wage Agreements in Ireland*. Dublin: Economic and Social Research Institute, Paper 104.

O'BRIEN, K. (1978), 'We Need a Social Contract, not a Confrontation', *Irish Times* (13 Nov.).

O'CARROLL, J. P., and MURPHY, J. A. (1983), eds., *De Valera and his Times*. Cork: Cork University Press.

O'CONNOR, J. (1973), *The Fiscal Crisis of the State*. New York: St. Martin's Press.

OFFE, C. (1975), 'The Theory of the Capitalist State and the Problem of Policy Formation', in Lindberg, Alford, Crouch, and Offe (1975).

—— (1981), 'The Attribution of Public Status to Interest Groups: Observations on the West German Case', in Berger, 1981b.

—— and RONGE, V. (1982), 'Theses on the Theory of the State', in A. Giddens and D. Held (eds.), *Class, Power and Conflict*. London: Macmillan.

—— and WIESENTHAL, H. (1980), 'Two Logics of Collective Action: Theoretical Notes on Social Class and Organisational Form', in M. Zeitlin (ed.), *Political Power and Social Theory*, vol. i. 67–115.

O'HIGGINS, P. (1979), *Irish Labour Law: Sword or Shield?*, Fourth Countess Markievicz Memorial Lecture. Dublin: Irish Association for Industrial Relations.

O'LEARY, C. (1979), *Irish Elections 1918–1977*. Dublin: Gill and Macmillan.

O'LEARY, J. (1982), 'Taxation: Some Implications for Incomes Policy', unpublished paper, Dublin Economics Workshop (22 Jan.).

OLSON, M. (1965), *The Logic of Collective Action*. Cambridge, Mass.: Harvard University Press.

—— (1982), *The Rise and Decline of Nations: Economic Growth, Stagflation and Social Rigidities*. New Haven, Conn., and London: Yale University Press.

O'MAHONY, D. (1964), *Industrial Relations in Ireland: The Background*. Dublin: Economic and Social Research Institute, Paper 19.

—— (1965), *Economic Aspects of Industrial Relations*. Dublin: Economic and Social Research Institute, Paper 24.

Organization for Economic Co-operation and Development (OECD) (1976), *Income Distribution in the OECD Countries* (Malcolm Sawyer). Paris: OECD.

—— (1977), *Towards Full Employment and Price Stability* (Paul McCracken). Paris: OECD.

—— (1978), *Wage Policies and Collective Bargaining: Developments in Finland, Ireland and Norway* (Dr. John Addison). Paris: OECD.

—— (1980), 'Collective Bargaining and Economic Policies', Report on a Meeting of Trade Union Experts, Paris (30 June–2 July).

—— (1982), *The Search for Consensus* (Martha Cooper). Paris: OECD.

ORRIDGE, A. (1977), 'The Irish Labour Party', in W. E. Paterson and A. H. Thomas (eds.), *Social Democratic Parties in Western Europe*. London: Croom Helm.

O'SULLIVAN, H. (1982), 'Jobs, Wages and Industrial Relations', Institute of Personnel Management Annual Conference, Galway (7 May).

—— (1983), 'Industrial Relations in the Public Sector', Junior Chamber seminar on 'Industrial Relations: The Way Ahead'.

PANIĆ, M. (1978), 'The Origin of Increasing Inflationary Tendencies in Contemporary Society', in Hirsch and Goldthorpe, 1978.

PANITCH, L. (1976), *Social Democracy and Industrial Militancy: The Labour Party, the Trade Unions and Incomes Policy 1945–74*. Cambridge: Cambridge University Press.

—— (1979), 'The Development of Corporatism in Liberal Democracies', in Schmitter and Lehmbruch, 1979.

—— (1980), 'Recent Theorisations of Corporatism: Reflections on a Growth Industry', *British Journal of Sociology*, 31/2.

—— (1981), 'Trade Unions and the State', *New Left Review*, 125.

PATTERSON, B. (1981), 'Change and Productivity Bargaining', in Pollock, 1981.

PEILLON, M. (1982), *Contemporary Irish Society*. Dublin: Gill and Macmillan.

—— (1984), *Strategies of State Mobilization in Irish Industrial Relations*, Ninth Countess Markievicz Memorial Lecture. Dublin: Irish Association for Industrial Relations.

PENNIMAN, H. R. (1978), ed., *Ireland at the Polls: The Dáil Elections of 1977*. Washington; DC: American Enterprise Institute.

—— and FARRELL, B. (forthcoming), eds., *Ireland at the Polls 1981–2*. Washington, DC: American Enterprise Institute.

PIZZORNO, A. (1978), 'Political Exchange and Collective Identity in Industrial Conflict', in Crouch and Pizzorno, 1978.

POLLOCK, H. (1981), ed., *Industrial Relations in Practice*. Dublin: O'Brien Press.

—— (1982), ed., *Reform of Industrial Relations*. Dublin: O'Brien Press.

POULANTZAS, N. (1973), *Political Power and Social Classes*. London: New Left Books.

PRONDZYNSKI, F. VON (1982), 'Unofficial Strikes: Myth and Reality', *Administration* 29/4, 400–11.

PRZEWORSKI, A. (1980a), 'The Material Bases of Consent: Economics and Politics in a Hegemonic System', in M. Zeitlin (ed.), *Political Power and Social Theory*, vol. i.

—— (1980b), 'Social Democracy as a Historical Phenomenon', *New Left Review*, 122.

—— (1985), *Capitalism and Social Democracy*. Cambridge: Cambridge University Press.

—— and WALLERSTEIN, M. (1982), 'The Structure of Class Conflict in Democratic Capitalist Societies', *American Political Science Review*, 76.

PUTTNAM, J. (1981), 'A New Day for Ireland', *National Geographic*, 159/4.

PYNE, P. (1969), 'The Third Sinn Féin Party: 1923–6', *Economic and Social Review*, 1/1, 29–50; 1/2, 229–57.

RABBITTE, P. (1983), 'Survival Management', Institute of Personnel Management Annual Conference, Galway (May).

RAFTERY, J. (1982), 'Patterns of Taxation and Public Expenditure: Towards a Corporatist Approach', in Kelly, O'Dowd, and Wickham, 1982.

RAYMOND, R. J. (1983), 'De Valera, Lemass and Irish Economic Development, 1933–48', in O'Carroll and Murphy, 1983.

REDMOND, M. (1982), *Ireland*. Netherlands: Kluwer.

REGINI, M. (1982), 'Changing Relationship Between Labour and the State in Italy: Towards a Neo-Corporatist System?' in Lehmbruch and Schmitter, 1982.

—— (1984), 'The Conditions for Political Exchange: How Concertation Emerged and Collapsed in Italy and Great Britain', in Goldthorpe, 1984.

—— and ESPING-ANDERSEN, G. (1980), 'Trade Union Strategies and Social Policy in Italy and Sweden', *West European Politics*, 3/1.

RICHARDSON, J. J. (1982), ed., *Policy Styles in Western Europe*. London: Allen and Unwin.

ROCHE, R. (1982), 'The High Cost of Complaining Irish Style', *Irish*

Journal of Business and Administrative Research (IBAR), 4/2, 159–87.

ROCHE, W. K. (1981), *Convention and Change in Irish Industrial Relations: Comparisons and Differentials*. Dublin: College of Industrial Relations.

—— (1982), 'Social Partnership and Political Control: State Strategy and Industrial Relations in Ireland', in Kelly, O'Dowd, and Wickham, 1982.

—— and LARRAGY, J. (n.d.), 'Patterns of Merger and Dissolution of Trade Unions in Ireland Since 1940', DUES Bulletin No. 2, Department of Industrial Relations, University College, Dublin.

—— —— (1987), 'The Trend of Unionisation in the Republic of Ireland', in T. Murphy, B. Hillery, and A. Kelly, (eds.), *Recent Trends in Irish Industrial Relations*. Dublin: University College, Dublin.

ROSE, R. (1980), ed., *Challenge to Governance: Studies in Overloaded Polities*. Beverly Hills and London: Sage.

ROTTMAN, D. B., and HANNAN, D. F. (1982), 'The Impact of State Taxation and Transfer Policies on Income Inequalities in the Republic of Ireland', in Kelly, O'Dowd, and Wickham, 1982.

—— and O'CONNELL, P. (1982a), 'The Changing Social Structure of Ireland', in Litton, 1982

—— —— (1982b), 'Economic Development and the Welfare State in Ireland: An Analysis of Public Finances', unpublished paper, Economic and Social Research Institute, Dublin.

—— HANNAN, D. F., HARDIMAN, N., and WILEY, M. M. (1982), *The Distribution of Income in the Republic of Ireland: A Study in Social Class and Family-Cycle Inequalities*. Dublin: Economic and Social Research Institute, Paper 109.

RUGGIE, J. G. (1982), 'International Regimes, Transactions and Change: Embedded Liberalism in the Postwar Economic Order', *International Organization*, 36.

RUMPF, E., and HEPBURN, A. C. (1977), *Nationalism and Socialism in Twentieth-Century Ireland*. Liverpool: Liverpool University Press.

RYAN, L. (1972), 'Fiscal Policy and Demand Management in Ireland, 1960–70', in A. Tait and J. Bristow (eds.), *Ireland: Problems of a Developing Economy*. Dublin: Institute of Public Administration.

—— (1982), 'Prospects for the Eighties', in Ryan et al., *The Economic and Social State of the Nation*. Dublin: Economic and Social Research Institute.

—— (1984), ed., *Irish Industry in the Eighties*. Dublin: Helicon/Confederation of Irish Industry.

SABEL, C. F. (1981), 'The Internal Politics of Trade Unions', in Berger, 1981b.

SACHS, J. D. (1980), 'The Changing Cyclical Behaviour of Wages and Prices 1890–1976', *American Economic Review*, 70.

—— (1985), 'Labour Markets and Comparative Macro-Economic

Performance', in M. Bruno and J. D. Sachs, *Economics of Worldwide Stagflation*. Oxford: Blackwell.

SACKS, P. M. (1976), *The Donegal Mafia*. New Haven, Conn.: Yale University Press.

SAMS, K. I. (1968), 'The Appeals Board of ICTU', *British Journal of Industrial Relations* 6/2.

SARTORI, G. (1976), *Parties and Party Systems*. Cambridge: Cambridge University Press.

SCASE, R. (1977), *Social Democracy in Capitalist Society*. London: Croom Helm.

SCHARPF, F. W. (1981), *The Political Economy of Inflation and Unemployment in Western Europe: An Outline*. Berlin: International Institute of Management.

—— (1984), 'Economic and Institutional Constraints of Full-Employment Strategies: Sweden, Austria and West Germany, 1973–82', in Goldthorpe, 1984.

SCHMIDT, M. (1981), 'The Role of Parties in Shaping Macroeconomic Policy', in Castles, 1981*b*.

—— (1982), 'Does Corporatism Matter? Economic Crises, Politics and Rates of Unemployment in Capitalist Democracies in the 1970s', in Lehmbruch and Schmitter, 1982.

SCHMITTER, P. C. (1974), 'Still the Century of Corporatism?' in Schmitter and Lehmbruch, 1979.

—— (1979), 'Modes of Interest Intermediation and Models of Societal Change in Western Europe', in Schmitter and Lehmbruch, 1979.

—— (1981), 'Interest Intermediation and Regime Governability', in Berger, 1981*b*.

—— (1982), 'Reflections on Where the Theory of Neo-Corporatism Has Gone and Where the Praxis of Neo-Corporatism May Be Going', in Lehmbruch and Schmitter, 1982.

—— and LEHMBRUCH, G. (1979), eds., *Trends Towards Corporatist Intermediation*. Beverly Hills and London: Sage.

—— and STREECK, W. (1981), *The Organisation of Business Interests: A Research Design*. Berlin: International Institute of Management.

SCHOLTEN, I. (1980), 'Does Consociationalism Exist? A Critique of the Dutch Experience', in R. Rose (ed.), *Electoral Competition: A Comparative Analysis*. Beverly Hills and London: Sage.

SCHONFIELD, A. (1965), *Modern Capitalism*. Oxford: Oxford University Press.

SCHREGLE, J. (1975), *Restructuring of the Irish Trade Union Movement: Memorandum Submitted to the Irish Congress of Trade Unions*. Geneva: International Labour Organisation.

SCHWERIN, D. S. (1979), 'The Limits of Organisation as a Response to Wage–Price Problems', in Rose, 1980.

—— (1980), *Corporatism and Protest: Organisational Politics in the Norwegian Trade Unions*. Kent, Ohio: Kent Popular Press.

SCITOVSKY, T. (1978), 'Market Power and Inflation', *Economica*, 45.

—— (1980), 'Can Capitalism Survive?—An Old Question in a New Setting', *American Economic Review*, 70.

SEXTON, J. J. (1981), 'The Changing Labour Force', in Sexton et al., *The Irish Economy and Society in the 1980s*. Dublin: Economic and Social Research Institute.

—— (1982), 'Sectoral changes in the labour force over the period 1961–80 with particular reference to public sector and services employment', ESRI *Quarterly Economic Commentary* (August).

SHALEV, M. (1978), 'Lies, Damned Lies and Strike Statistics', in Crouch and Pizzorno, 1978.

SHILLMAN, B. (1960), *Trade Unionism and Trade Disputes in Ireland*. Dublin: Dublin Press.

SINNOTT, R. (1978), 'The Electorate', in Penniman, 1978.

—— (forthcoming), 'The Voters, the Issues and the Party System', in H. Penniman and B. Farrell (eds.), *Ireland at the Polls 1981–82*. Washington, DC: American Enterprise Institute.

STEPHENS, J. D. (1979), *The Transition from Capitalism to Socialism*. London: Macmillan.

STEWART, E. (1975), 'Injunctions and the Right to Strike', *Irish Law Times and Solicitors' Journal* (Dec. 6).

—— (1978), 'Current Industrial Relations Law'. Dublin Association of Certified Accountants, Irish Region.

STEWART, J. C. (1976), 'Foreign Direct Investment and the Emergence of a Dual Economy', *Economic and Social Review*, 7/2, 173–97.

STREECK, W. (1982), 'Organisational Consequences of Neo-Corporatist Co-Operation of West German Labour Unions', in Lehmbruch and Schmitter, 1982.

—— (1984), 'Neo-Corporatist Industrial Relations and the Economic Crisis in West Germany', in Goldthorpe, 1984.

THUROW, L. (1980), *The Zero-Sum Society: Distribution and the Possibilities for Economic Change*. New York: Basic Books.

TRENCH, B., BARRY, G., BROWNE, V., O'TOOLE, F., and WHELAN, S. (1987), eds., *Magill Book of Irish Politics: February '87*. Dublin: Magill.

TUFTE, E. R. (1978), *Political Control of the Economy*. Princeton, NJ: Princeton University Press.

TUSSING, A. D. (1978), *Irish Educational Expenditures—Past, Present and Future*. Dublin: Economic and Social Research Institute, Paper 92.

UUSITALO, H. (1983), 'Incomes Policy in Finland: Economic and Social Effects in a Comparative Perspective', *Scandinavian Political Studies*, 6/1 (New Series), 1–25.

VISSER, J. (1984), *The Position of Central Confederations in the National*

Union Movements. Florence: European University Institute Working Paper No. 102.

WALLACE, J. (1982), *Industrial Relations in Limerick City and Environs: Final Report* (especially vol. iii). Limerick: NIHE.

WALSH, B. M. (1978), 'Labour Market Strategies', in Dowling and Durkan, 1978.

—— and O'TOOLE, A. (1973), *Women and Employment in Ireland: Results of a National Survey*. Dublin: Economic and Social Research Institute, Paper 69.

WALSH, K. M. (1983), 'The Measurement of Trade Union Membership in Four EEC Countries'. Brighton: University of Sussex Institute of Manpower Studies.

WHELAN, C. T. (1980), *Employment Conditions and Job Satisfaction: The Distribution, Perception and Evaluation of Job Rewards*. Dublin: Economic and Social Research Institute, Paper 101.

—— (1982), *Worker Priorities, Trust in Management and Prospects for Workers' Participation*. Dublin: Economic and Social Research Institute, Paper 111.

—— and WHELAN, B. J. (1984), *Social Mobility in the Republic of Ireland: A Comparative Perspective*. Dublin: Economic and Social Research Institute, Paper 116.

WHITAKER, T. K. (1979), 'Industrial Relations—Is There a Better Way?' *Administration*, 27/3, 282–93.

—— (1983a), 'From Protection to Free Trade: The Irish Experience', in id., *Interests*. Dublin: Institute of Public Administration.

—— (1983b), 'Financial Turning-Points', in id., *Interests*. Dublin: Institute of Public Administration.

—— (1983c), 'The Central Bank 1969–76: A Retrospect', in id., *Interests*. Dublin: Institute of Public Administration.

WHYTE, J. H. (1974), 'Ireland: Politics without Social Bases', in R. Rose (ed.), *Electoral Behaviour: A Comparative Handbook*. New York: Free Press.

—— (1980), *Church and State in Modern Ireland 1923–1979* (2nd edn.). Dublin: Gill and Macmillan.

WICKHAM, J. (1980), 'The Politics of Dependent Capitalism: International Capital and the Nation State'. in A. Morgan and B. Purdie (eds.), *Divided Nation, Divided Class*. London: Ink Links.

WINDMULLER, J. P. (1975), 'The Authority of National Trade Union Confederations: A Comparative Analysis', in D. B. Lipsey (ed.), *Union Power and Public Policy*. Ithaca, NY: Cornell University Institute for Labour Relations.

—— and GLADSTONE, A. (1984), eds., *Employers' Associations and Industrial Relations: A Comparative Study*. Oxford: Clarendon Press.

Index